CW00540303

"Peter Shore was a hero of mine when I entered Parliament. His commitment to democracy still resonates, along with his faith in an independent UK as an agent for good in the world. This biography is a must-read for all MPs."

KATE HOEY

"It's more than time for this excellent biography of Peter Shore, a great Labour figure. Today's party has much to learn from Shore's clear thinking on economics, industrial competitiveness and the EU distraction from its socialist purposes. It's wonderful to see a great minister brought back to life."

AUSTIN MITCHELL

"Of all the people involved in the Maastricht rebellion, Peter Shore stands out. I greatly admired his analysis, integrity and contribution, particularly on the economic front, and this outstanding biography emphasises that he was a man of immense political standing."

BILL CASH MP

"Peter Shore has been deserving of a biography to mark his contribution to the Labour governments of 1964–70 and 1974–79. This is a long overdue biography of an important politician."

LARRY ELLIOTT

"Peter Shore is a largely forgotten giant of British politics. I sat beside him in Parliament for many years. His powerful and lifelong case against what became the EU is now vindicated, and I predict his reputation will begin to grow again. This book will be an important part of that."
GEORGE GALLOWAY

"A superb study of an unjustly overlooked but principled and brilliant politician. If only we had someone of Shore's stature now."
ROD LIDDLE

"Peter Shore was a towering figure in Labour politics, and it is a delight to see this excellent biography being published."
JOHN MILLS

PETER SHORE
Labour's Forgotten Patriot

Kevin Hickson, Jasper Miles & Harry Taylor
Foreword by Bryan Gould

Biteback Publishing

First published in Great Britain in 2020 by
Biteback Publishing Ltd
Westminster Tower
3 Albert Embankment
London SE1 7SP
Copyright © Kevin Hickson, Jasper Miles and Harry Taylor 2020

ISBN 978-1-78590-473-8

10 9 8 7 6 5 4 3 2 1

A CIP catalogue record for this book is available from the British Library.

Set in Bulmer

Printed and bound in Great Britain by
CPI Group (UK) Ltd, Croydon CR0 4YY

MIX
Paper from
responsible sources
FSC® C020471

CONTENTS

FOREWORD

THIS EXCELLENT BIOGRAPHY OF one of the most under-rated British politicians of recent times is long overdue and all the more welcome for that reason. I could not help but think, given the timing of its publication in relation to other events, that the authors might well have echoed Wordsworth's impassioned appeal to Milton and exclaimed at some point, 'Peter Shore, thou shouldst be living at this hour!'

It is certainly the case that there is no one whose contribution to the debates and difficulties surrounding Brexit would have been more relevant and valuable. The terrain traversed by the authors shows conclusively how perceptively Peter Shore foresaw the issues that have since bubbled to the surface and that cannot now be denied.

No one could so convincingly have rebutted the many calumnies heaped upon those who, in the context of Brexit, dare to reflect and respond to British history, identity and aspirations. Peter Shore was a British patriot who refused to accept that such sentiments were the territory of the small-minded or bigoted, or that they were the exclusive property of the right wing in politics.

He correctly identified a determination to maintain control over the nation's own affairs and to remain true to our history as not just a central element in 'Britishness', but as inseparable from the self-government, social justice and democracy for which our forefathers had fought and made sacrifices, and that still matter to so many today.

No one reading this account of what Shore said and did on these matters can believe that, if he were alive today, the Labour Party would have shilly-shallied about giving effect to the people's judgement on Europe; a judgement that was made on their forty years of experience of an arrangement contrived in the interests of others and a form of government imposed on them step by step and by subterfuge.

Nor can anyone doubt that he would have derided a socialism that purported to find expression in a Europe dominated by unelected bureaucrats and bankers and dedicated to the interests of multinational corporations and the precepts of neoliberalism.

My own experience of working with and for Peter Shore accords exactly with the portrait of him painted by the authors. He was a man of charm and warmth and kindness – almost self-deprecating in his lack of bombast and posturing – but possessed of a sharp intellect, a determination not to budge from what he knew was right, and an instinct for getting to the heart of the matter.

I always assumed that those who did not know him well would have been taken aback at the unexpected passion and power of his oratory. He delivered, on occasion, some of the most powerful and effective political speeches I have ever heard – reflecting, I like to think, that Peter lived and felt his politics.

I remember to this day the sense of exhilaration and relief I felt when, after returning from a stint in Brussels with the Foreign Office and having concluded (I thought as an outlier) that the Common Market was against British interests, I heard Peter speak to a Labour conference and advance an analysis of what membership would mean that was exactly in line with my own.

For him, politics was not about scrabbling for votes but about the great questions of who we are as a people and how we should treat each other and organise ourselves for the common good.

This account of his contribution to British politics and British life correctly focuses on Peter Shore the man, as well as on Peter Shore the politician. I can only confirm the authors' conclusions.

My most enjoyable and inspiring times in politics were the congenial Sunday evenings my wife and I spent with like-minded friends and colleagues as guests of Liz and Peter Shore at their dinner table. That is when we were privileged to be given an insight into how he thought and what made him tick, and into what he thought it meant to be British.

The authors have provided us with a timely portrait and reminder of this kindly, thoughtful and passionate man.

Bryan Gould
January 2020

INTRODUCTION

WHEN ONE OF THE current authors interviewed Peter Shore in relation to his doctoral thesis on the IMF Crisis of 1976, in which he played a lead role, attention was placed on Shore's own alternative position to public spending cuts. Asked if his proposed import controls were legal under the Treaty of Rome, which the UK had accepted on becoming a member of the European Economic Community in 1973, he smiled and said that was all the more reason to impose them. Thus, in this anecdote lay the twin themes of Shore's political beliefs, namely a strong sense of patriotism which manifested itself principally in the form of opposition to European integration, and an interventionist economic policy designed to achieve higher rates of economic growth and the maintenance of full employment. That it was possible for a Labour government to have both was Shore's central contention.

Shore is now very much a neglected figure and, as Lord Morris has said, he is 'one of the forgotten men'.[1] That Shore has been overlooked is highlighted by the fact that he has not previously been the subject of a political biography. Indeed, in much of the literature his name is mentioned in passing only, present but a character in the background. On other occasions, authors have sought to dismiss his contribution and ability, such as John Golding, who considered him the 'Lone Ranger', lacking in direction and political nous.[2] Shore's biggest critic was Edward Pearce, who, in his biography of Denis Healey, considered Shore to be a 'placeman' that, in his opposition to 'In Place of Strife', had not known a 'placeman's place'. Pearce continued:

> Angular and thin to the point of emaciation, once compared to Smike … his politics were idiosyncratic and mixed, he was a conservative figure, attractive fleetingly to the left because of a hostility to what was then called the 'Common Market' of an unremitting, not to say obsessive, sort.

This did not abate even when he entered the Lords, bringing to a debate about juries his fervent support for a man selling sweets in ounces.[3] Elsewhere, Pearce wrote in a manner that suggested that Healey's doubts over European integration – disbelief in federal structures, distrust of the old upper classes of southern Europe and the possibility of honest municipal government south of the olive line – were unfortunate but acceptable, and Shore's objections no more than 'huddled, union jack keening'.[4] Some forms of Euroscepticism were acceptable; others, it seemed, were not. Pearce had himself once considered Shore to be good leadership material: 'In a moment of absence of mind I personally favoured the candidacy of Mr Peter Shore.'[5] However, he maintained that Shore should have been retained as shadow Chancellor, where Pearce felt he would have gone on to make a good opponent to Nigel Lawson.[6]

Still, others have looked favourably on Shore's character and politics. In 1993, by which time his position in the Labour Party had fallen to that of an unfashionable backbencher, the journalist Ian Aitken wrote:

> Nothing so accurately betrays the lofty and patronising attitude of true Eurofanatics towards those who do not share their enthusiasm than their reaction to Peter Shore. Never mind that he is an intellectual giant who towers over most of the people who sit in front of him on Labour's front bench. Never mind that he is one of the few remaining Labour MPs with top-level cabinet experience. He can be, and is, dismissed as an irrelevance because he has perversely refused to climb aboard Labour's belated European bandwagon.[7]

Dame Margaret Beckett MP considered that, while Shore has fallen from the public memory, 'that does not reflect in any way the standing he did have, the way in which he should be regarded'. Moreover, 'Peter was distinguished, highly intelligent, a bit chilly but a formidable and major intellectual figure in the Party.'[8] For someone who occupied several Cabinet positions, twice stood for the leadership of his party and was at the heart of the defining debates of the 1960s, '70s and '80s, it is worth re-evaluating his contribution both to the Labour Party and to British politics.

The lack of a Shore biography is a major omission in the literature on British political history. The relative dearth of references to him compared to other figures of his standing creates both a problem and an opportunity for would-be biographers. Much of the groundwork on which subsequent biographies can build has not been conducted, and this problem is compounded by the fact that Shore did not write his memoirs (although we do know that, if he had, they would have been called *The Record Straight*).[9] On the other hand, this important gap in the literature provides the opportunity to make a distinctive, original contribution to our shared knowledge of British political history. It is also timely. The Labour Party's move to the left in recent years is frequently compared with the early 1980s, when Shore was at the peak of his career. Moreover, the political, social and economic repercussions of the UK voting to leave the European Union in 2016, and the challenges this poses for the British political class – especially the Labour Party – results in Shore's politics having new relevance.

Positioning Shore within the Labour Party is also a challenge. Martin Crick's conclusion that 'Shore's own tradition of Labour politics was founded on an almost instinctive decency and honesty'[10] contains more than an element of truth – after all, he represented an impoverished constituency and it was evident that government action could benefit his constituents – but offers little in terms of positioning Shore on the right–left spectrum. The terms right and left (and centre) are useful journalistic shorthand for often complex realities. However, they also have meaning to those who use them at any given moment in time, even if those meanings are difficult to fathom to those outside the party. Essentially, at one point one wing will be in the ascendant and one declining. The term 'centre' is even harder to define, but if we see a political party as being like a bird with wings, there must also be a central body seeking to hold it together.[11]

Shore was loyal to the Labour Party and its current leadership for much of his career, but this was not a slavish loyalty. He disagreed with successive leaders on key issues of the day, such as with Hugh Gaitskell over unilateral nuclear disarmament (an issue on which he later changed his mind); with Harold Wilson on trade union reform; and with Jim Callaghan over the IMF Crisis. Positioning him is also challenging as he neither developed a socialist theory in the same fashion as Tony Crosland, nor garnered a following within the parliamentary party in the same way that Michael Foot or Roy Jenkins managed. Yet the lack of a 'Shoreite' body of work or grouping within the party should not prompt the dismissal of Shore's politics. In his publications, speeches and political achievements he represented a combination of qualities and values that are seldom embodied in one individual – a sincerely held British patriotism combined with an internationalism that transcended the European mainland; and a Keynesian and expansionist socialism to promote equality and individual liberty – all of which are different aspects of the Labour Party's makeup but rarely fused in the mind of one individual.

The conception of nationhood is a particularly interesting component of Shore's thinking. While post-Second World War Labour figures such as Clement Attlee, Ernie Bevin, Hugh Dalton and others were naturally patriotic, the notion in the Labour Party and more widely on the British left today has become sullied and tarnished; viewed as regressive, insidious and nativist. This change occurred in the latter part of the twentieth century and, therefore, as Shore's parliamentary career evolved, his values within the Labour Party became increasingly unfashionable. In part, it is why he is a neglected figure. His son emphasised this point: 'There's a Labour tradition that is captured by some of its other thinkers who have been written out of history ... a tradition that wasn't ashamed to say that "I'm patriotic", that strongly linked sovereignty with democratic self-government.'[12]

Shore was certainly not a right-wing figure in the Labour Party. He informed a Solidarity meeting that 'I speak to you as someone whose instinct and reason, whose philosophy and record have always been and will continue to be far nearer to the Left than to the Right of the

Party'.[13] Yet, while he had often adopted positions more associated with the left, it would also be a mistake to see him as 'of the left'. Instead it would be more accurate to view Shore as a man of the broad centre of the party. Throughout his career he aligned himself with quintessential figures of the centre such as Harold Wilson, who has rightly been seen as prioritising party unity above all else. Moreover, it was a centrism rooted in ideas. He was nuanced in his thinking about the root of socialism, and as a young man his opinions were formed by the anti-fascism of Arthur Koestler and the *News Chronicle*, and the Marxism of Harold Laski and John Strachey. His admiration for Stalin's Russia was tempered by Trotsky's *The Revolution Betrayed*, and later in life he would criticise the impracticality of the Marxist–Leninist creed, which he would associate with the Militant Tendency. By the end of the Second World War his thinking had been profoundly influenced by a particular reading of John Stuart Mill, stating: 'He, more than any other, convinced me that socialism was right. As devoted as he was to personal liberty, Mill acknowledged the area where personal freedom impinges on the freedom of others.'[14] The idea of the greatest good for the greatest number helped Shore resolve his conflicts with authority and discipline and he accepted what he described as a very British phenomenon: anti-authoritarianism tempered by the acceptance of discipline when the need for it has been agreed.[15]

Shore joined the Labour Party Research Department at the end of the Attlee era. There he was strongly influenced by such theorists of the welfare state as Richard Titmuss, Brian Abel-Smith, Peter Townsend and Michael Young. He began to be identified with the Bevanite left of the party, opposing Gaitskell both on general policy and on his proposals to redraft the party's commitment to wholesale public ownership.[16] In the 1960s, *The Observer* wrote that he was 'a man of the Centre who flirts with the Left without ever compromising himself too deeply',[17] while *The Economist* thought he was 'too intelligent to let his enthusiasm completely outrun his common sense'.[18] Indeed, this hostility to union leaders responsible for the 1978–79 'Winter of Discontent' was thought to place him on the party's right wing, and that impression was redoubled when he emerged as a multilateralist, expressing his opposition to unilateral nuclear disarmament at a time when Neil Kinnock was still committed to it. Also, he faced sustained efforts by the Militant Tendency to deselect him as he argued that the party must have clearly defined parameters. He was primarily seen as a figure of the right by this stage due to his decision to be joint chair of Labour Solidarity, a group firmly associated with the party's right wing. His innate patriotism was also at odds with many on the left of the party. As the Labour Party moved rightwards, first under Neil Kinnock, then John Smith and finally under Tony Blair, he grew more critical of the direction of travel, becoming further distanced from the leadership. His instincts were very much what would, from the mid-1990s, be described as 'Old Labour', with both his economic views and his Euroscepticism growing progressively distant from the mindset of those who now led the party. He was what David Goodhart was to later call a 'somewhere' in a party that was increasingly made up of 'anywheres' – at least in its upper echelons.[19]

Therefore, a case can be made that Shore remained rooted to much the same ideological territory that he had occupied since joining the party in 1948. While Aitken's assertion in the early 1990s that 'Shore has made his epic journey from right to left without moving even a toe muscle' was an exaggeration, he was correct to write, 'it is the party that has moved round him, not the other way round.'[20]

Given Shore's belief in parliamentary democracy, the sovereignty of Parliament, the historic rights of the British people and the exceptionalism of English history, BBC Radio 4 gave a succinct description of his politics. In early 1984, they considered that he came from the 'historical tradition of English radicalism, being close to the heart, if not the centre today, of the Labour Party ... a long-time Fabian-socialist'.[21]

A frequent theme of those we have interviewed and those who have written references to him is that he was a man of considerable distinction. He was clever, with an esteemed academic record, including being a member of the elite and secretive Cambridge Apostles, before serving as head of the Labour Party Research Department. He also wrote a number of works, such as *Leading the Left* and *Separate Ways*, which have been judged to be impressive and, as Anthony Howard assessed, his 'intellectual honesty' shone through in *Leading the Left*. However, as will be shown in subsequent chapters, combining a considerable intellect with the cut-and-thrust of politics did not come naturally. Consequently, there is some merit in Howard's assessment that 'Shore was always too much the don in politics to be a wholly effective operator', possessing 'that most fatal flaw in any politician, the gift of detachment'.[22] His powers of public speaking have also been widely noted. Aitken affirmed that Shore's desire to express his patriotism 'transformed him from a hesitant speaker into a genuine orator with distinct Churchillian cadences. Few MPs ... are so skilled at projecting intellectual power and controlled passion.'[23] Although not without political skill, as seen for instance in the way he fought off challenges from within his own constituency party, he fared badly in the two leadership contests in which he stood. He held to firm convictions, to the extent that his contemporary Roy Hattersley wrote that he 'was a man of principle who always (often to the consternation of his friends) refused to compromise',[24] and his principles were reinforced by his sense of loyalty, particularly to his party and country. Speaking in 1983, two years after the breakaway Social Democratic Party had emerged, he affirmed: 'the Labour Party has those title deeds to democratic socialism in this country. I will never renounce those title deeds and therefore I will never abandon the Labour Party.'[25] He always sought to defend what he saw as Britain's interests, something that stretched from his military service with the RAF at the end of the Second World War through to debates over whether Britain should join the euro currency prior to his death in 2001. Finally, although he has, as we will argue, clear ministerial achievements, they are not widely remembered to this day. After charting all of these developments in the main narrative of the book, we will offer an overall evaluation in the concluding chapter.

The coming chapters will follow a broadly chronological framework. Where there were several overlapping aspects, these have been split into separate chapters for clarity.

The key questions that the book addresses are:

- What motivated Shore in his approach to politics?
- What impact did Shore have?
- What is his lasting legacy?

Several sources have been utilised to write this biography, both primary and secondary, and the key primary sources are interviews and archives. Interviews have been conducted with a number of Shore's contemporaries inside and outside the Labour Party, while the main archival sources utilised are Shore's own papers, which are deposited at the London School of Economics, as well as the relevant government papers at the National Archives. Parliamentary reports (Hansard) and newspaper articles have also been of considerable benefit. This has been supplemented with the extensive use of published sources, including the memoirs and biographies of Shore's contemporaries, historical studies of the Labour Party and wider surveys of relevant periods in British political history.

We hope that the biography will fill a significant gap within the literature of British politics and political history, and will re-establish a forgotten but important figure who – in the context of Brexit – is once again highly relevant.

1

EARLY LIFE

YOUTH

PETER DAVID SHORE WAS born in the Two Bears Hotel in Great Yarmouth, Norfolk, on 20 May 1924. He was the youngest of Eleanor and Robert Norman Shore's three children. Robert was a teenage runaway turned Merchant Navy captain who served as a lieutenant in the Royal Naval Reserve during the Great War. By the time of Peter's birth, Robert was in his fourth year as the licensee of the hotel, which had previously been owned by his in-laws. He wasn't a natural hotelier; that was the preserve of his wife Eleanor's parents, who also owned a hotel in London. Whereas Robert was an adventurer, Eleanor was comfortably middle-class and reportedly never took up employment. Neither parent was remembered as political in any sense, though both shared an enduring patriotism.

The onset of the Great Depression would put an end to the family's time as hoteliers and to Peter's Norfolk childhood. Unemployment in

Britain shot up to 20 per cent by 1930 and the following year Robert Shore gave up his role as licensee and went back into the Merchant Navy. Unable to cope, Eleanor sent Peter and his brother Robert ahead to stay with relatives in Liverpool while she stayed with her daughter, Gwen, to wind up the family's Norfolk life.

With the hotel sold, Eleanor Shore headed north and moved her three children to the Mossley Hill area of Liverpool. Peter later revealed that the move from Norfolk to Merseyside had not been easy, but that he did not suffer as much as his older siblings.[1] Gwen and Robert were bullied for their accents while Peter, being the youngest, seems to have been more adaptable and suffered less. Neil Kinnock noticed in later years that when Peter became particularly passionate about a point he sometimes slipped back into Scouse phrasing.[2]

In Liverpool, Shore attended Quarry Bank High School in leafy Allerton. It is perhaps best remembered now as the school of a young John Lennon, though Lennon didn't achieve the same academic heights at the school as Shore had a generation previously. Quarry Bank was founded in 1921 and its first headmaster was a pioneering Old Etonian bachelor, Richard Fitzroy Bailey. Bailey had been an assistant head at the prestigious Shrewsbury School and modelled Quarry Bank along the same lines, with prefects and monitors largely responsible for pupil discipline, and the emphasis firmly on sport, nationalism and the Empire. Bailey was in charge throughout Shore's school years, a period in which Quarry Bank gained the reputation of being relaxed and liberal for its day, so much so that rumour held that no boy had ever been expelled. Not that Shore was ever in danger of such a move, as he was remembered there as 'a very nice boy, energetic and self-possessed'.[3]

Bailey focused on developing the boys' social consciousness by instilling into them an awareness of the unequal society in which they lived and how it was their duty to reach out to the poorest. It was no surprise that Shore, like most boys who went through Quarry Bank under Bailey's supervision, left with 'an affection for the school and a great respect for him'.[4]

Another future Labour MP, Bill Rodgers, was a fellow pupil at Quarry Bank, though four years Shore's junior. Although Rodgers didn't know Shore well at school, he remembered him as a prefect who cut a 'slight, rather shy figure'.[5] Shy he may have been, but that didn't stop Shore joining the Debating Society, having fostered a consuming interest in politics and history, and seeking political solutions to Europe's problems. Here he made his early speeches and began to develop his distinctive Churchillian speaking style. In a 1987 interview Shore reflected on those years:

> There was so obviously in the 1930s, the period of my boyhood, so much waste and human misery and lack of response to human needs that it seemed to me that a great effort of collective provision of services was required to meet those needs... Therefore, I asked what alternative political philosophies and political powers of action were available to us. Broadly these thoughts led me on the main road to socialism and the socialist solution.[6]

As a sixth former Shore read widely, including 'a great deal of Marx', but it wasn't Marx who appeared to have had a lasting influence on Shore, as he later explained:

> I found John Stuart Mill's *On Liberty* a most absorbing essay which

forced you all the time to think about distinctions between what he called 'self-regarding' and 'other-regarding' actions. In other words, between the legitimate area of self-fulfilment and self-advancement and the larger area where you had to consider yourself in relation to others, where your benefit might be the loss of benefit to them, your freedom might be an invasion of their freedom. It made me think about the working out of the balance in society between what was proper for collective action, and the advancement of collective freedom, and for one's own individual freedom. It seemed to set out the problem there in a more terse and dramatic way, better than I have seen it in any other work.[7]

Despite this absorption in politics and a developing social conscious-ness, Shore hadn't expressed any outward party political sympathies. Some of the boys had already nailed their colours by sixth form, be it Labour, Liberal, Conservative or Communist. But Shore wasn't a Tory nationalist like his younger brother, nor was he particularly en-amoured with the Liberals. The Labour Party, he thought, 'seemed lumbering and not all that attractive' at that time.[8] There was an almost natural draw to Communism, as there was for many on the British left in the 1930s, but Shore's reading drew him back from the possibility of becoming a Soviet fellow traveller. It was Arthur Koes-tler's *Darkness at Noon*, which Shore read as a sixteen-year-old, that had a powerful impact on him for its

remarkable critique, insight into and indictment of Stalin's Russia… It was rather important, because in socialism at that stage there were attractions from the revolutionary left, the communist left, the principal attraction to people of my generation being that they had been in the front line of resistance to right-wing dictatorships. That was their principal claim as it were. It was reading people like Koestler that, if the temptation did ever arise, showed me the answers to it. Also, other books on the left influenced me in the same direction, like Trotsky's *The Revolution Betrayed*, again from a different point of view, of course, but providing major insights into Soviet society and the obvious repression and tyranny which it was exercising.[9]

By the end of his sixth form education Shore appears to have fashioned the democratic socialist politics that would essentially stay with him for the rest of his life.

CAMBRIDGE, THE WAR AND LOVE

Richard Bailey had spotted an academic ability in Shore that led him to recommend that his student apply to Cambridge. As an ex-Cambridge man Bailey encouraged his brightest pupils to put themselves forward and Shore was awarded a scholarship to read History as an exhibitioner at King's College.

The famed British author and academic Noel Annan, then a Cambridge don, regarded Shore one of the intellectuals of the era, so, maybe unsurprisingly, Shore was invited to join the Apostles, 'perhaps the most distinguished secret society in the world' and so exclusive that it was known simply as 'the Society'.[10] The Apostles had been founded in 1820 with a sense of 'intimate brotherhood' and consisted of anywhere between six and twelve members – whose names were not disclosed – made up from among the brightest minds at Cambridge. How Shore came to join we cannot be sure, but he may well have been recommended by Annan or his former headmaster at Quarry Bank.

In his biography of John Maynard Keynes, Roy Harrod provided a snapshot of the Apostles:

> For the Society, truth was the paramount objective, and absolute intellectual integrity the means of achieving it. There was certainly a feeling that Apostles were different from ordinary mortals. For purposes of practical life, an Apostle had also, of course, to be an ordinary mortal; and it might be that he would set himself to plan and contrive in order to win position and influence in the world. That was a matter of indifference to the Society, not of reproach... As regards the ambitious, the saving clause would be that at heart they would be seeking to promote what they honestly believed to be a good cause.[11]

The Apostles were drawn almost exclusively from Trinity, though a small elite from further colleges including King's, of which Shore was considered one, were admitted. By the time of Shore's arrival Trinity had become 'the powerhouse of intellectual Marxism in Britain'.[12] Both Guy Burgess and Kim Philby, later exposed as Soviet spies, had read History at Trinity and were members of the Apostles before Shore's time. There is no evidence to show that Shore was implicated in pro-Soviet activities like some of his predecessor Apostles, nor does he seem to have been a terribly active Apostle at that. There was certainly some lingering suspicion, though. As we'll see later, Harold Wilson ordered extra background checks on Shore before bringing him into government, although this appears to have been, in the words of Neil Kinnock, 'an Oxford man's suspicion'.[13]

By this time Britain was in a state of total war and many young men had to suspend their university education to take part. Shore was desperate to do his bit and volunteered for the RAF in 1942, despite the high death rate; his eyes were set on becoming a pilot but, to his great annoyance, he failed to get his wings. Instead he held the rank of War Substantive Flying Officer in the Navigators of the RAF Volunteer Reserve. 'He thought the air force was wonderful,' remembers Shore's widow, Liz, 'except when they threw him out because he failed to put his wheels down. They moved him to Canada to retrain as a navigator and then he came home early. If the war in Europe hadn't have stopped when it did, he would have been dropping bombs on Germany.'[14] After returning from Canada, Shore was stationed in India for the last months of the war, and this experience fostered in him an enduring love of the Commonwealth and India in particular. Though Shore got through the war, his father Robert was torpedoed by a German U-boat and, despite surviving the initial hit and being rescued, died some days later.

Shore returned to Cambridge from India and became an active member of the Labour Club, but still without joining the Labour Party. Though Shore had his admirers and was generally recognised to be a talented thinker, he 'had no sense of how to pass exams' and did 'all the wrong things to pass a degree';[15] as a result he left Cambridge with a Third in History. Throughout his university career, he had spent more and more of his time reading tracts on economics and further hours with the Labour Club. He was also still linked to the Apostles, though after meeting his future wife he had little space left for 'the Society'.

THE LABOUR PARTY

In 1948 Peter Shore effectively got married twice; first to Elizabeth and second to the Labour Party. After Cambridge the Shores moved to London into a two-room flat just off All Saints Street, remembered fondly despite the bed bugs and the rats and Peter's papers strewn everywhere. While Peter sought work, he filled his spare time reading political works and policy papers. Only on holiday did Peter read fiction, and even then it was curated by Liz. Peter also developed a love for opera. The Shores' flat was one Tube stop away from Covent Garden and, despite knowing nothing about opera, they took advantage of the cheap seats and thus began a lifelong passion.

When Peter finally joined Labour, it was still the party of Attlee and the great reforming Labour government. Despite having some reservations, Shore said, 'When I began to think seriously about my activity in politics, quite clearly the obvious party to join was the Labour Party.'[16] He hunted for a parliamentary seat almost immediately and was adopted for the West Cornwall constituency of St Ives for the 1950 general election. St Ives had never (and has never yet) been won by a Labour candidate. Nevertheless, Shore increased Labour's share of the vote by 3.5 per cent to a respectable 30.7 per cent in a three-way contest, losing to the Conservative and National Liberal candidate Greville Howard, despite his campaign slogan 'Shore to Win!'

Though the result didn't take him to Westminster, it did give him more credibility in Labour circles. He didn't stand in the 1951 general election, instead concentrating on his new job in the Labour Research Department (LRD) in a position that would, Shore hoped, be stimulating in the short term, giving him a valuable insight into policy, while in the long term helping to clear the way to a safe parliamentary seat. In the

end, it took thirteen more years for Shore, and Labour, to be elected to
Parliament, a much longer apprenticeship than Shore had envisaged.
However, Labour's research department was described by Shore as

> a very important centre for thinking, largely because, with the excep-
> tion of the Fabian Society, which only publishes the individual views
> of its contributors, there is no other. You may get ideas and stimulus
> coming from well-informed, weekly papers of the left, and that is very
> helpful. But if you look around, there is no other place for the continu-
> ous thinking on the problems of democratic socialism and the practical
> problems of the society and the government of the day than in the
> Labour Party Research Department.[17]

Shore was working in the LRD as Labour left office with the demise
of Attlee's short-lived second government. After Labour's 1951 defeat
there was a lack of the kind of active and innovative leadership needed
in opposition. Even though many saw Attlee as old hat, he stubborn-
ly hung on to the leadership, mainly to stymie Herbert Morrison's
chances of replacing him. Andrew Thorpe writes:

> The years from 1951 to 1955 were to be one of the most dismal periods
> in the history of the Labour Party. From a position of potential strength,
> the party sank deeper and deeper into a mire of squabbling, with poor
> leadership and a lack of clear policy, in the face of an increasingly self-
> confident Conservative Party.[18]

Shore sought to inject some urgency into the Labour case. In 1952, he
wrote *The Real Nature of Conservatism*, exploring Conservatism as an
ideology, the Conservative Party's relationship with democracy and

'New Conservatism'. He also posed the question of why, in the era of universal suffrage, 'so large a portion of the electorate, many of whom are neither wealthy nor privileged, have been recruited for a cause which is not their own?' Shore's answer – that it rested on the development of propaganda techniques in manipulating public opinion and on irrational impulses in the shaping of political attitudes[19] – is unconvincing. He dissected recent Conservative statements and came to the conclusion that the 'New Conservatism' formed after the 1945 general election defeat had the same objectives as the 'Old Conservatism'. Consequently:

> The struggle against the New Conservatism is essentially a continuation of that against the Old. The Conservative Party today may be more intelligent, more sophisticated, better turned out than the pre-war Conservative Party; but it shares with it the same beliefs in authority, inequality and a class society. In the advance towards a socialist society these are the obstacles which must be overcome.[20]

Left-wing discontent was growing and by the time of the 1952 party conference the left won six out of the seven Constituency Labour Party (CLP) places on the National Executive Committee (NEC). In practice this meant very little, but it did heighten the sense of division within the party. Shore was identified (possibly by Harold Wilson) early on as being sympathetic to the Bevanites and began to attract support from the Labour left as a man to watch. Bill Rodgers gives us a vivid and important portrait of Shore in this period:

> During my Fabian time I found [Shore] a considerable political operator, with an unfailing device for making points to which people would listen. Pushing back a displaced lock of hair and raising his

voice, often with a half-laugh of amused discovery, he would draw attention to an apparent paradox or ask a sharp question. Such inter-ventions won him attention and respect, and I admired his skill while ungenerously resenting the reputation that it gave him for rather great-er wisdom than me.[21]

When the general secretary position of the Fabian Society became vacant in 1953, Rodgers, as assistant secretary, was a shoo-in. However, the Bevanites wanted to contest the position and, with the support of Harold Wilson, Richard Crossman, Ian Mikardo and Tommy Balogh, Shore was put forward against Rodgers. As expected, Rodgers won, but Shore took a respectable third of the vote and, according to the victorious candidate, 'appeared to bear no grudge'.[22] It all helped to build Shore's profile in the party and more doors began to open for him.

Next, he joined a group of mainly Oxford graduates, imaginatively called 'The Group', who met to discuss Labour matters over lunch. Although as a Cambridge man Shore was an outsider, he was invit-ed by its founders Dick Taverne and Bill Rodgers, which, despite his standing as the Bevanite candidate for the general secretary of the Fabian Society, shows that he was considered a rising star in the Labour Party, as well as a man of important and original ideas. It seems as if Taverne and Rodgers were attempting to poach Shore from the Bevanites and, although Shore met weekly with The Group, he quite quickly broke away when he entered what Rodgers termed 'the heart of the Wilson circle'.[23]

Despite being seen by some as a radical and a left-winger, Shore was viewed by others as an early Gaitskellite, and he certainly mixed in those circles. Through the war years Hugh Gaitskell had risen to become a high-ranking civil servant and entered the Attlee government

in February 1946. Four years later he was appointed Chancellor. His
first Budget imposed charges on glasses and dentures, which caused
the resignation of both Harold Wilson and Aneurin Bevan in 1951.
For the traditional Labour left, Gaitskell was a man who had no desire to
further extend socialism in Britain in a form they recognised; the best the
left could hope for was that he would consolidate the gains of the Attlee
government. He attacked the Bevanites, of which Shore was considered
a supporter, as 'a group of frustrated journalists' who undermined the
Attlee leadership and took direction from the *Daily Worker*, a paper of
the Communist Party of Great Britain. Gaitskell himself condemned
Attlee for not taking on the critical voices of the left and enjoyed the
support of right-wing union leaders Arthur Deakin (TGWU), Tom
Williamson (NUGMW) and William Lowther (NUM). Nevertheless,
Shore was excited both by the change of pace Gaitskell brought to the
leadership when he succeeded Attlee in 1955, as well as by his awareness
of the political implications of new technologies. Shore wrote:

> Unlike Attlee, Gaitskell was very much interested in personal and party
> projection. He did not confine his newspaper reading to *The Times*!
> Nor did he begin by scanning reports on play in the county and Test
> cricket matches. Indeed, Gaitskell kept a close watch on the papers and
> cultivated good relations not only with the parliamentary lobby but with
> newspaper editors as well. Sensibly, he recognised that the media was
> at the start of its TV revolution and that it was essential for a political
> leader to be able to use and command the new medium.[24]

Gaitskell recognised the moderniser in Shore and sent him to observe
the effect of television on the Rochdale by-election of February 1958.
The journalist and broadcaster Ludovic Kennedy was standing as the

Liberal candidate following the death of the sitting Conservative MP. Kennedy intended to use his television experience to increase coverage of the campaign and himself. Two debates between the candidates were broadcast by Granada Television and the BBC televised interviews with voters. Though Labour's Jack McCann won the seat with 22,133 votes, the Liberal candidate Kennedy gained 17,603, the highest Liberal vote for three decades. Shore believed television would change British politics and that the Labour Party had to act quickly to be ahead of the curve. He shared his thoughts with Tony Benn, who recorded in his diary: 'I found him very receptive to the general theme that television is the greatest and most important thing that has happened to British politics.'[25]

Shore now found himself allied to Benn as a moderniser of the party's campaigning who would bring it into the television age. They lunched regularly on the terrace of Parliament, discussing how to make the party a more effective campaigning machine, improve electoral strategy and tactics, and, most importantly, how to sell Hugh Gaitskell as a potential Prime Minister.[26] Douglas Jay and Dick Crossman were frequent visitors to both men and, as Crossman had a habit of surrounding himself with bright young people, Shore was clearly a man to watch for the future. Shore and Benn now met daily for morning coffee as the two acted as sounding boards for each other's ideas. Benn said of the morning meetings: 'It's the best part of the day and he always stimulates my mind immensely.'[27]

MEANS AND ENDS

However, rather rapidly Shore started to question his own trust in Gaitskell and began to move away from the ultra-modernising position proposed by the likes of Tony Crosland. Crosland took a revisionist line that looked beyond nationalisation as a means of reducing inequality. Gaitskell needed little persuasion, and indeed already had a reputation as a right-winger who now believed that the methods used by the Attlee government were unpalatable to the British electorate. The intellectual case for revisionism was made by Crosland in his major work, *The Future of Socialism* (1956).[28] He argued that the nature of the British economy had been so radically altered, both by longer-term trends (i.e. the transfer of power from business owners to managers, trade unions and the state) and the reforms of the 1945–51 Labour government, that Marxist analysis was now irrelevant – Britain had become post-capitalist. In order to make Britain into a more socialist country, there still needed to be a more decisive move in the direction of equality. However, it was thought that this could be achieved without further public ownership. Nationalisation was no longer a socialist priority: it was now a means to rather than the end goal of socialism, and not a particularly important one at that. Instead, a reduction in income and wealth inequalities could be achieved through fiscal measures, while the key to greater social equality was provided by comprehensive schools. Shore disagreed with this analysis and in his writings from this time tried to articulate an alternative model of socialism, one which continued to rely on the extension of public ownership.

Shore assisted the economist A. A. Rogow in his study of the industrial policies of the 1945–51 Labour government, published in 1955.[29] The study was a largely technical survey of the policies of the period and the obstacles to achieving the government's objectives. However, in its conclusion, the book allies firmly with the left. The government's policies, it says, amounted to a compromise between the forces of labour and capital, and the limits of its agenda were clear when it came to the nationalisation of steel. Industry was willing to accept the welfare state, but only because it drew a clear line between that and socialism – indeed, some commentators, not least on the radial left, felt that the welfare state was a way to keep workers content rather than transferring power from capital to labour. Consequently, by 1951 Britain had reached a condition of stalemate between socialism and capitalism: 'so viewed the welfare state represents an adjustment of conflicting social and economic interests which is acceptable to the major elements that comprise British society.'[30] There was growing pressure for further reform in a socialist direction from the grassroots of the party, 'to whom the welfare state brought material but not spiritual satisfaction'.[31] The Labour Party 'must reformulate its basic principles' in order to meet this challenge, Rogow's study concluded.[32]

Shore believed that an extension of public ownership was necessary for the pursuit of greater equality, and he believed that the capitalist sector remained too large: 'The continued existence of a capitalist sector of the present size cannot be reconciled with any significant further progress towards equality. For this reason, if no other, we cannot be content with fiscal remedies. It is necessary therefore to take another look at that old scarecrow, public ownership.'[33] He did not oppose the continued existence of a private sector, but thought that the public sector should be sufficiently large enough to set the direction of economic activity, rather than picking up unprofitable activities as the Attlee government had done.[34] The nation had its own interests, which often differed from those of industry: 'the nation has objectives in the economic field which are wider than, different from and sometimes opposed to those of industry'.[35] Moreover, the case for further public ownership was justified by the trend away from competition within the private sector. This was caused by growth in the size of corporations, a trend also noted by Crosland. But whereas Crosland felt that this allowed a more public-minded managerial class to pursue goals other than purely profit maximisation, for Shore it called into question the necessity for shareholders: 'The private shareholder has not only ceased to be indispensable to the economic system, he has become virtually functionless.'[36]

As Shore moved away from Gaitskell politically, he mischievously used the Leader of the Opposition's rhetoric to put forward radical policies that Gaitskell was then forced to water down. A key example of this was Shore's writing of the *Industry and Society* paper (1957) at Gaitskell's request. Shore said later: 'Since Gaitskell had himself claimed that "socialism is about equality" and that existing inequalities of wealth and income were unacceptable, the sooner private ownership was contracted and public ownership extended, the sooner would Gaitskell's own goal of greater equality be reached.'[37]

Shore's draft was unequivocal. Of large firms he wrote that they 'have clearly achieved an independent life and purpose of their own. So much so that one must ask the question: is there a case, in these large firms, for private ownership in its present form? Is there indeed, any case at all for private ownership of these firms?' For Shore, if shareholders no longer had control and capitalists no longer took risks, why should they be rewarded? He was also concerned that companies were amassing profits without reinvesting them. So, with no risk-taking nor reinvestment of profits, just what was the point of the capitalist? He noted:

in the past, socialist thinkers argued that the value of land increased steadily and automatically over the years, thus bringing to its owners a completely unearned increment. This led to the proposals for public ownership of land, or for tax measures designed to remove this unearned income ... it can fairly be said that many of the characteristics once ascribed to land are now possessed by the equity shares of industry.[38]

Shore's remedy was to take the top 500 companies into public ownership via gradual government share purchases, which meant there would be no sudden shock to the economy, but rather an incremental nationalisation. This wasn't the revisionist break from nationalisation that Gaitskell wanted, despite Shore framing it quite clearly on the leader's own statements. Gaitskell sent a heavily annotated copy of the draft to Crosland with instructions to revise the conclusions. Crosland was then neither an MP nor on the NEC, and few were made aware of the origins of the revisions at the time. Crosland watered down Shore's proposals to a mere government shareholding in the major companies, not full ownership, and the left saw this as a retreat from socialist principles. Under a future Gaitskell government, only road haulage and steel would be brought back into public ownership, having been privatised by the Conservatives, and private rented housing would be brought into municipal ownership.

Crosland's new but ambiguous conclusions allowed the report to be interpreted however the reader saw fit. Gaitskell and Crosland were able to quote the document and give the impression that they intended to nationalise little, whereas Michael Foot called it 'the most powerful, up-to-date statement of the case for public ownership issued officially by the Labour Party since 1945', although he changed his mind when he heard Bevan was cool about the document.[39] Some saw through Gaitskell's neutering of Shore's original draft. Crosland's amended version even managed to unite Jennie Lee, Herbert Morrison and Manny Shinwell, by no means natural political allies, who attacked the absence of a firm commitment to public ownership of the commanding heights of the economy, which they claimed demonstrated an ambivalence to traditional socialism. Lee fired that it was 'too pink, too blue, too yellow'[40] and *Tribune* also condemned the document.[41]

Nevertheless, the 1957 party conference adopted *Industry and Society* almost four to one. Gaitskell had managed to mute the dissent from the left by forming a sub-committee to consider the report, which included Ian Mikardo and Aneurin Bevan. Both were the most likely to criticise the final draft for its less than firm commitment to nationalisation, yet both displayed little more than a nonchalant attitude towards it.[42]

Crossman recorded in his diary that Shore's original document had been 'extensively redrafted by the office at Transport House, removing most of its radical trimmings and making it a great deal more reactionary'.[43] He also noted the reaction the report received:

> There was a good deal of indignation, not only among Tribune circles but also outside, in the constituencies and, even more important, in the Parliamentary Party, where what you might call the working-class elements had taken the occasion to assume that the Wykehamists were corrupting the Gospel by a too-clever-by-half intellectualism.[44]

Crossman's 'Wykehamists', a term referring to former pupils of Winchester College, were Gaitskell and his coterie of Crosland and Roy Jenkins. Furthermore, as the Gaitskellites put increased faith in opinion polls, to the cost of what Shore thought were key tenets of Labour's politics (nationalisation and Clause IV), Shore distanced himself from Gaitskell. He felt that polling was 'a powerful – too powerful – influence in [Gaitskell's] thinking and initiatives'.[45] Ultimately, though, Shore felt that Gaitskell 'was simply not on the same emotional wavelength, nor could he artificially contrive to be, as the majority of active Labour Party members'.[46] On top of this, Gaitskell had no connection to the working class. He was a product of the upper-middle-class elite, being public school and Oxbridge educated. This made it simpler, according to Shore, for him to become 'almost a hate figure, variously accused as a traitor to socialism, a "cold warrior" and a nuclear rearmer for which crimes he was berated and abused'.[47]

Shore's separation from the revisionists was also evidenced in his contribution to a set of essays edited by Norman MacKenzie, *Conviction*, published in 1958. The essayists wanted to see something more radical than revisionism, which they felt was too complacent about contemporary conditions. Far from being a post-capitalist era as Crosland had argued in *The Future of Socialism*,[48] it was in fact a stalemate situation, and a further push towards socialism was required.[49] Shore's essay can be regarded as a direct response to Crosland's thesis. Like Crosland, he drew on James Burnham's idea of the 'managerial revolution' to show that corporate ownership and control were becoming distinct, but argued that this was nothing to be complacent about since it created a new form of inequality: 'What we are witnessing', Shore wrote, 'is the rise of a new order which in certain respects is far closer to medieval society than to the capitalism of the past two hundred years. Indeed, the closest analogy to the modern corporation is a survival from pre-capitalist days – the Church.'[50] Shore did not 'want a society in which an elite, viewing the world through Board Room windows, makes the big decisions, collects the big rewards, while the mass of men deprived of power and responsibility dig their gardens or watch the telly'.[51] There was still much to be done, therefore, to bring about socialism in Britain. Shore in this period was clearly to the left in Labour circles.

CLAUSE IV CONTROVERSY

According to Benn, Shore had begun to sketch out some ideas for a book about modern mass society, though this was abandoned when a general election was announced for 8 October 1959. When the two men met to discuss Labour's prospects, both were pessimistic, and Benn told Shore that his chances in Halifax – the seat Shore had been selected for – were only 'slightly better than average'.[52] The general election saw the Conservative Party cruise to its third successive victory and Labour suffered a huge blow as Harold Macmillan increased his majority in the Commons.

After the defeat in 1959, Shore was very much seen as one of the modernisers with a bright future ahead of him. With Benn he formed the 1964 Club, 'to be based', according to Benn, 'on the simple objective of doing to the Party what we know has to be done – modernise and overhaul and make it a vehicle for progressive action in our society'. The club would include David Ennals, Anthony Howard, Ivan Yates, Gerald Kaufman, Shirley Williams, Reg Prentice and Dick Marsh, as well as Benn and Shore.[53]

Responding to the 1959 defeat, Gaitskell saw a solution in attacking some of the foundation stones of the Labour Party. Clause IV of the Labour Party's constitution committed it

To secure for the workers by hand or by brain the full fruits of their industry and the most equitable distribution thereof that may be possible upon the basis of the common ownership of the means of production, distribution, and exchange, and the best obtainable system of popular administration and control of each industry or service.[54]

Shore reflected later:

Hugh Gaitskell felt he had to react to three successive election defeats in a dramatic way and to show that the Labour Party was a modern party which wasn't stuck with old commitments, so he turned on Clause 4 as a symbolic representation or representative of Labour's past and he attempted to topple it. That would obviously have been a symbolic gesture of immense importance. But parties live by their faith and their history as much as they do by their requirements of the present... I thought it was a great mistake and actively opposed it.[55]

He tried to urge caution and asked that Gaitskell take more time to think the policy through but was ignored. 'He wasn't a good person to reconcile differences', remembered Shore; 'he was not a concilia-tor in any sense and his strength lay in his strong combative instinct and the feeling that he was right.'[56] As such, Gaitskell was loath to accept any counterargument and the move greatly antagonised divi-sions in the party, as Shore had warned. Wilson, considered by some as a possible successor to Gaitskell, famously remarked, 'We were being asked to take Genesis out of the Bible.'[57]

By the spring of 1960 Shore felt that the party leadership was in crisis. He thought the party was unable to connect with the younger generation of voters now emerging and if Labour lost this generation, he feared, the party would not survive long enough to be there when they sought a change from the Tories. Although Shore, as well as Benn, was at this point seen as being in the political centre of the party, he felt that Gaitskell was failing to lead a united socialist party. This could only result in further defeat, he thought, and Gaitskell was, in Shore's words, 'an authentic and unapologetic figure of the Right'.[58]

Shore now definitively moved towards Wilson and backed him in his unsuccessful leadership election bid in 1960, with Gaitskell winning two thirds of the vote. Shore admired Wilson's pronounced conviction in the use of state intervention to reduce inequality. Both believed in better commercial relations with the USSR and in combating the spread of Communism by supporting poorer nations who may be tempted to turn to Moscow.

Nevertheless, despite a growing distrust between Shore and Gaitskell, he was appointed head of the Labour Research Department following the 1959 election defeat. Though technically it was an NEC appointment, Gaitskell had to give his unofficial blessing. Shore noted that his 'relationship with Hugh Gaitskell went through different phases. He thought that I was rather over-radical, over-left and that was quite a problem because he tended to be a bit distrustful.'[59] Gaitskell had taken the advice of Crosland, who advised the Labour leader to make use of Shore's ability as a speech writer, but the Gaitskellites were wary; any paper or speech produced by Shore was sent to Crosland to be vetted first. Wilson's biographer Ben Pimlott referred to Shore as 'a one man Wilsonian fifth column within the ... Labour Party headquarters'.[60] But Shore was not anti-Gaitskell per se; he supported him against Anthony Greenwood in the 1961 leadership election and soon an issue arose that would ideologically unite them.

EUROPE

On the issue of Europe and the Common Market, Shore and Gaitskell were instinctively much closer. Shore later recalled:

> I became directly involved in the Britain and Europe question in 1961 when the then Prime Minister, Harold Macmillan, made his historic announcement that the UK – in total reversal of its policies pursued between 1945 and 1960 – was now applying to join the European Community (the Common Market) as a full member. The then leader of the Labour Party, Hugh Gaitskell, at once asked my colleague, David Ennals, the International Secretary, and myself, as head of the Labour Party Research Department, to examine the issues and present a preliminary paper for consideration by himself and his parliamentary colleagues. It was then, with a genuinely open mind but with the background knowledge of events that all thinking people of my age group possessed, that I read that basic document, the Rome Treaty – it was difficult then even to obtain a copy in the English language – and made my first preliminary analysis of its contents.[61]

Liz Shore remembered the Treaty of Rome as a huge document and trip hazard which lived on their bedroom floor for weeks as Peter analysed it page by page every night. There was even a standing joke in political circles that Peter was the only person to have read the document in full.[62]

Gaitskell, like Shore, was a British patriot and felt an unshakeable loyalty to the Commonwealth, and Shore had been struck by the unanimous opposition of Commonwealth socialist leaders to Europe at a meeting called by Gaitskell in the autumn of 1962. He was also

shocked by the terms of entry. The deterioration of relations with
the spokesmen of the six EEC countries had warned him off further,
despite being initially impressed by the political case made by Roy
Jenkins. Shore wrote the policy statement that lay behind Gaitskell's
party conference speech in Brighton,[63] in which Gaitskell warned
that entry into Europe would be 'selling the Commonwealth down
the river' and 'the end of a thousand years of history'.[64] In the stuffy
hall of the Brighton ice rink, Gaitskell's speech was uncompromising,
and George Brown commented that he sounded 'emotionally totally
opposed to Britain's having any involvement with the continent of
Europe'.[65] The speech caused friction with erstwhile Gaitskellites
and pro-Europeans Roy Jenkins and Tony Crosland. They found
the patriotic content unpalatable,[66] though what particularly irked
the pair was Gaitskell's reference to the sacrifices of Commonwealth
troops in the Great War: 'we, at least, do not intend to forget Vimy
Ridge and Gallipoli'.

However, on 4 January 1963 Gaitskell was rushed to hospital. He
died two weeks later, just four days before the resumption of Parliament. Shore later reflected that Gaitskell had numerous qualities
– 'honesty, courage, intelligence, reliability, judgement, loyalty and
industry' – and that he 'held firm to his principles and was intellectu-
ally convinced of the case for equality, liberty and international law'.
Strikingly, it was not these qualities, standards or principles, nor his
focus on the achievable rather than the ultimate goals, that marked
Gaitskell as a leader of the right; instead it was his inability to recognise and respect the other qualities of the left:

What was missing was the poetry, not the prose; the politics of the
heart, not the head; that special brand of romanticism and idealism that

motivates so much of the Labour movement; the belief in the infinite possibilities of improvement, the perfectibility of man, the brotherhood that should unite the human race: a glimpse of Jerusalem. And that special abomination for an economic and social system that sets man against man. The imagination to see, and the will to accomplish, a new society.[67]

Like most commentators, Shore believed that 'Gaitskell died at the height of his powers'.[68]

FINDING A SEAT

Gaitskell's death was a chance for Labour to regroup. Since its defeat in 1959 the party had been torn by divisions. According to Shore, Gaitskell was 'very much a right-wing intellectual' who 'persuaded himself that victory next time depended upon a dramatic and major renunciation of the Party's traditional commitment to "common ownership"'.[69] In Shore's view, it was the Common Market issue, which cut across the left–right divide within Labour, that won over most of the left but had split the Gaitskellites from top to bottom.

Only two men were ever in serious contention to replace Gaitskell: George Brown and the shadow Foreign Secretary, Harold Wilson. Jim Callaghan had reluctantly been persuaded to stand and, as expected, was eliminated in the first round, and Wilson won the second round with 144 votes to 103, in what was a decisive victory. 'The vote in part reflected', Shore thought, 'the traditional Left-versus-Right division in the Party but Wilson was able to gain support well outside his base on the Left by attracting a substantial part of the anti-Market vote and still others by his outstanding competence as a front-bench spokesman.'[70] Wilson inherited a fragile party but kept on the Gaitskellite shadow Cabinet, which avoided any immediate divisions.

Previously, both Shore and Crossman had been very supportive of Tony Benn in pushing for Labour to be at the forefront of television campaigning. Wilson took up the idea when he became leader and entrusted the venture to the three. Regular campaign meetings were held throughout 1963 to discuss an election strategy to win over a younger generation of voters. Crossman came over quite defeatist from the outset, though Benn and Shore believed Labour could win. Wilson shared Shore and Benn's enthusiasm and, as well as significant campaign planning, they drafted proposals for Wilson's first 100 days in Downing Street. The 'war book', as it came to be known, was 'a book of immediate action to be undertaken as soon as Labour comes to power', according to Benn's diary entry.[71] Shore drafted the document and was entrusted with passing it informally to Wilson. Shore, Benn and Crossman persuaded Wilson to set up a 'tactical high command' to consider day-to-day campaign matters; the group met every Wednesday and Shore attended as an advisor.

Shore truly made his name with rank-and-file Labour members at the 1963 party conference. He led with his idea of 'making public enterprise the agency for bringing growth to our lagging economy, instead of just nationalising dying industries',[72] and Benn recorded in his diary: 'I came home on the train with Peter Shore. It has really been his conference and the Chairman, Dai Davies, mentioned him by name when giving thanks just at the end. The next thing is to get Peter into the House, where he desperately wants to be.'[73] Benn considered Shore, as 1963 came to a close, one of the ablest people in the Labour Party.[74]

With the 1964 general election fast approaching, Shore's hopes that Wilson would find him a parliamentary seat were fading, and Tony Benn found his friend to be 'very depressed'.[75] Disagreements had also emerged in the inner circle over economic planning issues, which added to Shore's sense that he was losing Wilson's favour and, with that, his chances of a parliamentary seat. However, by mid-July Wilson was coming good for Shore and Benn records that Wilson was actively trying to secure a seat for him.

The first, though ultimately unsuccessful, sign of progress on this front was the forced retirement of Dick Mitchison in Kettering. At the age of seventy, the Kettering MP was, Wilson thought, too old to fight another general election and serve a possible four to five more years. Shore had the support of the Transport and General Workers Union but would need to speak to General Secretary Frank Cousins to ensure his candidature. He sought advice from Benn, who promised to get things moving in Shore's favour,[76] and Shore also urged Wilson to get Cousins to secure the nomination of Kettering's TGWU branch. With poor timing, the Shores decided to go to France on holiday. Benn was entrusted with making certain Shore's claim on the Kettering seat was followed through, but Shore still rang frequently from abroad for any update. The Shores' holiday was also nothing of the sort for Peter, as he drafted much of Labour's 1964 general election manifesto while away, handing a copy to Benn upon his return.[77]

Shore's workload, combined with the worry about his political future, took a heavy toll. While the manifesto was in its final drafting stage in September, Shore fell ill. As a Drafting Committee meeting came to a close at 2 a.m., Liz had to collect him; Benn noted in his diary that Shore looked 'very ill' and should have been in bed. On

11 September 1964, Benn was at Lime Grove for the television launch
of the manifesto. He recorded:

> I had to leave afterwards to take Peter Shore and Liz to Stepney where
> he had an important meeting with the Transport and General Workers
> Union delegates. It was a real shock to see him. His mind was working
> slowly, and he was slurring his words, and his left arm and leg were
> partially paralysed. I wondered if he had had a heart attack or a stroke,
> but Liz says it is a virus that has attacked his central nervous system. I
> had actually offered to speak in case he was too unfit for it, but I was
> not allowed into the meeting and I sat outside in the car.[78]

The following Tuesday Benn again took Shore to Stepney, where he
was adopted as Labour's candidate. 'I am delighted. Even though he is
clearly a sick man and will need at least a month's complete rest he will
be an MP at the end of it, whatever he does,' Benn said,[79] reflecting the
safety of the Stepney seat. The general election was held on 15 October
and Labour won with a majority of just four seats. Labour was back in
power after thirteen years and Shore was now an MP.

2

WILSON'S LAPDOG?

S HORE'S CLOSE ASSOCIATION WITH Harold Wilson turned out to be a mixed blessing in the 1964–70 parliament. On the one hand he owed his parliamentary seat to the leader's patronage, and this also allowed him to be at the centre of the government. But these clear advantages would also be a constraint, as Shore was seen as owing his position entirely to Wilson. He was, in the damning phrase of Denis Healey, 'Harold's lapdog'.[1] He was not to break free of this until he rebelled over industrial relations reform, which, as we will see, earned him some respect but also nearly cost him his position in the Cabinet. This chapter explores the nature of the Labour government of 1964–70 and Shore's personal involvement within it.

Shore's close association with Wilson was inevitably going to create tensions, since Wilson himself became a figure for criticism. Wilson had never been trusted by the Gaitskellites and the choice between Wilson and George Brown in 1963 was said to be one between 'a crook and a drunk'. Denis Healey was characteristically forthright in his critique of Wilson:

Since he had neither political principle nor much government experience to guide him, he did not give Cabinet the degree of leadership
which even a less ambitious prime minister should provide. He had no
sense of direction, and rarely looked more than a few months ahead.
His short-term opportunism, allied with a capacity for self-delusion
which made Walter Mitty appear unimaginative, often plunged the
government into chaos. Worse still, when things went wrong, he imagined everyone was conspiring against him. He believed in demons
and saw most of his colleagues in this role at one time or another.[2]

Shore was therefore criticised directly by those who felt he was not
up to the job, and also became a target for those who found fault with
Wilson indirectly. Upon becoming Prime Minister, Wilson appointed
Shore as his parliamentary private secretary, where he was part of the
inner circle of advisors at No. 10. Wilson's biographer, Ben Pimlott,
notes that the inner circle moved decisively to the left with Wilson's
election as Leader of the Opposition in 1963.[3] His close circle, or
'kitchen Cabinet', included Shore, the economist Tommy Balogh, Joe
Haines and Gerald Kaufman as press advisors, and Marcia Williams
as his private and political secretary. Another controversial character
was George Wigg, who had links to the security services. However,
on the election of the government the following year, the senior
Cabinet posts went to the Gaitskellites, with George Brown and
James Callaghan – whom Wilson had defeated in the 1963 leadership
contest – becoming the two senior economics ministers. In addition,
Denis Healey was appointed to Defence and the following year Roy
Jenkins was made Home Secretary. Shore felt that the new Cabinet
was a better mix than Gaitskell would have achieved by bringing in
Barbara Castle, Richard Crossman and (after a short period) Tony

Benn.[4] However, rivalry soon emerged between the real and 'kitchen' Cabinets. Pimlott believes that the civil service advice was also balanced against the kitchen Cabinet and, in the end, Wilson made up his own mind.[5] This chapter begins by analysing the economic record, which remains at the centre of assessments of this period of government.

THE ECONOMIC RECORD

In opposition, the Labour Party had struggled to come to terms with a more affluent society. With revisionists arguing that the economy had fundamentally changed,[6] the old reasons for public ownership were no longer relevant. Instead, the economy could now be effectively steered by the government of the day, committed to Keynesian economics. The left disagreed, claiming that public ownership was still fundamental to Labour's long-term objective of transforming Britain into a socialist country. However, both of these positions – which dominated Labour Party debate throughout the 1950s – were overtaken by unexpected events. Bevan, the standard-bearer of the left – at least until his 1957 conference U-turn on nuclear weapons – died in 1960. With Gaitskell's sudden death in 1963, the era of Gaitskellite-versus-Bevanite feuding had passed. Wilson had first come to prominence by resigning from the Labour government with Bevan, but had long abandoned his firm association with the left. However, equally, he did not embrace the revisionism of Gaitskell, standing against him for the leadership in 1960. Shore's close association with Wilson and Richard Crossman at this time led to him being viewed with considerable suspicion by the surviving Gaitskell supporters.

In place of the left–right arguments over nationalisation, Wilson articulated a technocratic form of socialism that was capable of appealing to the left and the right simultaneously, fostering a sense of party unity and suggesting that Labour would usher in a new radical era by unleashing the 'white heat' of the British scientific and technological revolution.[7] A new partnership between the state and the private sector would be forged, he said.[8] Wilson credits Shore with writing much of the 1964 and 1966 manifestos, which contained a series of commitments on the new approach to the economy,[9] and Shore also produced the initial draft of *Signposts for the Sixties*, an early articulation of this technocratic position that led to the 1964 manifesto. In these drafts, he drew on the ideas of J. K. Galbraith concerning private wealth and public squalor in the affluent society.[10] According to Shore, 'the theme of the whole thing may sound almost ironic in the light of more recent developments, but was really the need to correct the imbalances in our society'.[11] He also took the lead on drafting speeches for Wilson, including the famous 'white heat' speech.[12] Wilson's talk of the thirteen wasted Tory years fostered a sense of dynamism following Labour's triumph in 1964. The centrepiece of his new approach would be the National Plan, with an objective of raising economic growth over the course of the Labour government. Administrative reforms would also be introduced to facilitate this. The Treasury's dominance over economic policy was seen as a reason that the economy had not been modernised and, to redress this balance, there would be a new Department of Economic Affairs (DEA). This department would take responsibility for economic management, with the minister in charge taking the title of First Minister of State and therefore, in theory at least, taking precedence over the Chancellor. A new Ministry of Technology would also be established to harness science and technology. Despite later being seen as the victim of Treasury obstruction, at the time Shore believed that the 'remarkable thing was the ease with which the new departments were set up'.[13]

However, on coming to power the government was immediately faced with the dire state of Britain's international trading position: the balance of payments deficit was twice as big as was thought.[14] Wilson, First Secretary of State George Brown and Chancellor James Callaghan agreed that the parity of the pound should be maintained, and measures were put in place to protect sterling from devaluation. For critics this was the start of an erroneous policy whereby the National Plan was sacrificed, and Crosland was later to argue that the pound should have been devalued as quickly as possible in order to stimulate economic growth.[15]

The decision of the three senior ministers did receive some support from other Cabinet colleagues, however. Douglas Jay, also a committed Keynesian who in 1937 had penned one of the earliest statements of Labour Keynesianism, *The Socialist Case*,[16] argued that there was still no case for devaluation as late as July 1966.[17] The fact that it had become inevitable by November 1967 did not mean that it should have been done earlier, according to Jay; rather it was events in the intervening period which made it inevitable.[18] Peter Shore also argued against devaluation: 'a number of our colleagues thought that we should devalue from day one. Given the fact that we had a majority of about four it didn't seem to be a totally attractive idea and anyway we hadn't tried the corrective measures – import surcharge, export rebates and so on.'[19] It was necessary to allow time for the measures that had already been put in place to work. The risk, as Wilson saw it, of a policy of devaluation was primarily political.

Labour had overseen the devaluation of sterling the last time it was in power and to do it again would seriously undermine the party's economic credibility, especially as the pound was seen as a symbol of national prestige. Moreover, there was serious doubt that such a radical policy could be implemented, given that Labour had only a small parliamentary majority in 1964–66. Hence, devaluation was ruled out and became known as the 'great unmentionable', the elephant in the room that the Cabinet could not discuss. Shore and Jay also opposed devaluation at this time for a second reason. Namely, they felt that those who advocated devaluation were on the pro-European wing of the party and saw it as a preparatory step in leading the UK into the EEC.[20]

If the merits of devaluation were more finely balanced in 1964–65, then, critics have argued, the case for devaluation in 1966 was stronger. The election that year produced a much more comfortable Labour majority of ninety-six over all other parties. The kitchen Cabinet, including Shore, had urged Wilson to call the second election – inevitable after the 1964 result – in the autumn of 1965 and feared he had missed his chance.[21] However, the swing of 4.4 per cent in the Hull North by-election on 27 January 1966 justified Wilson's decision to delay.[22]

The increased majority may have strengthened Wilson's position, but there were to be no major subsequent Cabinet changes.[23] Of the kitchen Cabinet, Crossman felt that at this time the three most powerful members were Shore, Gerald Kaufman and Marcia Williams,[24] and while Kaufman and Williams stayed on in their existing positions, Shore became the parliamentary under-secretary at the Ministry of Technology. In January 1967 Shore moved to the same role within the DEA. At this stage, Wilson still regarded Shore as one of the 'brighter' MPs,[25] and Crossman said he was sorry that Shore had not been promoted to the Cabinet in this reshuffle.[26] Another result of the election was that the political case against devaluation was weakened, as there was now a comfortable majority in Parliament. Indeed, George Brown had gradually come around to the belief that devaluation was necessary. Comparatively, the precise timing of Shore's conversion to devaluation is somewhat ambiguous.

Tony Benn stated in his diary for 18 July 1966 that he and Shore differed on a number of issues, including devaluation. Shore was a 'parity man' and argued that in Cabinet Benn should oppose advocacy for devaluation.[27] Yet, Shore certainly changed his mind after the events of the summer of 1966, when the pound once again came under pressure and further deflationary measures were introduced, and in his own account of this period he argues that this would have been the right time to devalue:

> I think the case by the summer of 1966 was pretty clear. It was a great pity that we didn't devalue either then or even after, by February of 1967 or something like that. The trouble was that by accepting a kind of crude dampening down of the economy in the summer of '66 the National Plan lost all meaning and with it a lot of Labour's planning policy.[28]

Though depressing the value of the pound would have meant the defeat of the policy of the previous two years, it would have allowed the government to appear in control, choosing the timing of the devaluation. The failure to do so meant that further deflationary measures had to be taken. Eventually, the government was forced into devaluing the following year, in the face of further currency speculation. Pimlott

categorises the tensions within the Cabinet as less left/right and more
an anxiety between those who believed in caution and optimists who
thought devaluation pointed 'towards adventure and an open route
of almost limitless possibility'. This was reinforced by attitudes towards the EEC, with Eurosceptics falling into the former category
and pro-Europeans into the latter.[29]

On 29 August 1967 Shore was appointed to the Cabinet as Secretary of State for the DEA. Crossman noted in his diary that control
over economic policy had now moved decisively in favour of Shore
and Tony Crosland, who had been appointed president of the Board
of Trade on the same day following the reshuffle of the Cabinet, which
had involved the dismissal of Douglas Jay for holding Eurosceptic
views.[30] 'Power suddenly shifted to Shore and Crosland, the change
on the economic side is enormous', Crossman wrote.[31]

However, this neglected the fact that, although Shore had been appointed Secretary of State, Wilson had actually taken direct control
of economic affairs himself. Wilson told Crossman that this was a
personal test of his authority as Prime Minister: 'If I can't run the
economy well from the DEA, I'm no good. I was trained for this job
and now I've taken the powers to run the economy.'[32] Shore was therefore Secretary of State in name only. On 30 August, he rang Wilson to
ask what the respective roles of himself and the Prime Minister would
be. 'Defence in wartime was the best precedent for a Prime Minister
assuming strategic control of a department, assisted by a Secretary
of State,' Wilson replied.[33] The Prime Minister clearly intended to
have primary responsibility himself, with Shore as his agent only.
According to Kenneth Morgan, 'the essential power clearly lay in
the new alliance of convenience between the Prime Minister and the

Chancellor, who held confidential meetings every Monday evening to plan and plot the way ahead'.[34]

Shore was ideologically well suited to the role; as a planner he believed in the capacity and desirability of direct state control over the economy. For instance, he made announcements concerning the 'intermediate areas' in April 1969, which would roll out financial support to poorer parts of the UK that had not previously qualified for this support as 'development areas', intermediate areas being less poor than development areas but still affected by poverty.[35] Had he been allowed to do so, he would have used the powers of the DEA more extensively than they had been used under either of his predecessors: George Brown and Michael Stewart.

However, the direct role of Wilson, the Treasury's reassertion of its traditional control over economic matters and the growing pressure on the pound conspired to ensure that this would not happen. According to senior civil servant Leo Pliatzsky, the DEA was a failure: 'it was mourned for years afterwards by some of the younger enthusiasts who had served in it, but according to well-qualified opinions the department's role had been vitiated from the outset by the concept of creative tension'.[36] It was wound up in 1969, and Shore was therefore nominally in charge of a department whose days were numbered. Indeed, the post of First Secretary of State was first retained by Michael Stewart, who moved to the Foreign Office, and was then held by Barbara Castle until the end of the government, meaning Shore was denied the opportunity to be First Secretary of State by his mentor.

Shore did, however, continue to play a wider role in the affairs of the government. He noted that access to information on the state of the economy, previously unavailable to him, led immediately to his arguing that the pound should be devalued or tough import controls imposed without delay.[37] Indeed, this increased knowledge was the key factor in Shore changing his position on devaluation. He was involved in a secret government operation – Brutus – which was responsible for overseeing the devaluation,[38] with the special committee set up to oversee devaluation including Callaghan, Brown, Crosland, Healey, Stewart, Shore and George Thomson, the Commonwealth Secretary. According to Susan Crosland, Crossman was unaware that such a committee existed.[39] Instead, Crossman has Shore as one of only a small select group who were consulted.[40] The eventual devaluation came at great political cost, as the government's policy since 1964 had been defeated and Wilson's reputation damaged. Wilson appeared on television to tell viewers that 'the pound in your pocket' had not been devalued, while Callaghan was moved to the Home Office and Roy Jenkins took over at the Treasury. Crossman was scathing on Shore's winding-up on the economic debate in the Commons, 'once again totally ineffectively. He carries no guns, partly because he just hasn't got the feel of the House, but mainly because he's regarded as the PM's henchman at the DEA and not a full Cabinet Minister.'[41] Shore felt that the lesson was to oppose fixed exchange rates: 'it's one of the awful things about a fixed exchange rate that inevitably it comes under pressure'. In an attempt to defend the existing parity, the authorities must engage in a psychological battle with the speculators and when defeat happens it means a 'tremendous loss of confidence'.[42] However, the devaluation of 1967 did not stop further currency speculation and there was the risk of a second devaluation in 1968. Shore placed the blame firmly at Jenkins's door for this, due to his four-month delay to put together a 'credible package of public expenditure and taxes to back up and stabilise the new exchange rate'.[43] The government soldiered on until 1970, its national economic plan largely in tatters.

THE WIDER POLICY AGENDA

If the economic record was later to be seen as one of failure (though reappraisals of the economic record should also be noted),[44] the government appeared to have more solid successes in other aspects of domestic policy. In particular, the period is remembered for its liberalising legislation, often introduced in the form of backbench Bills but with the tacit or open support of the government. To its supporters this legislation made Britain more tolerant and civilised, while to its opponents it was granting licence to all sorts of undesirable behaviour and a new era of permissiveness.

In general, Shore was supportive of the legislation but was not one of the most prominent advocates for change. He voted in favour of all the liberalising measures, and on the death penalty he was a supporter of abolition. Despite being lobbied by constituents, especially when there were high-profile murders, he refused to support restoration, stating that his objection was not a moral one, but rather a refusal to accept that the evidence suggested it was a deterrent. He indicated, though, that he would be willing to support restoration if it was proven that it would deter murderers:

to me the basic argument about retention or abolition is whether the death penalty does, in fact, deter people from committing acts of murder. If the evidence did support it, then I think I should be

in favour of retaining it. But, in fact, the evidence that is available ...
strongly suggests that the death penalty has no such effect.[45]

He did argue, however, for tougher sentencing short of restoration.[46]

Shore also supported the legalisation of abortion, on the basis that
it would avoid the horrific examples of illegal abortions carried out by
untrained practitioners, with often severe consequences for the women
concerned. On 20 July 1967, Vera Houghton, the chairman of the Abortion Law Reform Association, wrote to Shore – and other supportive
MPs – to thank him for his 'consistent help'.[47] Although he was lobbied
by SPUC and the Catholic Parents and Electors Association, he confirmed that he would support a measure of reform. Writing to Rosalind
Caine, from the Stepney Townswomen's Guild (which favoured reform),
he said, 'while I should want to listen very carefully to the arguments on
both sides, and to study the actual wording of particular clauses you may
take it that I am generally in sympathy with a measure of reform'.[48] Similarly, he accepted divorce on the grounds that existing laws kept women
locked in abusive relationships, and on homosexuality Shore again supported reform, though his papers also show that he was concerned about
the availability of homosexual pornographic materials.[49]

If Shore was not one of the prominent social reformers of the period,
such as Roy Jenkins, he did play a much more active role in campaigns
on education. He was a member of the Public Schools Committee,
founded in 1964, which campaigned for the full integration of private
schools into the state system. Members included Richard Titmuss,
the academic Peter Townsend, Brian Abel-Smith, Tom Driberg and
Dick Taverne.[50] He was also a leading member of the Comprehensive
Schools Committee (CSC) alongside Caroline Benn and Townsend.[51]
Interestingly, Rhodes Boyson, a comprehensive school headmaster

who was to be a loyal Thatcherite minister in the 1980s, was also an active advocate for the schools at this time, although he was later to be a contributor to the Black Papers (a series of right-wing publications on education policy that challenged the prevailing consensus in favour of comprehensive schools and the alleged grip of left-wing educational practices) and eventually campaigned against such schools. Crosland, as Education Secretary, had issued Circular 10/65 encouraging local authorities to move over to the comprehensive school system, which was seen as an essential measure for bringing about greater social equality. The CSC cautiously welcomed the circular but believed that without adequate funding it would not have the desired effect.[52] However, Shore was also one of the Cabinet majority who voted to delay raising the school leaving age, despite it being a manifesto commitment, on the basis that it was now unaffordable given the country's economic problems. Crosland thought that of all those who voted against raising the school leaving age, Shore's position was the most difficult to comprehend: 'he's the only one that is un-understandable. Harold must be the Iron Prime Minister, Roy the Iron Chancellor. Dick Crossman is so crazy. Denis simply takes the vulgar view. Dick Marsh is becoming a total reactionary ... The others are simply unsound or second-rate.'[53]

Shore's approach to the constitution was very clear and strongly held. As was to be the case from 1974–79, in the late '60s he articulated a constitutionally conservative position and his views could be described, following Joseph Schumpeter's conception, as democratic elitist.[54] The Westminster Model of democracy worked well, he thought, because it produced strong government. Though Labour had been out of power for thirteen years following its defeat in 1951, it did not challenge the first-past-the-post system as the pendulum would eventually swing and the party would find itself back in power with a parliamentary majority. Anything that would constrain a Labour government and restrict its ability to implement social and economic reforms in the interests of the working class would therefore be unwelcome. Crossman records Shore as being supportive of his House of Lords reform proposals, which were designed to restrict the ability of the Lords to defeat or block the elected Commons but stopping short of abolition.[55]

Shore's position on Northern Ireland was also clear. For decades since the establishment of the Northern Ireland Parliament in 1921, the Protestant majority had effectively ruled unchecked by the constitutional measures designed to give the Catholic minority a voice. However, growing concern over civil rights abuses, including discrimination over employment, allocation of public housing and the drawing of constituency boundaries, led to mounting protests over the course of the 1960s. There was an affinity for the Catholic minority in Labour ranks, most notably from Harold Wilson himself. However, there was also a group of Labour parliamentarians who defended the Protestants. Callaghan was known to have Unionist sympathies and so too did Shore, who regarded Ulster as an integral part of the United Kingdom.

A major rift was to emerge between Shore and his political master over the issue of European integration. As chronicled in the previous chapter, Shore was very early on a staunch opponent of EEC entry, having produced the briefing paper that led to Gaitskell's 'end of a thousand years of history' speech in 1962. He was therefore always likely to be against subsequent attempts at European integration when George Brown was moved from the DEA to the Foreign Office and began approaching European leaders, despite the unanimous advice that membership was not in the national economic interest.[56]

This also resulted in a '*non*' from President de Gaulle, who feared that British entry would be a way for America to exert its influence over the EEC. At this stage, Shore became much more critical of Wilson over his speedy decision in 1967 to begin, in secret, preparations for a third application.[57] This was to lead to Britain's entry in 1973 following de Gaulle's departure from government in 1969. Shore argued in 1993 that Wilson's motivation was, initially at least, not a principled desire to enter the EEC but was rather the wish to outwit both Edward Heath and the pro-Europeans within the Cabinet, notably Jenkins.[58] However, on further reflection towards the end of his life, he revised this opinion to say that Wilson had been converted. This was partly due to the role of individuals such as Michael Palliser, who served as Wilson's joint private secretary and later permanent secretary at the Foreign and Commonwealth Office, but was mainly prompted by events including the problems encountered working with the Commonwealth, and the economic issues discussed previously. Wilson became 'a supporter of UK membership – reluctantly and without enthusiasm at any stage, the epitome and embodiment of the British attitude to the Common Market'.[59]

Shore was also a source of influence on Wilson at the time of the Vietnam War.[60] As we now know, Britain was urged by America to make a military contribution to the war in Vietnam. Wilson was in a very difficult position: on the one hand he was opposed to making any military contribution at all, believing that the war was likely to be protracted; however, he also felt that he could not make his opposition to the war known because Britain was dependent on the US for financial support. He therefore came under pressure both from President Johnson, who desperately wanted other countries to commit to the war effort in order to give the appearance that it was a combined international effort against Communism (as some did, including Australia and New Zealand), and conversely from peace protestors who wanted the Labour government to condemn the war. Shore was in the majority among the closest advisors to Wilson in arguing that Britain should not be involved. The one exception was George Wigg, who argued that 'the band of the Grenadier Guards marching in the streets of Saigon' would be a satisfactory symbol.[61] For Shore,

> it [was] hard to imagine any other Labour leader resisting very strong American pressure so successfully ... Enormous efforts were made by the Foreign Office, the Treasury, the Americans to get Britain wholly to identify with the war and express this with a military presence. Harold did give support, but he never sent a single soldier.[62]

Developments in Africa also posed challenges for the government at this time. The Cabinet was divided over selling arms to South Africa, with Healey recording that the Cabinet majority was initially in favour of sales to the country immediately or after a short delay. Only eight originally opposed the idea, including Shore. However, after debate, the majority swung the other way and Wilson informed the House of Commons that the ban on arms would remain in force.[63]

TROUBLE AND STRIFE

The period since 1945 had been a relatively harmonious one for Britain's industrial relations. The Labour government of 1945–51 had removed controversial legislation imposed after the General Strike, and the incoming Conservative government had not sought to impose restrictive measures. However, the economic downturn in the mid-1960s resulted in more strike action, most notably the Seamen's Strike of 1966. The previous year a Royal Commission had been established, releasing its Donovan Report in 1968. This report called for a new approach to strikes but stopped short of legal sanctions. Meanwhile, Wilson had become concerned over the political effects of being closely associated with the trade unions. He set up a small group to work on the issue, led by Barbara Castle but including Shore, Tony Benn and her parliamentary private secretary (PPS), Harold Walker. Castle also received advice from Bill McCarthy of Nuffield College, Oxford.[64] The group had a clear Bevanite feel to it, the Bevanites having argued in the 1950s against leaving wages to free negotiation between employers and employees, believing that there needed to be a national strategy as part of wider government planning. A more interventionist policy to end free collective bargaining was therefore in keeping with the left's longer-term position.

Castle then produced the infamous 'In Place of Strife' proposals, which sought to impose on the unions new legal restrictions for the first time since the end of the Second World War. The matter split the Cabinet. The opponents of reform included a broad range of ministers from across Labour's political spectrum, the most vocal being Callaghan, who regarded himself as representing the trade unions' interests. Callaghan had come from a union background and felt that those who wanted reform did not understand the unions:[65] 'From the moment I set eyes on it I knew that such a proposal, which ran counter to the whole history of the trade union movement and to the ethos of the Donovan Report, could not succeed,' he said.[66] In Cabinet, support steadily drifted away, including that from Roy Jenkins, who had initially supported the paper. Shore, seeing the scale of opposition to the proposals and how divisive the issue had become, moved to outright opposition from 5 June, when the TUC voted overwhelmingly against them.[67] He made a strong statement in Cabinet on 17 June, which Pimlott believed helped to tip the 'wobbling middle' against the proposals.[68] For some, including Crossman, this was the first time Shore had distinguished himself in Cabinet: 'Peter spoke with tremendous strength. Everybody in Cabinet agreed that it was the first time he had ever said anything which had a real effect.'[69] Wilson, however, was furious. He told Benn that Shore 'had been a great disappointment' and that 'Barbara and I will never forget Peter's speech on industrial relations'.[70] The Prime Minister felt betrayed by the man he had promoted and Benn felt that it was clearly Wilson's desire to sack Shore at this point.[71] According to Crossman, Wilson said, 'I over-promoted him, he's no good'.[72] On 2 July, Crossman records Wilson as saying that 'he must deal with some other failures' and mentioning Shore again.[73] In a further Cabinet reshuffle, Shore was moved to minister without portfolio and Crossman, previously a close ally of Shore's, remarked in his diary that he did not deserve a Cabinet post at all.[74] In later life, Shore believed that the real failure had been to enforce the prices and incomes policy which led to 'a very poor substitute policy', namely 'In Place of Strife'.[75] Castle's proposals had been, he thought, 'a brave new policy and it was pressed with reckless courage … to the point where it was painfully clear that there was no majority for it in either the PLP or the Cabinet'.[76]

DEFEAT

In May 1970, Wilson responded to an apparent revival in the party's opinion poll ratings and called a general election. Shore was used as minister without portfolio to draft the manifesto once again, meaning he had played a central part in the writing of three consecutive manifestos. The inner circle running the campaign comprised Wilson, Callaghan, Shore, Balogh and Will Camp, a public relations man from British Steel, with whom Shore was to form a lasting friendship.[77] However, bad economic news during the campaign led to the return of the Conservatives under Edward Heath.

For many within the Labour Party the experience in office between 1964 and 1970 was negative, and the economy did not live up to the hopes of the National Plan. Tony Crosland did not hold back on the economic record, noting that, 'in 1970, unemployment was higher, inflation more rapid and the rate of growth lower than when the Conservatives left office in 1964'.[78] As Kenneth Morgan put it, 'a government run by a trained economist, and containing such powerful minds as Jenkins, Crosland, Healey, Jay and Shore had been unable to transform the economy'.[79] Shore, in contrast, felt that there were clear successes in the government's economic record, including regional policies and educational reforms. However, the main problem was the failure – despite schemes by the Ministry of Technology designed to encourage them to do so – of businesses to invest. This 'left in most of our minds the question "How do you motivate British industry to a policy of sustained industrial expansion?" I'm not sure whether any of us yet knows the answer to that.'[80] In sharp contrast to the emerging New Right, Shore remained firmly committed to the principles of government regulation and coordination of the economy. Historians have come to view the economic record more favourably than contemporaries and there were clear legislative achievements in terms of socially liberal reforms. However, welfare, education and housing (with the rapid development of high-rise tower blocks) were at best more mixed, and the record on foreign policy was only subsequently viewed more favourably, especially in relation to the Vietnam War.[81]

For Shore personally, the period was also mixed. On the one hand he could use his experience and connections to be immediately at the centre of the government, while on the other he was held back by his patron and widely viewed with suspicion by critics and opponents of Wilson. However, on Europe he had once again established his independence of mind, which had led to a distancing between himself and Wilson. He had first set out his own stall in Cabinet on the issue of industrial relations reform and his stock had risen by the end of the government. Yet it was to be in the 1970s that he would become one of the more distinguished members of the Labour Party's upper echelons.

3

THE CHARGE INTO EUROPE
AND THE 1975 REFERENDUM

THE THIRD, SUCCESSFUL APPLICATION for British membership of the EEC under the Conservative Prime Minister Edward Heath exposed the divisions within the Labour Party. Labour's manifesto for the 1970 general election, while emphasising that British and Commonwealth interests needed to be safeguarded, asserted that the forthcoming negotiations would be 'pressed with determination'.[1] However, in opposition, the party's position shifted from one of seeking membership towards one of scepticism, pledging in 1973 to renegotiate the Conservative government's terms of entry and to put the whole issue of Britain's membership in the EEC to the people, using either a general election or a referendum. It was a policy that enabled Wilson (who was in favour of membership but without the zeal of the committed pro-Europeans) to hold the party together in opposition to membership on Conservative terms. Simultaneously, the approach allowed Wilson to complain that Britain was entering 'on the wrong terms', but not that he was opposed to the principle of membership. After all, Wilson had led the failed second attempt at membership, and the Conservatives could claim that they had 'picked up the hand' that had already been prepared by their predecessors. Callaghan, who as Foreign Secretary led the renegotiation, adopted a similar view to Wilson while, for Shore, it was in the 1970s that his anti-Europeanism and rhetorical ability came to the fore, as he was a gifted public speaker and was able to popularise the anti-European message. His political standing increased and *The Times* considered him 'the most formidable anti-European member of the PLP'.[2]

ENTERING THE COMMON MARKET

Shore reflected on Wilson's change of attitude towards Europe, considering that Wilson, like Macmillan, became increasingly pessimistic about the prospects before the UK. The Commonwealth had become more and more demanding and critical of Britain, and the issue of anti-racism dominated its agenda. Also, the problems with the British economy, such as the balance of payments and the sterling crisis, convinced Wilson that Britain's future lay in Europe.[3] However, for the likes of Roy Jenkins, the leading Labour pro-Marketeer, the change in policy to one of opposing membership led to him resigning as deputy leader. In the last Labour government, Jenkins had been able to advocate for membership from his influential position as Home Secretary, and then after devaluation as Chancellor. Indeed, unknown to Cabinet as a whole, a subcommittee of Labour's leading Europhiles had been set up in 1969 with the task of preparing positions and papers for a renewed British application should Labour have won the 1970 election.[4] It was Jenkins who led the sixty-nine Labour rebels who voted with the Conservative government to take the UK into the Common Market, with Jay reflecting: 'The truth was that, by this time, with extremists like Jenkins and Rodgers, the pro-Market doctrine had become a religion, transcending all other loyalties'.[5]

Shore had been an anti-European from the 1950s. He damned Britain's first application under Macmillan in *Entitled to Know*, comparing Britain to

> an ageing virgin who had resisted all advances in her youth [and] had, at last, brought herself to the moment of delicious surrender: one by one the garments had been taken away, the unheard of liberties had been taken. Naked, defenceless and loving, she awaits the final embrace – only to be told that she is not yet ready or fit for union![6]

At the end of March 1970, Shore delivered a significant speech pouring the coldest water on the whole idea of the EEC, declaring that the electorate, not the politicians, must decide. He had 'no patience with those who, in their eagerness for membership, resent our resolve to put all the facts involved to the British people before decisions are taken. This decision, above all others, is one that politicians alone cannot take.'[7]

Given that his comments were made in the run-up to a general election, they caused some consternation with Wilson and the Foreign Secretary Michael Stewart. Benn noted that Shore was pleased with the reaction to his speech, believing 'very strongly, that the Common Market is an illusion and politically it will be advantageous if it is clear that some members of the government have reservations about entry'.[8] Shore apologised for failing to consult Stewart but not on the substance of his speech. He argued that he

> merely drew attention to the undeniable fact that the EEC was not simply

an enlarged free trade area but was a community which involved its members in a commitment to a closer and more intimate relationship with fellow members than with outside countries ... It could not be maintained that it was wrong to remind public opinion of this essential fact.

Shore was instructed to make it clear that the government's declared purpose was to join the EEC if acceptable terms could be obtained.[9] He did so, in a somewhat grudging fashion, five weeks later.[10]

After the 1970 general election Shore left the front bench, believing that Labour's opposition to the Common Market was bound to be muted at best. His perspective was that, by January 1970, after the transitional period, 'the original Six had gone solid on the tax arrangements, the CAP ... The effect was that we were about to negotiate from a position of having already capitulated.'[11] Therefore, it was better to rally against the Heath government from outside of the shadow Cabinet, where he would be free to voice his clear opposition. Shore joined the cross-party Common Market Safeguards Campaign (CMSC) and Jay records that the CMSC steadily recruited both from within politics and from outside, 'to counter the efforts of the European Movement to insinuate that no anti-Marketeers were quite respectable'.[12] Shore told the Oxford University Labour Club that the Conservative government had 'capitulated', and that Britain had suffered an 'unmitigated defeat' in the face of 'the cold, hard assertion of the French national interests' against British interests, accepting the whole financial and agricultural system of the Six. Moreover, if the pro-Europeans were unable to persuade people by the arguments of fear, 'then there are the arguments of greed. If we join, it is said we will be much richer than we are today.' He also noted that, if it was merely an argument about wealth, then Britain should apply to join the United States.[13]

Shore joined an unofficial anti-Market group of Labour MPs, known as the Peart Group, along with others such as Jay, Eric Deakins, John Gilbert, Nigel Spearing and Stanley Clinton-Davis. For Jay, the membership was not the Tribunite left but from the centre or right of centre of the party.[14] Shore accused Geoffrey Rippon, Heath's chief negotiator, of being 'outwitted, out-generalled and out-faced'. The love-in had to stop, he thought, and agreement had been reached only by abandoning vital British and Commonwealth interests.[15] At the Special Labour Party conference arranged in July 1971, which convened to discuss the party's attitude towards Heath's terms, Shore spoke with passion and to high approval. Appearing on the balcony, he said with immense conviction:

> For what we have been persuaded, or our negotiators have been per-
> suaded to concede, is the abandonment of the 120-year-old policy of
> cheap food for this country, a switch of supply from traditional low-
> cost suppliers to the high-cost, inefficient farms of Western Europe;
> Britain to withdraw from the two preferential areas of which she is a
> member in trade, from EFTA and from the Commonwealth, to go into
> the third club, the Common Market, which takes only 20 per cent of
> her trade; and to liberate for the first time since 1939, the movement
> of capital, the movement of firms out of Britain into Western Europe.[16]

Shore went on to argue:

> Do not be depressed by these feeble voices which convince you, or
> seek to convince you, first, that you have no capacity to solve your
> own problems; secondly, that the world of tomorrow is a world of vast
> aggregates, regional blocs from which it is death to be excluded, it is

not; thirdly, do not fear, you have the power to stop this act of madness and to change the history of this country and to insist that we shall make arrangements for our future that are right — not for the CBI and for Edward Heath, but for the people of Britain.[17]

Wilson supposedly muttered 'Churchillian' at Shore's fixity, intensity and rhetorical ability.[18] It was one of the turning points of his career, bringing him back into the forefront of the party and national politics; it helped get him elected to the shadow Cabinet later that year, and it finally shrugged off the 'poodle' tag. In October 1971 Shore became Labour's spokesman on Europe, gaining 105 votes in the shadow Cabinet elections. From this position, Shore was able to lead the opposition to Rippon. He also led in the famous October debate on the White Paper, outlining the agreed terms; took apart the Treaty of Accession when it was published in January 1972; and then mounted a sustained assault during the whole prolonged debate on the floor of the House, on the European Economic Community's Bill that brought the treaty into effect from 1 January 1973. Shore could not see how the Conservative government could maintain that there would be no loss of essential national sovereignty. The transfer of power would be to the non-elected institutions of the Community, such as the Commission, the Council of Ministers and the Committee of Permanent Representatives.

SHORE'S EUROSCEPTICISM

Alongside Shore's ministerial responsibilities, he published articles, fleshing out in detail his opposition to the Common Market, the inadequacy of the pro-European arguments and how Britain should approach withdrawal. Writing in the *New Statesman* in 1971, he dismissed the arguments of the pro-Marketeers. For Shore, the Marketeers were not motivated by the 'modest coordination of foreign and defence policies but a full-blown West-European state – the United States of Europe – with a government and a directly elected parliament into which the existing separate nation states would merge'. This would, he said, involve a 'massive transfer of political and economic power from the nation states to Europe'. Shore identified two arguments that had considerable force on the left: firstly, there was 'the traditional socialist/liberal hostility to what is seen as the war-like European nation-state – a hostility fed by the still-green memory of two world wars'; while secondly, and very different from the first, there was 'the desire to establish a new world power centre in Western Europe, able to match the power of the USA and the USSR'.[19]

The pro-Marketeers had misread the post-Second World War situation, as the 'relative power of Britain, France, Italy and Germany in relation to the Russian and American super-powers has been so great that it is virtually inconceivable that any European nation could now threaten the peace of the world'. Moreover, while past national antagonisms had been based on an 'economic system in which the prosperity of one nation could, in fact, be secured only at the expense of another', economic prosperity was now based on trade without serious conflict with its neighbours.[20] Shore then assessed how a West European state would operate as a new world power, considering that such a state would have to match its power with that of the other super-powers, including in terms of nuclear arsenals. For the British, the question remained as to whether they would be willing to accept the decisions, such as on war and peace, made by a European government and a parliament in which Britain had only a small minority of members. Besides, at a time when there was an increasing concern with the remoteness of decision-making in Britain, the transfer of power from the nation state to a federal Europe would exacerbate the problem. In the UK, there was no sense of shared history and destiny with the Six.[21]

Membership of the EEC, although not solely to blame, had caused higher food prices through an external tariff encouraging the import of European foodstuffs, and therefore had led to inflation. This had consequences for economic policy, as membership was 'geared to the assumption that we would gain a trading account. If we do not, we have nothing with which to finance the known and major deficit items.'[22] Withdrawing from the Treaty of Accession would relieve the inflationary burdens and costly food prices of the Common Agricultural Policy (CAP), a system of subsidies to farmers that critics felt was supporting inefficient continental farming, as well as the upcoming contribution towards the European Communities Budget. 'But perhaps the greatest gain of all would be that we shall be able once more to conduct our own relations in trade, investment and other matters with the rest of the world', thought Shore. The Commonwealth, as a multi-racial, multi-religious global association including the least and most prosperous nations with a shared history, still had considerable potential. A free trade relationship with mainland Europe would help to dispel the idea that a regional West European bloc was the solution to current problems.[23]

Writing in *Europe: The Way Back*, Shore outlined that the purpose of the Labour movement was to bring economic forces within the ambit of democratic control and decision-making, therefore furthering socialist ends. On the other hand, the Common Market sought to remove decision-making authority from its member states. This view reiterated the comments Shore had made at the 1972 Labour Party conference: he had not 'come into socialist politics in this country to connive in the dismantling of the power of the British people as represented in their parliament and in their government'.[24] The objective of the EEC was to remove the economic power acquired by states in the postwar period and this was mirrored in the *laissez-faire* principles of the Rome Treaty, 'a contemporary Magna Carta of business freedoms, liberating commerce and industry throughout the Community from state intervention and public control'. As such, British socialists in favour of a deepening relationship had committed to the steady erosion of state and democratic power. Shore thought they also had to stop confusing the internationalism of socialism with the desire to build a West European state. Instead, it was important to turn 'to the task of strengthening, defending and improving what already exists: democracy in Britain', and realise that 'for 400 years, our interests in commerce, the flow of our money, our trade and our people has been oceanic, not continental'.[25] What mattered was the will of a nation to be self-governing and free; there was no need for socialists to apologise for upholding this view. He noted:

Indeed nothing is more extraordinary in this long argument about Europe than that so many pro-Marketeers who have themselves for the previous twenty-five years passionately espoused the cause of self-government throughout the world, should now dismiss as without value for Britain what they still regard as the greatest prize for the rest of mankind! And it is sheer muddle-headedness for such people to fail to distinguish between the legitimate and praiseworthy desire by a people to rule themselves in freedom with the reprehensible and illegitimate desire of one nation to rule and dominate another.[26]

For Shore, the media, the Foreign Office, the Cabinet Office, industry and the professions, including academia, had led the charge into Europe, and therefore any attempt to renegotiate the terms of entry and membership, or to leave, was going to be met by a reluctant and resistant elite. After rejecting the 'wrecking tactic' of the deliberate blocking of policies, Shore identified two aims of the renegotiations: that the law of the Community must cease to have effect in Britain except where Parliament wishes and so decides it, and that those provisions that are repealed are those that it is essential to our own interests to remove, and at the same time are those that exert the maximum pressure on the Community to negotiate new terms.[27] A phased approach to negotiations would prove most fruitful, Shore thought. It would be required that all Community decisions, and thus all British ministers on the Council of Ministers, be brought under the direct control of the House of Commons, resulting in no policy, regulation or directive being accepted unless the minister had obtained the prior consent of the House.[28] Still, it is notable that this would only prevent new policies from being agreed, leaving existing Community laws untouched.

Consequently, in Phase One, it was necessary to 'repeal, amend or suspend the European Communities Act', the 'Act that gave to the Community the right to make laws for Britain'. Shore identified several features of the Act to which he was opposed. For example, Clause 2 (1), which provided all Community legislation in the future, as well as in the past, to be self-enacting and in need of no further parliamentary process. According to Shore, the clause 'negates the sovereignty of the Parliament, surrenders the rights of the British people and betrays the whole democratic process in Britain.'[29] Moreover, he deemed that it was necessary to repeal sub-clause 2 (3), which authorised the payment of monies and taxes to the EEC; curtail sub-clause 2 (4), as that had given authority to the provisions of Community law over the conflicting provisions of UK law; and limit the jurisdiction of the European Court in Clause 3 of the Act. Shore also opposed clauses in the European Communities Act that had transferred economic powers to the EEC and wanted to redress the payment formula of the CAP.

Phase Two would involve removing Britain from the CAP (as it was burdensome and kept prices up), the financing of the £2,000 million-a-year EEC Budget, and ensuring that trade arrangements with the EEC considered the Commonwealth countries. After all, Shore noted that 'there can be no gain, only loss, for us to have to raise tariffs against Commonwealth countries with whom we have long enjoyed mutual tariff preferences'.[30] Lastly, there was the question of future Community law and Community decision-making that impacted on the living standards, welfare and employment of British people. For Shore, there was a large and growing 'no-go area' excluding UK law and policy, where the 'writ of the Community alone runs'. This had implications for a Labour government that 'could not possibly allow its regional and industrial policies to be made or unmade by the Brussels Commission'.[31] The objective of Phase Two was to encourage the Community to re-examine itself, to reject the federalist ambitions of Monnet, and to move towards 'the British conception of a much looser and much more democratic grouping of European states who prize and retain their contacts with other continents'. A successful British renegotiation would be measured by substantially changing the nature of the Community, preserving British and Commonwealth interests and reasserting the authority of British democracy.[32]

Finally, Phase Three would be determined by whether negotiations were a success or a failure. If negotiations failed, then Britain would withdraw from the EEC, re-join the European Free Trade Association (EFTA), and ensure that aspects of our EEC arrangements were mutually agreeable to all sides, including the Commonwealth. The attraction of a Europe based on free trade and cooperation for Britain was definite, having nothing to do with the caricature of 'narrow nationalism', insular introversion, or the dislike of foreigners with which pro-Marketeers sometimes seek to discredit their opponents. The framework of Western Europe involved not an enlargement but a reduction in Britain's area of contact, influence and concern, while the Commonwealth provided the country with close and continuing contact with governments and people not in one affluent half-continent, but throughout the world. Importantly, the matter would be put to the people as, 'it is right for the most basic constitutional reason that membership involves – even on the terms put forward above – a substantial change in the power of the British Parliament and a commitment on Foreign Policy of a kind that requires a positive act of consent'.[33]

SHORE AND THE RENEGOTIATION

After Enoch Powell had spoken about the possible need for a Labour government due to the commitment to hold a referendum, Wilson was swift to state that there were no circumstances in which he would work with Powell behind the scenes. However, Shore took a different view, stating that it was 'almost inconceivable that he or any other politician should receive so massive a rebuke for advancing the proposition that, in the last resort and on a matter of profound importance, he would put the interests of his own country before that of his party and that of the Common Market'.[34] The Labour Party came to power in March 1974, committed to renegotiating the terms of British membership in the EEC and putting the whole issue to the people, and the position of Trade Secretary provided an ideal platform from which Shore could continue his campaign against the EEC. However, the renegotiation would fall far short of the process he had envisaged in *Europe: The Way Back*. In April, Shore informed Jay that 'the mood was changing' within Cabinet, that weaker ministers, under pressure from the Foreign Office, were turning soft. By June, Jay records that Shore had given him a depressing account of discussions within the government: while Shore and Hart had secured some gains on trade and aid, Fred Peart on the CAP had collapsed. Shore remained confident that the anti-Marketeers in the Cabinet would stand together and reserve the right to attack the final settlement when it was reached. However, others had shifted, such as Prentice and Morris, and aside from Shore, only Foot, Benn, Castle and William Ross were completely firm.[35]

Whitehall believed that while Wilson and Callaghan wanted a successful renegotiation, Benn and Shore did not.[36] Callaghan was flanked on the one side by Roy Hattersley, a longstanding and active pro-Marketeer, and on the other by Shore, with the objective to provide a balanced view.[37] King wrote that 'what one did, the other assiduously tried to undo'.[38] However, the Turkish invasion of Cyprus on 20 July meant that Callaghan and Hattersley were unable to attend the Council of Ministers meeting on 22 July; Britain was a guarantor of power, meaning Callaghan, as Foreign Secretary, and Hattersley, as minister of state at the Foreign Office, had to focus their time on Cyprus. Consequently, Shore represented the government alone and duly caused some consternation by blocking progress on trade negotiations for commodities, as well as by raising the issue of energy policy, in contravention of the brief that had been agreed inter-departmentally in Whitehall. Although Callaghan was to resolve the energy policy in September, Wall comments that Shore's behaviour 'brought to the fore the whole issue of Britain's commitment to the principles of the Community and tested the tolerance of Britain's European partners'. It would be the only occasion that Shore represented the government in Brussels by himself.[39]

While Shore emphasised Britain's unique role within the Commonwealth and the benefit of cheaper food from outside the Common Market, it must have come as a disappointment when, as Trade Secretary in August 1974, he toured Australia and New Zealand only to find them relaxed about British membership. Shore delivered a series of barnstorming speeches in opposition to membership, looking forward to the day when the British people 'can face the future without any necessity of joining a particular trading bloc'. Wilson contacted Shore, reminding him to abide by the agreed statements. On his return to the UK, he told the Cabinet that, 'for the most part, Australian Ministers appeared not to care strongly one way or the other'. In New Zealand, he found opinion 'frankly very concerned' about the CAP but, even there, 'they did not press their views too hard'.[40]

Later in 1974, Shore began to agitate against the provisions of the Common Commercial Tariff. Britain was to make a further move towards this, impacting on third countries (those not in the EEC), together with an additional 20 per cent reduction in the tariff on imports from the rest of the Community. In a minute to Wilson of 1 November, Shore proposed that the government should make the further reduction in tariffs on imports from the Six, but not implement the next move towards imposing the Common Commercial Tariff on third countries. He argued that this 'would carry us a step further towards the goal of European free trade while avoiding tariff increases on goods from the Commonwealth and other third countries which it is in our interest to avoid'. Shore foresaw that 'some will argue that it would constitute a breach of the Treaty and would have adverse consequences on our whole relationship with the Six', but 'there have been occasions in the past when Community obligations have been delayed.'[41] In Cabinet Healey and Callaghan rounded on Shore's proposal, believing them to have minimal practical benefits, and arguing that the other member states would never agree. The matter was discussed again on 2 December, but Shore was outmanoeuvred. Wilson sided with Callaghan and Healey, taking the view that Britain should honour her treaty obligations and, instead, encouraged Shore to make a statement that the British government would not ask for a deferral. As a result, Shore called a press conference at which he roundly denounced the European Community.[42]

When the Cabinet met on 18 March 1975, seven ministers voted against the renegotiated terms: Benn, Castle, Foot, Ross, John Silkin, Eric Varley and Shore. Judith Hart, the minister for overseas development, also registered her opposition, though she was not permitted to attend Cabinet. Shore argued that continued membership was 'disadvantageous to us materially, to the powers of Parliament and to the unity of the United Kingdom and in relation to the kind of world we wished to see'.[43] Saunders charts the actions of Labour's anti-Europeans, writing that once

collective responsibility [had] lapsed, the so-called "Dissenting Ministers" held a press conference in the Grand Committee Room of the
House, where they were joined by more than eighty Labour MPs. A
total of 129 MPs signed an Early Day Motion demanding withdrawal,
which was followed by a motion to the NEC demanding that Labour
campaign for a No vote.[44]

Had the motion succeeded, it would have placed all the resources of
the Labour Party at the disposal of the 'Out' campaign. After the special conference in April, which had voted by a majority of two-to-one
in favour of withdrawal, Benn attempted to commit the NEC to campaign to leave. However, Shore and Foot were reluctant to bring down
the government over the issue of Europe. As Saunders notes, 'had the
NEC instructed the party to campaign against the Labour government,
the survival of the Wilson administration would have been in doubt'.[45]

SHORE AND THE 1975 REFERENDUM

Wilson encouraged Shore to come out strongly against EEC
membership in the 1975 referendum campaign, saying 'that it would
make him or break him'.[46] As it transpired, the referendum helped
to make him: he made numerous speeches across the country and
was one of the leading figures representing the 'Out' campaign from
the Labour Party. Other Labour figures included Castle, Foot and
Benn. Where the referendum was concerned, Shore felt that he had
a different approach to Benn, aiming 'to stress what unified the anti-
Marketeers',[47] and indeed he shared a platform with Conservatives
such as Enoch Powell and Scottish Nationalists like Douglas Henderson.

Michael Cockerell's *How We Fell for Europe* reported that Labour's anti-Common Market Cabinet ministers turned away from a meeting of the cross-party National Referendum Committee, at which Powell was present, when they realised it was being filmed.[48] In contrast to Shore, Benn placed greater emphasis on the freedom to implement socialism outside of the Common Market and refused to share a platform with Powell.

The anti-Marketeers from across the political spectrum faced an uphill struggle against the weight of the major political parties, British industry and the media. Moreover, they were portrayed as a rag-tag bunch from the fringes of British politics and society. The *Evening Standard* produced a cartoon titled 'Join the professionals', showing a march containing Shore, Benn, Powell, Foot, the National Front, Scottish Nationalists, Ulster Unionists and the Communist Party of Great Britain. Shore differed from the others portrayed in the cartoon as he was one of the few leading members who could be regarded as a moderate, and an establishment figure, meaning he was well-placed to lead an effective and influential campaign. However, his integrity and dislike of political manoeuvring – two traits that would hinder his leadership ambitions in the 1980s – prompted both admiration and frustration among fellow campaigners. Castle was impressed by his ability to master the arguments, especially before the Oxford Union debate on Europe, in which he casually jotted 'down a few ideas' that were to become probably his most famous speech, known for both its passion and coherence. She also noted that he was 'the keeper of our EEC conscience as well as of the archives of the detailed issues involved'.[49] Still, Castle complained about his lack of attention to the practical details of organisation, particularly his indifference towards the National Referendum Campaign.[50] She became angry that Shore was not using his department to provide the information that she and others needed, and this led her to doubt whether Shore had 'an emollient enough temperament' to lead the party.[51]

Shore gave a notable speech at the Oxford Union Debating Society, broadcast live on television, in which he carefully dismantled the economic, political and historical arguments for membership, finishing by accusing the pro-Europeans of fearmongering.[52] *How We Fell for Europe* supports this view, making clear that the use of 'fear' was a deliberate tactic of the 'In' campaign. Shore also identified that the loss of confidence and nerve in 'the high places in society' had encouraged support for and ultimately membership of the Common Market, which, in turn, had drained the 'self-confidence, the morale and the unity of our people'.[53] He would later state that fear reinforced the loss of confidence: 'in the Referendum campaign the main argument used against us wasn't an argument at all, it was the fear of freedom, of being out on our own. That is absolute nonsense, and the fact that this fear operates so powerfully is an indication of our loss of confidence.'[54]

Throughout the referendum campaign he attacked the 'In' campaign at its source through a combination of rhetorical force, intellectualism and patriotism. The Conservatives, who at this time were more pro-European than the Labour Party, supported membership, though according to Shore this was because it would 'weaken a Labour government's ability to control the economy in the interests of the whole people'. Indeed, it was thought that membership would result in 'a weakening of the whole historical drive of the Labour Movement to win economic democracy alongside political democracy'.[55] While at first Britain would be treated 'with tolerant patronage' in the

Common Market, it would change to that of 'growing impatience; finally with rigour and severity by our new masters and creditors in Brussels'. In a phrase reminiscent of William Pitt the Younger, Shore said that 'the British anti-Market solution is to save ourselves by our own exertions'.[56] At the core of Shore's argument was the loss of sovereignty. As he put it:

> Have we so abandoned confidence in ourselves and hope in our future that we are ready to submit to the presumptuous powers of the Brussels' authorities, to surrender to them not just our legitimate economic interests, but the basic right of our Parliament and people to decide the policies, to make the laws and levy the taxes on our land?[57]

The economic growth enjoyed by the Six was not merely a consequence of rebuilding from a low base, but was also the stimulus provided by the dismantling of trade barriers. They also benefited from large agricultural populations that offered a reserve army of labour. Britain, by contrast, possessed no such reserve and had well-established trade patterns outside of Europe. Shore stressed that he was not an isolationist (a position he dismissed as 'great folly') but he did deny that the future lay with regional blocs. At a time when Europe was losing its pre-eminence, he argued, it made sense to be flexible in making trade arrangements, working, where appropriate, with oil producers in the Middle East or with new partners in Asia and Latin America.[58] Shore, like Powell, argued for a Free Trade Area for the whole of Western Europe and increased access to the British market for overseas producers. He was prepared to cooperate functionally with the EEC on such matters as Concorde, and other high-technology industries, but it was not in the UK's overall interest in trade and economic growth to become a member. After all, the horizons of Britain had never been set by Western Europe.

> Our trade, our energies, our wealth and our people have flowed out not in the main across the Channel but across the Atlantic and to all the countries and continents of the world, including, of course, the countries of the Commonwealth and the great English-speaking continents of North America and Australasia. In these links we have found both our security and our prosperity, and there they will rest in the future.[59]

Shore continued, arguing that it was Britain's nerve that was being tested:

> For what the advocates of membership are saying, insistently and in-sidiously, is that we are finished as a country; that the long and famous story of the British nation and people has ended; that we are now so weak and powerless that we must accept terms and conditions, penalties and limitations, almost as though we had suffered defeat in war; that though we have the right to vote on June 5 we have no option in fact but to remain in the Common Market cage.[60]

Butler and Kitzinger, in their formative study of the 1975 referendum, perceptively wrote that, had the referendum been held on whether Britain should join the Common Market rather than remain in it, the result may well have been different. After three years of membership, the vote was a statement in favour of the status quo, not for new departures; it was a desire to avoid the disruption of leaving.[61]

The scale of the two-to-one majority in favour of remaining in the Common Market meant that, at least for the foreseeable future, Britain had resolved its place in Europe. Shore indicated that, while he was disappointed by the result, he accepted that it was binding on the government and therefore on himself.[62] As later chapters in this book will show, however, he would quickly return to the matter.

CONCLUSION

The period 1970–75 and the issue of Europe helped Shore to increase his standing within the Parliamentary Labour Party (PLP), firstly from the back benches and then from the shadow Cabinet, critiquing the Heath government's application. As one commentator remarked, 'it is given to few politicians whose lamps burn low in early career to make a comeback. Shore has done so.'[63] In government he took an active part in the renegotiations, and then played a leading role in the referendum campaign, and he commanded respect as he was prepared to master the minutiae of Common Market legislation. Still, it is unclear whether his increased stature within the PLP translated into increased popularity with the public; in a poll conducted during the 1975 referendum campaign on public attitudes to leading figures on both sides of the debate, he had only a +3 rating. This was higher than other leading 'Out' campaigners – Powell (+2), Foot (-9), Benn (-15) and Ian Paisley (-59) – but significantly lower than the pro-Marketeers. Cabinet colleagues such as Shirley Williams (+25) and Roy Jenkins (+25) had much higher positive ratings, as did Conservative proponents of membership such as Heath (+21) and Whitelaw (+25).[64] However, this mixed polling did not prevent *The Observer* writing that 'Shore emerged from the episode with greater credit than any other politician, with the possible exception of Ted Heath'.[65]

Shore judged that, in joining the EEC, Heath had betrayed the British people, having lied to them about the costs of membership, as well as the loss of sovereignty and democratic control. Reflecting on events, Shore considered the Heath–Rippon application and negotiation to be a 'surrender'[66] and, moreover, that Heath had betrayed British national independence and the country's extensive global network of political, economic and military alliances. The central purpose of the Heath government had been 'to end [our] separate, island history and to immerse it for ever in a Union with its continental neighbours.'[67] The episode highlighted how the 'patriotic card' was available to the Labour Party as well as the Conservatives, and evident in Shore's stance was a proud belief in the achievements of the British people, alongside optimism in what they could achieve in the future. It was a form of left-wing patriotism that distinguished him from many of his contemporaries, who had concluded that Britain's future lay inside the European Community and, later in his career, it is this that would set him apart from the mainstream of the Labour Party. 'The British disease, if there is such a thing,' reflected Shore in 1974, 'is gloom about being British.'[68]

Certainly, individuals such as Shore and Jay, who vehemently opposed membership of the Common Market, were deemed to have done so as a result of their nationalism and xenophobia, and they were therefore viewed as 'little Englanders'. Heath accused the anti-Europeans of being 'frightened about the big wide world', deeming that, 'for people like Peter Shore international brotherhood stops at Margate'.[69] Anthony King, in his analysis of the 1975 referendum, expanded on this theme. He wrote, 'the fact is that, like many

Conservative opponents of the Common Market, they could not bear the idea of foreigners making decisions affecting the lives of ordinary British citizens; they could not bear the fact that Britain no longer had a large role to play in world affairs'.[70] However, Shore argued that he had the full scale of Britain's international commitments in mind, and his vision of the country's world role and future bore remarkable similarities to Churchill's notion of Britain at the meeting point of concentric circles. The internationalism of Shore and Jay was not, in fact, constrained to one continent; Britain's world role was global, they thought, with interests and relationships across the whole of the English-speaking world. Those relationships would be reduced if Britain entered the Common Market and therefore membership signalled a tragic parting of the ways.

Shore's critique of the Common Market was not like others on the left, who viewed it as a 'capitalist club', and the fact that business favoured membership was enough to condemn the idea. Instead, Shore, along with Jay, offered a full and well-rounded objection to membership, combining the economic costs with the consequences for the British labour movement, democracy, sovereignty and Britain's world role. Butler and Kitzinger concluded that the referendum verdict 'must be kept in perspective. It was unequivocal but it was also unenthusiastic. Support for membership was wide, but it did not run deep.'[71] In short, the electorate's attitudes towards European integration were fluid, not fixed, and if there was a change in circumstances, their opinion would duly change. There was nothing to assume that Britain's membership of the EEC would be permanently accepted.

4

THE TERMS OF TRADE 1974–76

EDWARD HEATH'S DECISION TO call a snap general election on the question of 'Who Governs Britain?' backfired as the Labour Party found itself back in office after just four years in opposition. However, its lack of a parliamentary majority meant that a second election would not be too far away and, indeed, it took place in October of the same year. This time, the result was a parliamentary majority for Labour of just three seats. This precarious position, combined with the ascendancy of the party's left-wing faction, was to shape its approach in government for the next five years.

The previous chapter dealt at length with the primary concern of Shore's political life at this time: Europe. The purpose of this chapter is to explore Shore's record as a Cabinet minister between the February 1974 general election and the so-called IMF Crisis, when Britain appeared on the verge of bankruptcy and had to apply for a loan to the International Monetary Fund, which reached its final stages in December 1976. Throughout this time Shore served in the Cabinet as Secretary of State for Trade, although Wilson's decision to appoint Shore to Trade was opposed by Roy Jenkins, given that the role would impact on Britain's trading relationship with the EEC.[1] However, Wilson went ahead with the appointment, thus demonstrating his confidence in Shore's abilities. For Bernard Donoughue, the Cabinet formed by Wilson in 1974 was very strong, including Shore, but a combination of events and the 'deadweight of Labour's antique ideological commitments' were to ensure that it would not, ultimately, succeed.[2]

THE RISE OF THE LABOUR LEFT

Shore was not to repeat the role he had adopted in 1964, 1966 and again in 1970 as the principal author of the Labour manifesto. This is partly because, following defeat in the 1970 election, the Labour left had become ascendant.[3] In power, the left had seen Wilson as their man but got little in return. Consequently, after 1970 the left argued that a future Labour government's economic policy needed to be more radical. It came to dominate the NEC, which took control of policy-making, and had numerous successes at the annual party conference. The left pursued a more radical economic agenda, which included greater controls over the movement of capital, goods and services, and more extensive public ownership.

One key influence on what was to become known as Labour's Alternative Economic Strategy (AES) was Stuart Holland, who argued that the traditional distinction between the micro and macro economies, upon which Keynesian economics depended, was no longer valid since companies had grown to such a size that they could effectively determine their own prices and avoid the regulations of governments that still thought in terms of a competitive market economy. This 'mesoeconomy' necessitated more extensive public ownership, not in the form of the traditional nationalised industry but in competitive public enterprise.[4] Another key influence was the Cambridge Economic Policy Group, which argued for import controls.[5] These ideas were developed into *Labour's Programme 1973*,[6] which in turn formed the foundations of Labour's manifestos the following year.

The Labour Party therefore went into the 1974 elections with a more radical agenda than at any time since 1945. The leadership did not share the left's enthusiasm for the policies and several of them were removed in the final versions of the manifesto. However, Labour's precarious parliamentary position and the economic problems the new government faced allowed the leadership to abandon numerous other commitments that had been made in opposition. As we will see, following further defeat in 1979, the left accused the leadership of betrayal, pursued the AES with more vigour and sought to implement rule changes that would ensure such 'betrayal' could not happen again.

The Labour right was pushed onto the defensive after the 1970 defeat. Tony Crosland argued that the central economic failure of the Wilson administration, of which he had been a part, was the lack of political will to promote economic growth. All of the means were at hand, but the government had refused to use them. There was no need for a shift leftwards and the theories that underpinned the AES were flawed. All a future Labour government needed to do was to pursue Keynesian demand management and the rest would fall into place. It should not get sidetracked either by concerning itself with the parity of sterling, as Wilson had done, or by being diverted into industrial planning policies along the lines of the National Plan. More extensive public ownership was not required.[7]

Shore occupied a middle way between these two arguments. He believed, and so too did Crosland, that a more radical policy was needed at the time of the IMF Crisis, making a sustained critique of Denis Healey's economic policy. Although associated with the left-wing group between 1974 and 1976, Shore was not an advocate of the AES and never would be. His position, which he articulated at the time of the IMF Crisis and again as shadow Chancellor, is best characterised as one of radical Keynesianism. He believed that the state should have the capacity to steer the national economy, if necessary by resorting to limited and selective protectionist measures.

TROUBLED TIMES

One issue for which Peter Shore had responsibility at this time was the attempts by Freddie Laker to start running a low-cost transatlantic airline.[8] Laker had been involved in various business ventures in the aviation industry and his initial application for *Skytrain* was submitted in June 1971. However, the project was bogged down in legal wrangling from that point until Shore revoked the licence on 29 July 1975, for which Laker took the government to the High Court and won the case. The government appealed, but the appeal court also ruled in Laker's favour. Lord Denning, the judge presiding over the case, decided that the government had the right to change the existing legislation but that it must do so through changes to the Act on the floor of the House of Commons, whereas Shore had simply issued a White Paper. Laker's venture was initially successful; he received a knighthood in 1978 and was highly regarded by Margaret Thatcher. However, in 1982 Laker's company went bankrupt in what was seen as the biggest corporate failure ever to have occurred in Britain. In the context of the transition from the postwar social democratic consensus to the New Right, Shore could be seen as someone resisting the emergence of more competitive markets. However, defence for Shore comes from Norman Tebbit, who, reading Denning's findings when appointed parliamentary under-secretary for trade in 1979, summoned the relevant officials and confirmed that Shore had been legally correct. However, Shore chose not to take the case to the House of Lords. Tebbit comments that 'Peter Shore had made a sensible political decision not to fly in the face of public opinion, although I believed he would have had a good chance of winning if the case had gone right through to the House of Lords'.[9] Tebbit also believed that the weaknesses of Laker's business model were already apparent on the Conservatives coming to power in 1979.[10]

Apart from the Laker case, the other two matters that occupied Shore in the Trade Department were the European 'renegotiations' (the subject of the previous chapter) and the wider economic debate that would dominate the Cabinet's attention for the period of Labour government in the 1970s.[11]

The primary lesson that should be drawn from the experiences of economic management during the Labour government in the '60s, according to Shore, was that fixed exchange rates did not work. Indeed, by the time Labour came back to power in 1974 the fixed exchange rate system, Bretton Woods, had collapsed. For those who had been in government up to four years previously, this was seen as an advantage at first, since Labour could get on with its domestic economic plans unimpeded by the need to maintain the parity of sterling. However, they were soon to appreciate that a problematic floating exchange rate also had the capacity to blow the government off course.

Labour was able to quickly resolve the industrial unrest that had caused Heath to call the election. Seemingly having forgotten his own attempts to impose legal constraints on the ability of trade unions to strike, Wilson argued that the blame for the industrial unrest of 1973–74 must go to Heath. Wilson, in contrast, could work with the unions more harmoniously. A pay settlement of 35 per cent was reached with the striking miners on 6 March, which resolved the immediate unrest and the three-day week was ended the following day. On 31 July, the government repealed the Industrial Relations Act of 1971, which had been particularly controversial due to its creation of an industrial relations court, which was an attempt to restrict the ability of trade unions to strike. This caused unrest and the Social Contract was therefore devised, whereby the government would seek to implement social reforms that would benefit the working class in return for pay restraint by the unions. The agreement was to last until the autumn/winter of 1978/79, when the whole thing was to come crashing down spectacularly in the Winter of Discontent.

Meanwhile, Tony Benn had got to work on the AES proposals but received short shrift from Wilson and Denis Healey. He had also established worker cooperatives for the *Scottish Daily News* and the Meriden Motorcycle Company, though these were later to be seen as failures of the cooperative approach. Benn had earned the distrust of many of his Cabinet colleagues early on in the government, and after the referendum he was moved to Energy. Shore remained personally close to Benn in this period, although the strains that would lead to them parting company in the early 1980s were starting to show. Shore was sceptical of Benn's economic approach and cannot be seen as being on the left at this time, despite the existence of a 'left group' that included both Benn and Shore.[12]

In contrast, the government's approach was to adopt Keynesian fiscal expansion, and Healey outlined this position in a speech to the Confederation of British Industry (CBI) on 14 May 1974. His Budget that March had increased spending and taxation, albeit with reduced subsidies to the nationalised industries. In July, Healey announced extra measures that increased the Public Sector Borrowing Requirement by £200 million, which was to grow to a further £800 million in November 1974. The government also acquired shares in British Leyland and Burmah Oil.

However, at this point the government's approach changed. There were principally two reasons for this, the first domestic and the second international. The government became more focused on the problem of inflation, which had increased dramatically in 1974-75. It was felt that a key reason for this was the rise in wages; the miners were given a further 35 per cent increase on 13 February 1975 and figures showed that the average wage rise in 1974 had been 29 per cent. Realising both the dangers to the survival of the Labour government and the damage to the living standards of trade union members, Jack Jones (Transport and General Workers Union) advocated pay restraint. The new agreement was a £6 flat rate policy, with no increases for higher earners. The left objected but the party and the TUC agreed, and inflation fell to 16.5 per cent in 1976.

The second domestic issue the government faced was a rising public sector borrowing requirement (PSBR). As we have seen, the government's own policies in 1974 had added to this, but it was decided from early 1975 that the PSBR must be cut. The Public Expenditure White Paper, which was published in February 1975, was the first clear statement that the government would seek to reduce the deficit in the public finances, and the Budget on 15 April cut spending by £1,100 million, which had a deflationary effect on the economy. This led *The Times* to argue that the postwar orthodoxy had been broken.[13] A key measure for making further reductions would be the implementation of 'cash limits', which would impose a nominal figure on each major item of capital expenditure. Finally, Wilson announced that Cabinet committees could not overrule the Treasury, meaning that spending ministers seeking to oppose cuts would have to make their case in full Cabinet, reducing the chances of success.

Healey then announced in December 1975 that he would be applying for a stand-by facility from the International Monetary Fund (IMF), who insisted that the government needed to do more to cut public spending and the deficit. This brings us to the international situation. The Labour government had embarked on its expansionist fiscal stance in 1974 with the support of the IMF. At that time its main worry had been the slowing down in the world economy following the formation of OPEC and the quadrupling of oil prices, meaning governments needed to seek to reflate national economies. The IMF was still committed to a Keynesian economic approach, but its attitude changed (seemingly under the influence of US and German central banks) to being primarily concerned with inflation and public sector debt. It was to adopt a more hard-line position from the end of 1975.

The tensions within the Cabinet were exposed that December. Healey argued that there had to be a reduction in public spending in order to free up resources for the private sector; there would be no cuts for the immediate financial year (1976/77) but there would need to be reductions of £1 billion in the following year and £2.4 billion in

1978-79. The case for making resources available to the private sector was to be repeated in 1976 and was no doubt influenced by the then fashionable 'crowding out' thesis of Bacon and Eltis, which stated that the wealth-consuming public sector took vital resources away from the wealth-creating private sector, and that this was the cause of Britain's long-term economic decline.[14] It is notable that, some years later, when Shore was shadow Chancellor, a sympathetic account of his economic policy by Bryan Gould, John Mills and Shaun Stewart – on the one hand more radical than Healey's had been, yet on the other rejecting the alternative economic strategy (AES) – debunked the crowding out thesis.[15] Benn opposed the December cuts, proposing the AES instead, and Crosland also began to distance himself from the Treasury's position, tentatively having argued in May 1975 that 'the party's over' in terms of local government expenditure.[16] At this juncture, Shore was broadly in line with the Treasury's position, believing that public finances needed to brought under greater control.

Therefore, by the spring of 1976 there had already been a clear shift in the government's economic policy. However, if they felt that things had turned a corner, they were to be disappointed. The critical events of 1976 began in early March, when the Bank of England sold sterling and the following day cut interest rates. It was to lead to a rapid decline in the value of the currency to $1.70 by the time of the autumn party conference. The extent to which this was a deliberate policy of depreciation that went wrong, or the result of incompetence and indecision, is debatable, and the Treasury was certainly divided on the issue. Douglas Wass, as first permanent secretary, argued in favour of depreciation as the solution to Britain's economic problems. A lower valued pound would boost exports, he thought. This was a recurring theme in subsequent economic policy debates and Shore felt that it was central to his economic policy as shadow Chancellor, with some of those closest to him, such as John Mills, becoming long-term advocates.[17] Others in the Treasury and the Bank of England opposed the measure, believing it would get out of hand since the currency markets would develop their own momentum.

While the Keynesians were supportive of depreciation, others continued to argue against it, and Edmund Dell suggested that Healey was in the latter group.[18] The idea that a small nudge in the parity of sterling could be affected was wrong; a larger fall would be required. However, this would be inflationary, as it would significantly increase the value of imports, and the Social Contract would therefore be put at risk from the extension of the incomes policy that would be required to halt inflationary pressures. More cuts to public spending would also be needed in order to free up resources for investment in exports. Healey placed the blame firmly at the door of the Bank, and the Bank placed it at the Treasury.[19] What is clear is that this was a botched devaluation, which precipitated the economic crisis of later that year. It also posed questions for Shore's preferred economic policy, based as it was on a lower pound.

THE LEADERSHIP CONTEST

At this point Wilson announced his resignation, informing his Cabinet on 16 March 1976. It had not been anticipated. According to Bernard Donoughue, Marcia Williams 'came out of her room looking very fraught and took Peter Shore to one side – I heard him loudly gasp: "no!"'[20] Conspiracy theories began to circulate, but the reality seemed much more straightforward: Wilson looked, to his closest aides, exhausted, and he was beginning to suffer from ill health. His decision also seemed to come as less of a shock to Jim Callaghan, who had been tipped off in advance. Wilson had come back in 1974 without the ambition that he had in the 1960s, and even to his critics, such as Healey, he did not have any of the sense of paranoia of that earlier time.[21] He had decided that Callaghan should be his successor, promoting him to Foreign Secretary, from which position he would go on to become the only person ever to hold the top four offices of state.

In the leadership race following Wilson's departure, any hopes that Benn had of Shore supporting him were lost when Shore declared for Michael Foot.[22] Other candidates were not particularly serious contenders: Healey had just managed to upset his parliamentary colleagues in debates over public spending cuts on 10 March; Jenkins was far too pro-European to attract support across the party; and Crosland had never been one for courting support from parliamentary colleagues. For Shore, Foot had the right approach on Europe. He was also a distinguished parliamentarian and Shore was eventually to support Foot once again in 1980.

The first-round results were announced on 25 March. Foot topped the poll of MPs – who at this time still elected the leader without a wider vote of party members – with ninety votes. Callaghan was a clear second with eighty-four, while Jenkins obtained fifty-six, less than he expected, and immediately withdrew. Benn secured thirty-seven votes, which was more than was predicted, and also immediately withdrew, urging his supporters to vote for Foot in the second round. Healey fared badly with just thirty votes and Crosland came last with a mere seventeen. With Benn and Jenkins having withdrawn and Crosland eliminated, Healey decided to continue. In the second round Callaghan came first with 141, compared to Foot's

133 and Healey's thirty-eight. Finally, Callaghan got 176 and Foot 137. Jenkins agreed to leave British politics that autumn to become president of the European Commission in 1977, only to return four years later to lead the Social Democratic Party (SDP). The left did well in the contest, showing the changing nature of the Parliamentary Labour Party, but Callaghan was able to appeal to those on the right and the trade union centre. Indeed, the ensuing reshuffle marked a decisive shift to the right. Healey had expressed a strong interest in being Foreign Secretary and Crosland for the Treasury. However, Callaghan felt that Healey couldn't be moved in the immediate context of economic instability, while Foot urged Callaghan to make Shore the Foreign Secretary instead.[23] Yet, this could have been equally as divisive as giving the role to Jenkins, because both he and Shore held strong, though opposing, views on Europe. Callaghan has said that he liked Shore and that, apart from the different opinions on the EEC in the referendum the previous year, there was no significant difference of opinion between them: 'Peter's opposition to Common Market membership was one of the few political differences we had. In later years we usually found ourselves on the same side, and I admired greatly his dislike of cant and humbug, his scorn for the impractical, and his eloquence, which at its best was as grandiloquent as Churchill's.'[24] Overall, as Kenneth Morgan notes, Callaghan's Cabinet was more to the right than Wilson's had been: 'Wilson had an old loyalty to the Bevanite past; Callaghan had none whatsoever.'[25] Given that Shore was a one-time Bevanite this may suggest that his position would be weakened and, indeed, this seemed to be the case when he was replaced at Trade by Edmund Dell, instead becoming Secretary of State for Environment. However, Shore was to play a much greater role in Cabinet from now on.

CAP IN HAND

The leadership contest was a mere interlude in the mounting economic crisis. One of Callaghan's first meetings was with Healey, and records how shocked he was by the scale of the attempt to defend sterling since early March. Healey announced that he may need to approach the IMF once more and the following day, 6 April 1976, he announced his next Budget. There would be no further cuts to public spending, but cash limits would be rolled out. This pacified the Cabinet but seems to have disappointed the markets. A further year of pay policy was also announced, and although the measures already taken were having an impact on the PSBR and on inflation, the lack of market confidence led to further falls in the value of the pound. An international loan was agreed totalling $5.3 billion, which had to be repaid by the end of the year.

The decision was taken to introduce further expenditure cuts in July 1976 and led to what Healey described as 'an appallingly difficult series of meetings with my Cabinet colleagues'.[26] The Economic Strategy Committee of Cabinet met on 2 July and the majority were opposed to Healey's demand for £1 billion of cuts. Crosland made the Keynesian case against cutting at a time of economic downturn but was unable to play a significant role at this time due to his Foreign Office commitments. Benn made the case once more for the AES and, while Shore was not supportive of this, he was to resist cuts in his Environment Department Budget, namely to transport and housing. In this he was supported by Crosland, much to Callaghan's annoyance.[27] By the end of the month Healey had managed to obtain cuts of £1 billion, plus another £1 billion from increased employers' national insurance contributions. As the Environment Department was a high-spending one, Shore had to bear the burden of these latest cuts (along with Shirley Williams, who had responsibility for food subsidies). Critics on the left argued that this would lead to unemployment and social distress, while those on the right said it was too little too late.

Relative calm during August was followed by an avalanche in September. The pound fell dramatically, and Healey was forced to apply to the IMF for a loan, contending that the government would have to stick to its painful public expenditure plans. The scenes of Healey being booed at the September party conference only added to the sense of mounting chaos. Callaghan tried to calm the markets by appearing to endorse monetarism in his conference speech, and Healey raised interest rates on 7 October, but only after threatening to resign when Callaghan had initially refused to back him. Callaghan began a flurry of international negotiations from October onwards and the IMF delegation arrived on 1 November. They argued that cuts would be required amounting to £3 billion in 1977/78 and £4 billion in the following financial year.

The Cabinet debates of July were merely a taster of what was to come in November and December. At the Economic Strategy Cabinet Committee meeting on 3 November, Shore made his case for selective import constraints. For him, the PSBR was secondary to the lack of growth, and he believed that the government could carry international opinion for import controls.[28] The first key Cabinet debate took place on 23 November, notwithstanding the fact that the previous evening two dissenting groups of ministers (the social democrats and the left-wing group) had met privately, with the latter meeting taking place in Shore's office. This group included Shore, Benn, Foot, Silkin, Stan Orme and Albert Booth, but to see it as united would be a mistake.

Foot played a relatively small role in Cabinet debates, being keen to support Callaghan in his attempt to preserve the unity – indeed the very existence – of the government. Furthermore, Benn called for the AES, while Shore had a more moderate alternative strategy, privately arguing against Benn's proposals. Meanwhile, Silkin was closer to Shore in advocating a 'soft left' position. In Cabinet the next day, Callaghan called for unity and stressed the need to avoid leaks, with Healey setting out the economic position and making the case for cuts. This was opposed by Crosland, who thought there was no economic need for cuts, and in this he was backed by Hattersley. Shore also spoke against cuts, saying, 'we are being asked to bite the bullet but in fact we'll blow our political brains out'.[29]

The best prospect for defeating the IMF package of cuts would have been for the two dissenting groups to have worked together. The possibility of this was raised when, on 24 November, Crosland and Hattersley brought forward a proposal for limited import deposits, moving them closer to Shore's position. However, there appears to have been little attempt to form a common front, and Shore said that he was not approached at this time.[30] Certainly, Shore and Crosland had never been especially close, going back to the 1950s when Crosland had been a firm ally of Gaitskell and Shore had been closer to Wilson. In the early 1970s, Susan Crosland recorded Tony as saying that 'Peter Shore is a nice man but his economic theories are not what one wants at this moment', on hearing that it might be Shore or himself who was to be appointed shadow Chancellor following Jenkins's resignation.[31] In fact it was to be Healey, with whom they were now both in fierce disagreement. Political rivalries between the two camps may explain this in part, and talks between David Hill and Frances Morrell, advisors to Crosland and Benn respectively, failed to make progress, perhaps due to the tendency for Benn to argue for the full AES package rather than seeking a wider alliance based around a softer proposal. The two groups began to splinter. Some of the social democrats believed that Crosland's negotiating position (which was effectively to tell the IMF to go away and threaten to withdraw troops from Germany and Cyprus in order to pressurise the Americans) was unrealistic. Others feared that import controls would strain relations with the EEC and would possibly even be illegal under the Treaty of Rome. Some of those who had previously been associated with Crosland's position began to drift away, including Harold Lever, Bill Rodgers and Shirley Williams.

Moreover, Healey believed that the three alternative policies presented to Cabinet in detail on 1 and 2 December were all flawed.[32] On 1 December, Benn had put forward his case for the AES once more. However, it appears that ministers had been furnished with critical questions and the case was deemed to have fallen apart. Shore then presented his paper.[33] The choice, he said, was between deflation and an alternative policy, and the Chancellor's proposals, he suggested, would be a 'political tomb' for the government.[34] He argued that import controls were needed as a short-term measure to cure the current account deficit, but he opposed the AES for calling for controls over a long period, which would not allow domestic industry to regenerate. His approach was consistent with the EEC and GATT (Article XII) rules, which allowed temporary import restrictions in times of economic urgency. Moreover, the OECD trade pledge, which the government had twice reaffirmed, stated that surplus countries should act in such a way that stimulated international trade. As they were not doing so, the government should not feel compelled by international economic obligations, Shore said. It was thought that other countries may follow Britain's lead on this, as they too were in deficit – most likely Italy but also possibly France, Australia, New Zealand and Canada, who were all experiencing balance of payments problems. The IMF would accept such proposals, Shore argued. He believed that this would result in a surplus of £4 billion by 1978, accepting that the June stand-by would have to be repaid, but that a three-month extension should be requested. However, Cabinet rejected Shore's proposals on the basis that he had misunderstood the strength of feeling in America, Germany and the IMF; without the loan, Britain was facing a position of bankruptcy.[35] Moreover, his proposed measures would in themselves have a deflationary impact and would lead to retaliation, and some Cabinet members argued that the reaction of the EEC would need to be considered. Crosland then made his case against cuts, but this also failed to carry the Cabinet.

Callaghan decided – perhaps what he was all along going to do – to support Healey. He squared the package of cuts with the trade union leaders and informed Crosland privately. Then, in Cabinet the next day, Callaghan announced his decision.[36] He was followed by Crosland, who said he would support the Prime Minister even though he thought it was the wrong policy, whereas Shore objected by asking if it was right that a Cabinet minister could support a policy he admitted was wrong.[37] Another said that Crosland had 'collapsed like a pack of cards'.[38] Shore and Benn continued to state their opposition to the package, but the majority was now in favour.

Further acrimonious negotiations took place over the following days, with Healey at one point threatening to call a general election if the IMF did not back down. The IMF director, Johan Witteveen, had demanded an extra £1 billion of cuts and Healey responded saying he could 'go take a running leap'.[39] Healey had not had a Prime

Ministerial sanction for threatening an election on the basis of the
IMF versus the government, but Callaghan said that he was 'quite
happy that he should have done so' as this was the time to be very
tough in the negotiations.[40] Eventually an agreement was reached and
was put to Cabinet on 6 December.[41] Cabinet debated where cuts
should fall in what Benn described as an 'agonising process',[42] with
Shore agreeing to cut the budgets of the water authorities as part of
the wider package of cuts. On the same day, the left-wing ministers
met again. Foot said that he would not be resigning and the others
present – including Shore – took the same stance.[43] The following
day, Callaghan appeared to lose his temper over possible resignations
and Foot intervened to stress that the left-wingers were willing to
support the decisions taken over the past week.[44] On 15 December
the Letter of Intent (the agreement with the IMF) was published.[45]
Press coverage would be highly critical, they knew, but international
opinion was favourable. The loan was granted, and the economic
position improved dramatically in 1977. Indeed, the speed of the recovery was so marked that some questioned whether the crisis had
been real at all.

Healey later admitted in his memoirs that the crisis could have
been avoided because the Treasury forecasts were incorrect.[46] The
PSBR was not as bad as was thought at the time, which would appear
to support the arguments of Healey's opponents. However, Healey
would maintain that it demonstrated the power of the international
currency markets. No doubt had Crosland lived beyond the end of
that government he would have been critical on the same grounds as
he had been in 1964–70: the absence of political will. Had Crosland
or Shore been appointed Chancellor instead of Healey, the response
of the government may well have been different. Certainly, some years

later, as shadow Chancellor, Shore argued that a more radical policy than that pursued by Healey should be adopted and that this was possible without going for the AES. However, the inability of Shore and Crosland to work together and to maintain the support of a section of the Cabinet ultimately allowed Healey's position to win out.

The legacy of this episode is open to interpretation. In one view, the speedy recovery of the economy in 1977 appeared to justify the decisions taken in December 1976, meaning the effects were therefore both political and long-term. Indeed, the lurch to the left after 1979 was in part inspired by the events of 1976, when the government was accused of betraying its manifesto commitments and imposing measures that hurt the working class most. However, the longer-term effects of the crisis may be that faith was lost in the capacity of governments to act in the face of what was to become known as globalisation. Certainly, subsequent events, including the defeat of the Mitterrand government's socialist economic policy and then the forced withdrawal from the Exchange Rate Mechanism in 1992, led New Labour to believe that it had to adopt a policy of seemingly tight fiscal rules and an independent central bank. Those who wanted Britain to be part of the European single currency seemed only too willing to accept such constraints on fiscal policy, yet both of these positions undermined the central Keynesian belief in the autonomy of the central state over economic policy.

For Shore personally, the IMF Crisis considerably increased his standing within the Cabinet. He had set out his own economic theory, one which challenged the Chancellor and was taken much more seriously than the AES advocated by Benn, and the fact that Shore ultimately lost this debate was not fatal. It is recognised that in debates over economic policy it is very difficult to defeat the Chancellor in

Cabinet, given that his/her economic case is supported by the civil servants in the Treasury, and that the arguments of his/her opponents can also be subjected to Cabinet scrutiny. The Chancellor's position is unassailable if backed by the Prime Minister. Therefore, Shore's defeat on the policy was less significant than the increased profile he found within the Cabinet from making his case. Shore had come out of the IMF Crisis stronger than when he went into it – stronger, in fact, once his mentor had vacated the stage.

5

THE DEATH OF DEMOCRATIC
SOCIALISM? 1976–79

THE CALLAGHAN PREMIERSHIP WAS a tumultuous
period in British politics, with the death of democratic socialism widely proclaimed. For many, the final years of the Labour
government were the painful demise of the postwar consensus,
which finally ended in 1979 with the election of Margaret Thatcher.
Bookended as it was by the IMF Crisis and the Winter of Discontent,
few positive achievements were listed by critics of the government:
for the right, it was more than ample evidence of the failure of social
democracy,[1] whereas, for the left, it also proved that Labour's attempt
at managed capitalism had failed and only a 'truer' form of socialism could be a future Labour government's policy.[2] The decision
of the 'gang of four' to establish a new political party also reduced
the numbers who were willing to defend the Labour government. It
was only years later that an attempt to restore the reputation of the
Wilson–Callaghan governments was made.[3] This chapter seeks to
revisit that era, in which Shore played a central role. It begins with a

discussion of his ministerial achievements and then goes on to look at his contribution to the wider policy debates and political direction of those tumultuous years.

ENVIRONMENT SECRETARY

The Department of the Environment emerged rebranded as the Whitehall department, with new responsibilities ascribed to it that did not fit into any other portfolio. It therefore acquired responsibility for a wide range of policies; these may not have necessarily cohered, but they did consume large amounts of public spending – for instance, housing and public transport. Certainly, concern with the natural environment was not as great then as it has since become.

It was while serving as Secretary of State for the Environment that Shore suffered a personal loss, when one of his sons, Piers, was found dead from a drug overdose on Friday 9 September 1977. Piers had been living in a squat and had become addicted to drugs. In the memorial service at All Saints, Putney, on 16 September, Trevor Huddleston described him as 'a very amusing boy, popular and well loved', and went on to say that 'those who are loving and generous are also vulnerable'.[4] It was an event which clearly left a lasting legacy on Peter and Liz Shore, and although it did not appear to affect Shore's ministerial work at the time, it may have contributed to his later depression.

On becoming Secretary of State, Shore decided that he did not wish to have a political advisor. He had taken over the role from Tony Crosland, who had been promoted to Foreign Secretary, and

Crosland's political assistant, David Lipsey, had moved with him. Lipsey was asked to persuade Shore that he needed to be replaced,[5] but Shore remained opposed to the idea – it was not in the British tradition and he believed that the civil service was suspicious of the idea of political advisors. After a while, however, Shore asked if he had anyone in mind. Lipsey recommended Jack Straw, who had been political advisor to Barbara Castle but now found himself out of work following Callaghan's decision to dismiss her as one of his first acts in No. 10. Straw had the advantage, Lipsey felt, of being a Eurosceptic. Shore was convinced and Straw was appointed, although he later had to stand down as he had been selected for the Blackburn constituency to replace Castle. He was to be succeeded by David Cowling, who was later to work for the BBC. Cowling speaks very highly of Shore and felt that his ministerial record was one with clear successes,[6] although he notes that he himself was supportive of European integration at this time and made Shore aware of it. Still, he was appointed anyway and the issue was not discussed again, which is surely a sign of Shore's tolerance of opinion diversity. Indeed, Cowling says that he was given much encouragement in the role. Shore's longstanding friend Brian Abel-Smith also took up an advisory role,[7] while as his PPS Shore initially employed John Prescott. However, Prescott decided to become part of the delegation to the European Assembly and was to be replaced by Bryan Gould. Yet this, too, did not last long because, although not a ministerial position, the PPS is meant to obey the party whip; Gould nonetheless rebelled against the imposition of a duty on imported food that included New Zealand lamb, and was sacked. As a mark of his disapproval of this decision, Shore refused to take on another

PPS for the rest of his time in office,[8] showing a clear sense of loyalty to Gould, and those who worked closely with Shore throughout his career also felt a strong sense of loyalty towards him.

If his advisors held Shore in high regard, Sir John Hunt, the Cabinet Secretary, did not. Shore, he said, 'does not always give the impression of being a happy man at the Department of the Environment and suggested that his strength lay in intellectual argument rather than executive decision-making in a department of 70,000 people'. However, it is notable that Hunt made observations on a number of Cabinet ministers, often going beyond a formal assessment of their administrative capabilities.[9] Comparatively, Bernard Donoughue felt that the ministers who performed best in this government were those who employed special advisors, as it allowed them to engage in debates outside of their ministerial brief, such as Shore on the IMF Crisis.[10] Overall, he felt that Shore was 'an endearing and independent-minded maverick from the right' of the party.[11] Indeed, Lord Morris believes that Shore was a respected and thoughtful member of the Cabinet,[12] while, according to Bill Rodgers, Callaghan took Shore seriously as a member of the Cabinet and gave him increased status.[13]

One decision made by Callaghan to which Shore objected was the separation of transport policy from the Department of the Environment in order to create an additional Cabinet post for Rodgers. Lipsey felt that Shore had inherited a distinctive and radical transport policy from Crosland, which was to divert funds away from rail subsidies, disproportionately benefiting the middle classes, towards the local buses upon which the working classes largely relied. Shore published Crosland's transport paper unaltered.[14] However, the ministerial reorganisation meant that there was no time for him to develop his own transport policy, and he expressed his unhappiness with this privately.[15] Other areas of policy therefore predominated, and Shore obtained two Bills in the Queen's speech in November 1977: the Housing Bill, which would give extra help to first-time buyers; and the Inner Cities Bill.[16] These two areas, housing and inner cities, were the priority issues for Shore.

Labour was moving in the direction of allowing tenants greater control over their houses through residents' associations, which would allow them to make alterations to their properties – something that had been previously denied in the postwar town planners' uniformity. Shore argued that there should be a Tenant's Charter[17] and, in a speech to the Institute of Housing in Harrogate on 23 June 1978, he put forward that the expectations of tenants had increased at the same time that councils had become more distant landlords. Residents, he thought, were demanding more choice and local councils needed to respond to this: 'it is a sign of health in a society that people should demand and expect a choice'. Shore also suggested that tenants should be more involved in the decisions affecting their housing and should have greater rights to do so. Social and physical environments needed to be improved, in particular by moving away from high-rise blocks, in a recognition of a problem created by the 1960s desire to build high.[18] A further area of discussion was the local government rates, with reference to the Layfield Report of 1976. Shore believed that there was no perfect system of local government finance, but that retention of the rates was the least bad option, whereas a poll tax would create widespread opposition.[19] In the end, those living in tied cottages were given more rights.[20] Shore also steered the Housing (Homeless Persons) Bill through the Commons, which became law in July 1977 despite opposition from the Conservatives and some on his own side, who believed that the priority attached to housing the homeless would allow some to queue-jump and would reward irresponsibility.[21]

However, the most controversial issue was ownership. There was growing pressure to allow council tenants to purchase their own homes and the policy was popular among Labour voters living in council houses. However, there was also considerable opposition from the Labour left, who believed that the policy was pandering to materialism. Shore attempted to steer a course through this stormy political sea, and the issue was on the agenda within the department as soon as he took up the role of Secretary of State. He stated that there was a need to review the policy as a possible source of revenue given the government's programme of cuts.[22] In September 1976, Shore issued guidance on housing tenure, which included measures to allow for cheaper mortgages, and local authorities were encouraged to sell their houses to tenants at full value and in such a way that would not deplete social housing stock 'locality by locality'.[23] This was a tentative step in the direction of home ownership, but disappointed those in the government who wanted to move more decisively down the path of selling council houses. According to Donoughue, Shore failed to support the 'right to buy' and therefore missed a political opportunity.[24] The Policy Unit had been developing such a strategy, but

> when Peter Shore finally drafted an official statement on the government's position on the sale of council houses in late 1978 it was phrased in a way which would delight a few thousand activists on the Labour left and alienate the hundreds of thousands of council tenant voters who wanted more freedom.[25]

However, this assessment overlooks the fact that Callaghan was also of the view that the sale of council houses would divide the party.[26] For his part, Tony Crosland had been a cautious supporter of council house sales, but recognised that if it was pushed through it could become another Clause IV moment, splitting the Labour Party.[27] Shore's view on this was therefore no different from his Cabinet colleagues, seeking to balance the views of voters with those of the party. Shore's more tentative approach can also be seen as far sighted, in that he identified the social housing crisis that would emerge following eighteen years of Conservative government; both Conservative and Labour governments since 1979 had failed to build anywhere near enough social housing.

Thatcher took credit for the policy, which she implemented immediately on coming to power. However, this fails to grasp the level of opposition Shore faced from within his own party as he allowed the civil service to develop policy proposals and mooted the idea in speeches. It was certainly true that the Conservative Party was willing to move much more rapidly in this area;[28] it had made tentative moves in this direction in the 1960s, but there was a stronger sense of purpose in the 1970s. A report for the Conservatives was produced on this area ahead of the 1974 elections, and then, in 1976, *The Right Approach* advocated the sale of council houses to tenants. The policy was contained in the 1979 manifesto and was quickly enacted. Indeed, Michael Heseltine, Shore's Conservative successor, did not need to discuss the policy with the Prime Minister after coming to power; the decision had been made: there would be a right of tenants of more than three years to purchase their home at a specially discounted price. After the fall of the Labour government, Shore declared much more fully his support for council house sales, saying that people had aspirations and that Labour must facilitate them: 'socialism and a little prosperity have unlocked aspirations which cannot, and should not, be denied'. Those owning their own homes had increased since 1945 to 59 per cent by 1980, 'and all the surveys show that many of the remaining 41 per cent would like to do so'.[29] Later, he confessed that his policy in government had been wrong on this issue: 'I totally misjudged the policy of selling council houses. It had a dramatic effect.'[30]

Shore's other principal policy concern at this time was to recreate the inner cities. Here Donoughue argued that Shore 'mastered the appalling complexities of the inner city problem and made as much progress to redistribute resources towards these run-down areas as was possible within the constraints of public expenditure'.[31] For his advisor David Cowling, the inner-cities policy was a principled priority. Too much emphasis had been placed on new towns and Shore announced that the new towns expansion would be halted.[32] In February 1977, Shore spoke at the 'Save Our Cities' conference in Bristol. He said his aims would be to attract businesses back into the inner cities, improve the social and physical environment and relieve immediate social stress.[33] He produced a White Paper on Inner Cities in June 1977,[34] and this resulted in the Inner Urban Areas Bill, which received its second reading in the Commons on 9 February 1978[35] and became law later that year. The legislation gave special attention to 'partnership areas' requiring special assistance based on need. Considerable funding was secured, especially given the wider budgetary constraints, and Shore began to make a series of speeches and press releases where the new funding was announced from May 1977 onwards.[36]

Although the policy was rolled out nationally, London was a particularly strong focus, especially in Tower Hamlets where exceptionally poor housing had survived. The slums would be cleared and replaced with modern housing with gardens in what was a radical policy, especially at times of fiscal restraint. There had been considerable focus over the past two decades on new towns, but the problems of the inner cities were acute, meaning that the housing conditions of the inner-city working class were dire. Shore had in mind a new model of what the cities should look like, with considerably improved housing and open recreational spaces.

It is clear that Shore regarded this as a matter of social justice and that there was a clear sense of momentum. However, with the change of government in 1979, Shore's policy was redirected. In place of the new housing, funding was diverted to the building of high-rise office blocks to accommodate the newly expanded banking sector. He told his son Cris that it felt great to switch on the tap to help these areas but was frustrating after 1979 to see the Docklands Corporation – where Shore had invested £17 million in 1977[37] – buying up the land and being unable to do anything about it in opposition.[38] For many years poverty coexisted with the newfound affluence of the banks, with local residents benefiting little, if at all, from the new world that Thatcher was unleashing.

Shore also advocated relaxing planning laws in order to allow for industrial development. Denis Healey regarded this as part of a wider shift in government policy in favour of industry through the National Economic Development Council (NEDC).[39] He himself increased spending on training schemes and Shirley Williams began to shift education policy towards the needs of industry. Sixteen projects were developed, including silicon chip technology, and Healey regarded this as a successful period of partnership between government and industry, although it was soon to be eclipsed by the free-market agenda of Thatcherism. Shore was also keen to protect national heritage, with

Battle Abbey being purchased, or 'saved for the nation' as he put it,[40] as well as funding being announced to restore historical buildings.[41]

The importance of nuclear power was also recognised by Shore. However, when faced with a decision to build a new facility at Windscale he rejected pressures to have the measure rushed through without full consultation.[42] He argued that such an important matter should be subject to a full public inquiry: 'I welcome this debate because I believe that the matters covered by the Windscale report go far beyond those normally raised by a planning inquiry and because it is right that these matters should be debated in this House'.[43] The inquiry opened in June 1977,[44] and the following March Shore reported on the findings to Parliament.

Shore's tenure in Environment was an interesting one. Few ministerial records are unblemished, and one must also take into account the constraints that ministers and governments face, both political and economic. Shore could have legislated for council house sales, but this neglects to consider the growing power of the left within the Labour Party at this time. His policy on the inner cities was certainly bold and correct; despite the fiscal constraints he did manage to secure funding and, had the government survived, it would have improved the conditions for some of the poorest in society. However, this was not to be as the minority government limped on in the face of dire conditions.

MINORITY GOVERNMENT

The Callaghan government lost its parliamentary majority in March 1977 and faced a no confidence vote. Callaghan entered into talks with the Liberal Party, now under the leadership of David Steel,[45] and, in return for adopting certain Liberal policies, the Labour government would be supported by the party in votes in the House of Commons. The agreement included consultation with the Liberals before each piece of legislation was put before the House, a system of proportional representation for the European parliamentary elections, and pushing ahead with devolution to Scotland and Wales.[46]

For the majority of the Cabinet there was no alternative to the pact, but four ministers objected.[47] One of these was Shore, who felt that the agreement was dangerous, and he disagreed with direct elections to the European Parliament, especially under proportional representation, which he felt eroded the principle of the sovereignty of the Westminster Parliament.[48] Devolution would lead, he thought, to a 'Europe of the regions', as the EEC sought ultimately to destroy national loyalties.[49] Other dissenting ministers were Tony Benn and Stan Orme from the left of the party, who feared the further dilution of the socialist intent of the 1974 manifestos, and – surprisingly – Bruce Millan, the Scottish Secretary, who said that, although he recognised there was no alternative under the circumstances, a pact would be very risky and so he could not support it.[50] The government won the no confidence vote by 322 to 298, with all the Liberal MPs voting in support of the government. The pact allowed Labour to stay in power for another year until it was dissolved on 7 September 1978. It can be regarded (as Shore himself came to believe) as being more successful for the Labour Party than for the Liberals, not just because it helped keep Labour in power, but also because it was seen as highlighting the negotiating skills of the Prime Minister as the Liberals secured very little from it.[51] The experience of the Lib–Lab Pact was a generally unhappy one, nonetheless, as Labour ministers resented the required consultations with their Liberal Party counterparts. Healey, in particular, was highly critical of the Liberals' economic affairs spokesman, John Pardoe;[52] indeed, Shore had the same 'shadow' in the pact and felt that Pardoe had no proper role to fulfil.[53] Shore's opposition to dealing with the Liberals was also a product of his experience in his constituency, where he believed the Liberal Party to be 'vile'.[54] To David Lipsey, Shore had nothing in common with the Liberals: he believed in two-party politics, with Labour as the representatives of the working class, and that this should not be diluted by alliances with a third party.[55] In addition, he thought the Liberal Party said different things locally and nationally and could not be trusted.

Following the ending of the Lib–Lab Pact, the Labour government staggered on, seeking deals with the Ulster Unionists and the Scottish and Welsh Nationalists. The price was parliamentary constituencies of the same size as the rest of the UK for Ulster. Shore felt that this was a perfectly legitimate request, once again confirming his strong Unionism, which had first been demonstrated at the time of the decision in 1969 to send troops to Northern Ireland.[56] The Nationalists wanted to progress devolution, though to this Shore was opposed.

The episode highlights Shore's constitutional conservatism. In the annual Nye Bevan lecture on 5 December 1976, Shore rebutted the 'elective dictatorship' thesis articulated by Lord Hailsham and defended the doctrine of parliamentary sovereignty unimpeded by written constitutions that shifted power from Parliament to the courts. According to Shore, it was this reality of parliamentary sovereignty that had allowed for the peaceful evolution of British society, unlike many continental countries which had suffered political upheaval.[57] Shore was a defender of the monarchy[58] and was opposed to proportional representation, to elections to the European

Parliament and to devolution. The latter of these was likely to take up considerable legislative time, he thought, and the corresponding proposals on greater devolution to England were of 'anaesthetising boredom'.[59] A further example of Shore's constitutional conservatism at this time was a Cabinet debate over the reform of Freedom of Information legislation, which had been proposed in Parliament by the Liberal MP Clement Freud. Shore believed that this was a charter for the paranoid and would weaken the role of the MP by giving greater power to the courts – he had not become an MP to give power away to the judiciary.[60] He was backed by the likes of Tony Benn, but some were more inclined to support the legislation. In Cabinet, Shore opposed reforms to liberalise the Official Secrets Act,[61] although, following the controversy over the publication of Crossman's diaries, the civil service attempted to restrict the publication of ministerial memoirs in the form of the Radcliffe Report. Bernard Donoughue regarded this as an attempt by the civil service to bounce the Prime Minister into a decision to restrict the rights of ministers, and Shore was one of those who opposed it on liberal grounds.[62] Finally, after the 1979 vote of no confidence, the Cabinet met to draw up its manifesto commitments. Benn proposed abolition of the House of Lords on the basis that it was undemocratic and a feudal relic. However, Shore argued passionately for not including this proposal in the manifesto on the basis that there was never any agreement on what would replace it.[63]

The economy had improved since the calamitous events at the end of 1976, but there were still significant challenges. For backbench MP and Shore's former PPS Bryan Gould, the problem was that Healey had allowed the pound to rise in 1977, meaning that the potential gains of devaluation had been lost.[64] Gould was close to Shore,

and this narrative fitted in to the subsequent economic policy that
Shore proposed as shadow Chancellor: that an overvalued pound
was responsible for Britain's economic troubles and that this in turn
reflected the strength of the UK banking sector over its manufacturing sector. Shore returned to his preferred policy of selective import
controls in Cabinet[65] and also proposed tax changes that were met
with support from the Chancellor, but which were dismissed by the
Prime Minister. The proposals argued that mortgage tax relief should
be withdrawn for 150,000 taxpayers who earned over two and a half
times the average wage. Healey felt this was a sensible proposal since
the 'existing provision was grossly regressive; it distorted the housing
market and meant that a tiny minority of wealthier people paid far
less in interest on their mortgages than the rest of the population'.
However, Callaghan felt that it would lose votes. The consequence
was that 'the rich are still able to pay far less interest than the poor in
borrowing for their houses'.[66]

   Britain's relationship with the EEC also took up a lot of Shore's
attention at this time, as in all other periods. Though the referendum had
been meant to settle the issue, it was not long before further disputes
arose as the EEC sought to move towards the closer integration of
its member states. Without the support of his Cabinet, Wilson had
agreed to a number of proposals while at the European Summit in
December 1975, which were to incur the wrath of the Eurosceptics.[67]
This included direct elections, but there was also the decision to
introduce a new passport for the 'European Community'. On hearing
of this, Shore erupted. Benn states that after breaking for lunch
the Cabinet reconvened and a number of new maroon-coloured
passports had been distributed. On seeing them Shore remarked,
'We don't have to have these passports, do we? Surely we can keep

our British ones if we want.' On being told that this was not possible, he exclaimed, 'My children and grandchildren *forced* to abandon the old British passport!' According to Tony Benn he was 'boiling with rage' and Benn has said that he himself very much agreed with Shore. Bruce Millan, however, spoke against them, saying that it was a peculiar middle-class concern as most of the working class did not have passports.[68]

The third area of disagreement over European integration at this time concerned plans for closer economic and monetary integration. Roy Jenkins, now President of the European Commission, was a keen advocate for this policy. However, in the Cabinet Shore objected on the basis that it was a step towards a federal Europe; he believed that the policy was wrong in principle and could not work.[69] In the end, the government avoided committing itself to closer monetary union. In addition, the EEC also argued that Britain should relax its controls on capital movements, asserting that its balance of payments problems were now resolved. Shore remarked that it was crazy for them to say this at the same time that the IMF was arguing for greater budgetary restraint in order to restore its financial position.[70]

As the government wore on, the major issue became industrial relations. Shore was not a particularly strong advocate for the trade unions, and according to Lord Lipsey this reflected his statism. If the government wanted to impose a pay policy, Shore thought, the unions should accept it in the national interest.[71] However, he was also a supporter of greater workplace democracy. For example, the Report of the Committee of Inquiry on Industrial Democracy, chaired by Alan Bullock, proposed a number of measures on how to introduce industrial democracy and was split, with a minority report proposing a different set of recommendations. Shore expressed his view privately that the report lacked clarity, attesting that employee representatives should be directly elected.[72]

The Social Contract had survived the IMF Crisis and the cuts leading up to it. However, the public sector unions were becoming restless when Callaghan insisted on a 5 per cent pay norm. Some, including Shore, argued for a slightly higher pay norm, believing that 5 per cent would mean a cut in living standards.[73] The government's policy applied only to the public sector, and its inability to determine wages in the private sector was demonstrated when Ford workers got 17 per cent. This lit the fuse for public sector workers going on strike. Shore was in the thick of this in the expansive Environment Department, with local authority manual workers bringing among the most forthright of pay demands at 40 per cent.[74] For Donoughue, Shore was 'enigmatic' at this time. Some Cabinet members (not Shore, he felt) were playing politics ahead of a future leadership contest, to be held once the government fell, and many were constrained by their sponsorship from different trade unions.[75] By January 1979 the pay norm had risen to 10 per cent, but Shore and David Ennals (Health) proposed 15 per cent.[76] 'The reality was that there were too many marshmallows and too few vertebrae in Jim's Cabinet,' Donoughue thought,[77] though it is notable that he had previously recommended that Shore be sacked from the Cabinet along with other ministers whom he deemed to be underperforming.[78] Cabinet debated whether there could be a state of emergency, and some on the left ruled out having such draconian legislation, even for emergency workers. However, Benn records in his diary that Shore was one of those who argued in favour, saying that the police had managed to secure better pay and conditions despite not having the right to strike.[79] Shore thought that gravediggers lacked 'a sense of common humanity' and asked their trade union representatives, 'What about the dignity of the dead?'[80] In one incident Shore turned on Dennis Skinner, MP for Bolsover since 1970 and a figure firmly associated with the left wing of the Labour Party. Shore had begged the striking gravediggers, 'whatever their grievance, to reconsider their action, to understand the distress being caused to the bereaved, and the deep offence being caused to the overwhelming mass of our people, and to return to work'. Skinner thought this hypocrisy, since the government could achieve this by granting the strikers what they demanded. However, Shore was having none of it: 'hypocrisy – no; death is not hypocrisy, nor is human grief. Nor is the sense of common humanity that people have when they share these experiences. Therefore, some sense of common fellowship and decency between members of the same community ought to come across.'[81]

Callaghan says in his memoirs that his instincts were to invoke a state of emergency, but he was persuaded that the measure would have little direct practical benefit while also inflaming passions.[82] He therefore felt that the best option would be to seek to pacify the unions. On his return from an international conference in Guadeloupe, at which he was seen swimming in the warm sunshine, he sought to play down fears of 'mounting chaos' – which was promptly reported in the press as 'crisis, what crisis?'. For some, Callaghan seemed to lose his finely tuned political antennae, but Shore believed that it was simply the Prime Minister saying in his own 'imperturbable "Uncle Jim" way that "I am not panicking, nor should you"'.[83] For the Conservatives under Margaret Thatcher, this showed the extent to which the trade unions were now out of control, and Peregrine Worsthorne sought to capture the mood, arguing that what people wanted was the smack of firm government.[84] The Labour Party had been elected in 1974 on the basis that it could govern effectively through a deal with the trade unions, but by early 1979 all that lay in ruins. The left sought to place the blame on the failures of government policy and Callaghan's decision to impose an overly restrictive pay norm on the public sector. However, Shore strongly defended Callaghan's actions. Indeed, if anything he felt Callaghan should have gone further. For him, reflecting later in his book, *Leading the Left*, Callaghan's failure had not been being too strict but rather not being strict enough:

> It was a nightmare. No one, in their wildest dreams, could have predicted such a collective barbarity in advance of the actual event ... Callaghan was certainly not to blame for the Winter of Discontent ... If fault there was, it was that the government was altogether too conciliatory ... The armed forces should have been deployed to clear the refuse, dig the graves, ensure the water and other essential supplies. They were not.[85]

Shore was placed on a secret committee of ministers and civil servants (GEN 158), chaired by Merlyn Rees, the role of which was to coordinate the government's response to the strikes and to keep essential services running.[86]

The devolution referenda were held and lost on 1 March 1979. In Wales there was a clear majority against a Welsh Assembly of 79.74 per cent to 20.26 per cent, whereas in Scotland there was a narrow majority in favour, of 51.62 per cent to 48.38 per cent. However, a Labour unionist amendment by George Cunningham, that 40 per cent of the total registered electorate had to agree to devolution, meant that the referendum was lost. The nationalists switched their support to the Conservatives, believing that this would be the best way to secure devolution (after all, it would have been carried in Scotland if not for the Labour amendment), and also because the Conservatives had embraced devolution in their 1974 manifestos. However, it should be stated that they were unlikely to get it under Margaret Thatcher, who was an instinctive unionist and had presided over a cautious move against devolution in her party.[87] The Liberal Party also voted against the government, prompting Michael Foot to ridicule David Steel in his summing up of the no confidence debate. In the end Labour lost by one vote.

The timing of the election was therefore taken out of the hands of the Labour government. Had Callaghan been able to limp on a little longer he may have fared slightly better, and certainly there are those who argued that had Callaghan called a snap election in the autumn of 1978 he may well have won. The Cabinet had met in July the previous year to discuss the timing of the election, and at that point Shore believed that the matter should be left to Callaghan's discretion, though he was personally in favour of delaying the election until the following spring – a view, according to Kenneth Morgan, shared by Callaghan, Foot, David Owen and probably Healey.[88] The economy had improved slightly and Labour had nudged ahead in the opinion polls over the summer. Some felt that Callaghan had to call the election in the autumn, but he announced, quoting the words of a music hall song at the party conference, that he would not be doing so. It was unlikely that Callaghan would have secured an improved parliamentary position in any case; during the 1979 election campaign he told activists that every thirty years or so there is a sea change in British politics and that this was one such moment.[89] He remained more popular in the opinion polls than Thatcher in terms of personal rating, but Labour was clearly unpopular and suffered a significant election defeat.

The period was hardly a heroic one in British political history. However, if governments are judged in terms of the constraints they face and the context in which they operate – as these authors think they should be – then the 1974–79 government could be considered a limited success. Lacking a parliamentary majority for much of its existence, with a strongly divided parliamentary party and Cabinet and facing mounting economic problems and industrial unrest, the government did have achievements. Shore found ministerial successes and made significant contributions to Cabinet discussions, and by the end of its term in office he was considered among the top flight of Labour politicians. Not that this would do him any favours within the party, though, as the left began to accuse the government of betrayal.

6

THE SHADOW CABINET AND THE 1980 LEADERSHIP CONTEST

SHADOW FOREIGN SECRETARY AND THE 1980 LABOUR LEADERSHIP

SHORE RECEIVED 145,000 VOTES for the National Executive Committee of the Labour Party in 1978, a figure that rose to 217,000 in October 1979. His stock within the PLP was rising and his contemporaries state that his standing within the shadow Cabinet under Callaghan was high. According to one minister, his influence grew in Cabinet when Callaghan started to cultivate him.

> Jim built him up greatly, partly to split Benn off. He realised that if he could carry him, Peter's common sense and judgement would keep him clear of Tony. So he elevated him, often he would have him speak third after himself and Denis. He treated him as rather more than a departmental figure, as someone whose views on a lot of things were worth hearing.[1]

In the shadow Cabinet election in June 1979, Healey was top, Silkin second and Shore third. Callaghan told David Owen, Foreign Secretary between 1977 and 1979 who was later to be a founding member of the Social Democratic Party, that he wanted to appoint Shore as shadow Foreign Secretary because he wished the parliamentary party to have a choice in the leadership election. For Owen, Callaghan was exalting Shore in order for him to take Foot's place 'as leader of the centre left', and Callaghan liked Shore and 'recognised in him his own robust patriotism'. Indeed, Shore needed the international experience that he would gain as Foreign Secretary if the party was going to see him as a credible challenger. It had been noticeable in the previous Cabinet that Callaghan had taken the trouble to ensure he carried Shore's support, and now he was allowing Shore to promote his own chances.[2]

As Foreign Secretary Shore performed powerfully, condemning the Soviet invasion of Afghanistan and supporting the United States administration and Mrs Thatcher in a boycott of the Moscow Olympics. According to Shore, the Soviet Union had breached international law and flouted international opinion; it had violated the independence of a small neighbouring state, and therefore for the world community to send their athletes would be interpreted as international acceptance and approval of the Soviet Union and its policies. He was outraged at the idea of British athletes competing in the Moscow Olympics while the Soviet Union denied its citizens fundamental human rights. The Labour Party's position was to oppose a boycott, on the basis that it would jeopardise the détente between the countries. When the matter came to the House of Commons it was a free vote; Shore indicated that he would have been happier supporting the government's boycott, but its inability to consult the British Olympics Committee and lack of agreement with Britain's allies over alternative sites for the games meant he would advise Labour MPs to abstain. The government motion calling for a British boycott was supported by 315 votes to 147. The official opposition amendment did not mention a boycott but merely expressed the belief that an effective response to the Soviet invasion could only be achieved by securing substantial common agreement among the governments and sporting authorities of Western Europe, the USA and elsewhere. The amendment was defeated by 305 votes to 188.[3] Dalyell believed that in his vehement support for the United States and Margaret Thatcher in boycotting the Moscow Olympics, Shore had hampered his leadership hopes: 'It was annoyance over this episode that helped to persuade many on the Left to pressurise Shore's hitherto chief leadership backer, Michael Foot, to stand as party leader'.[4] Besides, Shore's criticism of the trade union leaders and position on the 'Winter of Discontent' placed him in opposition to the Labour left.

In September 1980, Shore made a notable speech titled 'The Stalemate Society', which was interpreted as a personal manifesto. The essence of the 'stalemate society' was between capital and labour, noting that the power of the state, representing the whole community, had become increasingly confined. Important social developments had to be considered: the passing of ownership from private to public hands and, in the private sector, the increasing share ownership not by individuals but by financial institutions. Shore resurrected the idea of a comprehensive national economic plan, selective import controls to guard British industries and the democratisation of decision-making in industry, as the running of industry was much too important and difficult for management alone.[5] In response to the 'stalemate society' speech, *The Times* judged, 'he is more of a self-generating theorist than anyone active at the top of the party since Mr Anthony Crosland'.[6]

The timing of Callaghan's resignation, shortly after the 1980 conference which had voted for the principle of an electoral college to appoint a new party leader, was a deliberate attempt to ensure that the new leader would be elected under the old system, as it was feared by Benn's opponents that the electoral college system would favour him. For a time, it looked like Shore would be the leading contender against the right's Healey, and when *The Times* profiled him he was thought 'the most likely to succeed' Callaghan.[7] Bryan Gould wrote in his memoirs that Shore was

> regarded as a strong candidate, particularly in the light of the expectation that Michael Foot would not stand. In that case, it was reckoned, Peter had a good chance of emerging as the left's candidate who would survive to face Denis Healey.[8]

Jack Straw echoed Gould's analysis: 'Peter seemed the obvious choice as party leader. He had the intellectual weight and the ministerial experience. He cared about the party, nurtured his east London constituency, had none of the baggage of Denis Healey, and seemed more likely to win an election than Michael Foot, considerable though Michael's reputation was at the time.'[9] He announced his decision to stand on Thursday 16 October, a day after Callaghan had announced his resignation.

Shore's purpose was to 'unite the Party and to rally the country around radical and workable socialist policies'. He deemed that 'a change of course is vital if we are to rescue our economy, improve our physical and social environment, solve the great problem of the Common Market and play a more constructive part in achieving peace,

justice and security in an increasingly dangerous world.' Shore also criticised his rival, Healey, for his performance as Labour Chancellor: 'The
experience of the last Labour government was not an entirely happy
one in terms of economic policy. There were changes and different policies in the economy which the government could have pursued.' Shore
was not prepared to depart from the views he had expressed then,[10]
and Nick Butler interpreted Shore's criticism of Healey as suggesting
that he 'let the Party and the agenda down by just doing day-to-day
management, keeping things together'. Butler went on to say that Shore
'felt that Healey was not a proper economist, [he was] someone who
lacked a theory, and while he was clever and got things done, he did so
without analysis'. On the other hand, 'Peter liked to have a theory and
his was Keynesianism'.[11] Criticising the economic policies of the last
Labour government, Shore considered that it had to be much bolder:

> The economic policy of the next Labour government must be very
> different from that of the last. The failure to sustain expansion, the re-
> peated occasions that governments have been 'blown off course' is the
> root cause of our long relative economic decline and the loss of self-
> confidence that we have suffered. We will need both a strong political will
> and a strong economic policy if we are to succeed. All other policies must
> be subordinated to expansion and pointed to this end: the management of
> the currency, the movement of capital, the decision of investors, the own-
> ership and control of industry and the scope of collective bargaining.[12]

The next Labour government would have to tackle unemployment,
poverty and the decline of inner-city areas, prevent the continued
collapse of industries, and halt the contraction of community services. It would have to restore a sense of community, something

Shore considered to be a central principle of socialism, in place of the New Right's emphasis on individualism. Indeed, part of Shore's appeal to the PLP was linked to the position he adopted during the debates over the IMF loan: an alternative expansionist economic strategy in opposition to the Healey programme of public spending cuts. He continued to argue for a substantial devaluation of sterling, a significant reduction in interest rates, the abandonment of money supply targets, increased public spending, selective import controls, an overriding priority given to full employment, and a voluntary incomes policy. Shore also envisaged a thriving private sector. As such, *The Times* wrote, 'it is, to a large extent, a restatement of Crosland's belief that egalitarianism can only be achieved in any real sense when there is a surplus of wealth being made'.[13] On the EEC, Shore's long-standing Euroscepticism had some appeal to the Labour left, and he argued that Britain must try to negotiate the restoration of Parliament's supremacy, resulting in a return of self-government, and only secede if that became impossible. After all, he reasoned, Britain had many friends in the Commonwealth, North America and elsewhere. Meanwhile, on defence, he had moved away from the position he had adopted in the 1950s in support of CND, and he was now pro-NATO and anti-unilateralist, believing that Britain should maintain a deterrent for as long as the USSR had a nuclear arsenal.

A few months before the leadership contest, *The Observer* considered that the PLP was divided three ways: there were about sixty-five in the Tribune Group on the left, around seventy in the Manifesto Group on the right, and about 133 uncommitted in the centre. In a three-horse race, Shore's supporters believed that he could attract up to twenty-five votes from the first group, not more than ten from the second and up to 100 from the third – though not necessarily on the first ballot. If Michael Foot were to run, however, that would severely damage, and probably scupper, his chances.[14] Shore returned to the issue of the groupings within the PLP in an interview with Radio 4, noting that, while he was not a member of Tribune or the Manifesto Groups, he had come third in the most recent shadow Cabinet elections 'without any block or organised support', indicating that he had support from across the party. Indeed, Shore believed that he would gather support from the left and centre of the party, although he expected the right to blanch at the sight of his name on the ballot paper.[15]

Shore was under the impression that Foot, his long-time friend, would not stand, as there was an agreement in place that they would not stand against each other. Indeed, the events on Friday 17 October reinforced this view, and Straw's account of that day is revealing: 'I was with Peter in his Commons room. Michael came in and told Peter that on the following Monday he would announce his support for Peter. He didn't want to do it there and then, as he had to give an important lecture on Jonathan Swift in Dublin the following day.'[16] However, Foot was coming under increasing pressure to announce his candidature, and over that weekend received numerous representations from his supporters, claiming that Shore could not defeat Healey. Chris Mullin and Stuart Holland drew up a list of twenty left-wing MPs who would support Foot but would not vote for Shore. Holland judged that Shore's failure to commit himself to conference resolutions, either to leave the Common Market or to renounce nuclear weapons, meant he was not a proper standard-bearer of the left.[17] By Sunday 19 October Foot had succumbed to pressure and decided to stand. He told Shore on the Monday that he was going to make an announcement, but rather than a statement in favour of Shore, he was going to announce his candidature. Certainly, those around Foot deemed that Shore was unable to defeat Healey and the only viable 'stop-Healey' candidate was Foot, and while the weight of representation made to Foot over that weekend influenced his decision, it also suggested that Foot, too, doubted whether Shore could defeat Healey.

Shore accepted Foot's decision but naturally felt aggrieved, as, in practice, it meant that his potential support from the left of the PLP would go to Foot. John Silkin's decision to stand also affected Shore's chances; while Silkin was in favour of extending common ownership, was against controlling incomes as a policy and considered that Britain should offer its nuclear weapons to the UN Security Council, and was therefore to the left, he shared Shore's anti-EEC sentiment. Consequently, Shore's position was squeezed by both Foot and Silkin. He felt that he could not withdraw, having acquired promises of support, but once Foot announced his candidature 'my campaign had come to a juddering stop'.[18] In the last election held under the old system, Shore won the backing of thirty-two MPs. As Silkin (thirty-eight MPs) and Shore between them had fewer votes than Foot (eighty-three MPs), under the rules of the exhaustive ballot they both dropped out. Reflecting a few years later, Shore affirmed that he had no sense of being cheated out of the leadership:

> I've never believed that if Michael Foot had withdrawn or had not taken a part in that election, that I would have been the Leader … I think I'd have got a very decent vote but I think that the leadership would have gone, probably, almost certainly, to Denis Healey at that time.[19]

As the 'stop Healey' candidate, Foot defeated Healey in the runoff on 10 November by 139 votes to 129. Whether Shore, if Foot had not stood, could have beaten Healey is open to debate. Straw wrote, 'with Michael's support, he would have beaten Denis Healey',[20] and Gould held that 'many good judges thought Peter might have the beating of Denis'.[21] Indeed, there are arguments in favour of this view. Shore was radical in his approach to Europe and was to the left of Healey on the economy, and therefore it is very likely that he would have been able to attract the support of the Labour left. Also, he did not have the political baggage of Healey, who was tainted by the policies he had pursued as Chancellor in the 1974–79 Labour government. However, Healey remained an influential figure with a considerable support base within the party, whereas Shore, who had standing and was well-respected, lacked a body of support within the PLP. In addition, Healey's more pragmatic approach contrasted with Shore's ardent scepticism, and for Shirley Williams, while she agreed with him on many things, she could not accept his opposition to the EEC.[22] Whether the left would have gravitated to Shore with the same enthusiasm with which they greeted Foot is also open to question, as he had previously been critical of them and was never 'of the left'. In terms of character, both men were very different, as Shore lacked Healey's natural gravitas. Indeed, Stanley Clinton-Davis, who had worked with Shore at the Department of Trade, deemed him 'too cerebral rather than a magnetic person … Peter was not shy, but he would not mirror himself or put himself forward – not a self-aggrandising man.'[23] Similarly, Gould noted that Shore 'was not a natural campaigner and organising support did not come easily to him'.[24] It would be these reticent features along with his principles and sincerity that prevented Shore from reaching the top.

Indeed, Shore encouraged his supporters to transfer their backing to Foot. This raises an interesting question: why did Shore, having been scuppered by Foot, encourage MPs to vote for him over Healey? Shore admired Foot politically, and the pair enjoyed a close relationship that went back several decades. Moreover, Foot's leadership held out the prospect of a more Keynesian economic policy, and therefore it was more in tune with what Shore was proposing. This meant that Foot would have had to rely on Shore's economic judgement. On the other hand, Healey would have been much more rigid in his analysis and, given their history over the IMF Crisis, in which they had different views on policy, Healey would have been less likely to promote Shore and his judgement in the shadow Cabinet. Indeed, in *Leading the Left* Shore looked favourably towards Foot, as he was the only candidate in the election who would not have been forced to fight a further election when the electoral college was established due to the strong support he had on the left of the party. Moreover, Foot was well-respected in the constituencies due to his long history of radicalism, and he enjoyed a close relationship with the trade unions. Importantly, by winning the leadership, he stopped Tony Benn, who was seen to be too far to the left. Thus, in Shore's judgement, the election of Foot as party leader had helped to save the Labour Party.[25]

SHADOW CHANCELLOR

Foot gave Shore the shadow Chancellor brief. The appointment reflected Shore's standing within the party and his economic ability and was a consolation prize for Foot's behaviour in the leadership contest. According to Straw, who was brought into Shore's frontbench team along with Bob Sheldon (a former Treasury minister) and Robin

Cook, Peter 'was rewarded for his loyalty'.[26] The team's purpose was to work on Labour's alternative economic policy and from the outset of Shore's time as shadow Chancellor he laid out an economic strategy that emphasised regulation and a competitive devaluation of sterling. In the foreword to *Monetarism or Prosperity?* Shore wrote that the central purpose of economic policy was the expansion of national wealth and the growth of the economy: 'economic expansion, not inflation, not the exchange rate, not the size of the public sector borrowing requirement, not the level of public expenditure and certainly not the fulfilment of paper targets for the growth of money supply, should be the central purpose of economic policy'.[27]

There was also an ethical dimension to economic growth, namely the weakening of social and psychological obstacles, the reduction in fear of unemployment, and tackling the defeatist attitude that had intensified. Key to this was a 'competitive exchange rate', for 'without a positive policy for the exchange rate, nothing will come right: and the great flow of North Sea Oil, which perversely is impoverishing rather than enriching us, makes this all the more urgent'.[28] The un-competitiveness of British industry had firstly been caused by unemployment, and, secondly, by the government's attempt to 'squeeze inflation out of the economy' through monetarist policies. Shore dismissed the monetarist doctrines of the Conservatives: the policies, philosophy and political purpose of the government to reject the whole postwar period of full employment and state involvement as an aberration was an attempt to return to Victorian Britain, he thought. For Shore, there was no economic salvation to be found in 'the academic dreaming of Professors Milton Friedman and von Hayek – the Dr Strangeloves of economic policy'.[29]

Shore accepted that devaluation would push up import prices, but

Labour's relationship with the trade unions would enable a Labour government to avoid the escalation of pay settlements seen in 1979. In addition, the expansion of the economy would ensure that devaluation did not disrupt workers' living standards.[30] However, a Labour government would also have to consider the balance of payments problem – the same problem that had afflicted successive postwar governments. While increased demand would assist British industry, it would also lead to the purchase of foreign goods, and 'we cannot allow excessive import penetration to continue to destroy Britain's industry'. Britain would be unable to contribute to world economic growth 'if, through our continued inability to match imports with exports, we are forced to cut imports by running our own economy at half-speed'. Shore linked the balance of payments problem with the Common Market, arguing that Britain had a £4,000 million deficit per annum in manufacturing goods, obligations to buy expensive food under the CAP and the significant budgetary contribution. Shore finished his speech on a patriotic note:

> For Britain, success in trading, balance in trade, is a matter of survival. Our 55 million people cannot be sustained in these islands unless we succeed, unless we earn our national living. No British Government can or will tolerate the situation in which the Nation itself ceases to be viable and our own people, in ever increasing numbers, are forced into idleness at home or to emigrate to near and distant lands.[31]

In February 1982, Shore launched 'a new national argument', a 'new think-in as well as a talk-in' about the economic problems that had beset the nation. Its objective was to challenge the Conservative government narrative that 'there is no alternative', that the postwar era was a mistake and that the government was unable to resolve economic problems. On the contrary, Shore stressed that the government could achieve economic growth and full employment. In November 1982, Shore and the Labour treasury team produced a seventy-page document entitled *Programme for Recovery*. The report set out how aggregate demand could safely be expanded without the country falling over a cliff, as the followers of 'there is no alternative' (TINA) policies so stridently argued it would. The figures were put through the Treasury economic model, and Shore's team were sure they stacked up.[32]

Programme for Recovery planned to devalue sterling by 30 per cent over two years, supported by other measures such as public sector investment, cuts in VAT and the National Insurance Surcharge, price controls and the introduction of some import controls. Low real-wage growth was an implicit assumption, although it was not clear how this was to be achieved.[33] According to Mark Wickham-Jones, Shore accepted that the difficulties of securing full employment were 'formidable', requiring 2.5 million new jobs.

> Nevertheless, with 4 per cent growth per year, unemployment could be reduced to under a million. Reflation would come before intervention because it would take time to get any industrial measures up and running. Shore accepted that eventually planning agreements with companies would be needed, but he did not share the antipathetic attitude to industry of left wingers. Unlike supporters of the AES, he did not conceive of them as mechanisms that would allow the government to impose its will on firms. Reversing the argument made for them, he claimed that planning agreements would help a government identify and meet the needs of the economy and individual companies. [34]

However, *Programme for Recovery* was not endorsed by the NEC, nor was it published by the party. Despite its cool reception, the document served another purpose, namely challenging those who favoured the AES. Austin Mitchell noted that Shore's strategy differed from the AES, 'using expansionary Keynesianism and the dynamics of the market through devaluation as a stimulus to growth where the Alternative Economic Strategy was *dirigiste*, centring on controls, managed trade and the use of the power of the state'.[35] According to Straw,

> [the] document [aimed] to gain credibility for our approach, which was being ripped apart by both the Tories and the newly created SDP. To a degree, it succeeded but at a high price. The *Sunday Times* spotted that, to achieve the growth rate needed, we'd assumed that sterling would have to depreciate by 10 per cent. Labour to devalue by 10 per cent was an irresistible headline and a damaging one.[36]

Shore's role as shadow Chancellor was to challenge the Thatcherite narrative that 'there was no alternative', restating arguments that governments could do things as they had from 1945 to 1979, and emphasising the things that a Labour government would have done differently. Writing in *Renewal*, he sought to defend the social and economic system introduced by the Attlee government, outlining the advancements in living standards that the postwar settlement had delivered for working people.[37] Pugh judged that Shore had written a 'remarkably frank eulogy of both Labour and Conservative governments after 1945'. Moreover, it was said that he had displayed the greatest awareness of the fact that if Labour was to defend the postwar settlement, it had to 'exploit the fears of all sections of society who suffer from Conservative attempts to demolish it'.[38]

Shore's task as shadow Chancellor was set against a backdrop of party in-fighting, the breakaway SDP and the electoral appeal of Thatcherism. Therefore, to a certain extent, Shore's economic policy was made on the run. However, Shore's Keynesian approach stressed the resumption of government responsibility for unemployment, employment and a commitment to sustained prosperity. Interestingly, during the drafting of Labour's general election manifesto on 11 May 1983, Shore presented the only dissenting voice. Most shadow ministers did not seem bothered to put up a fight for what the opinion polls suggested was a hopeless attempt to win the election.[39] Shore criticised both the pedestrian language and the content of the draft without any success[40] and Golding writes that while others were prepared for the left to take the blame, Shore 'expressed the heretical view that manifestos were meant to win elections'.[41]

SOLIDARITY

Shore was involved with 'Solidarity', an organisation created by Labour moderates to oppose the Labour left, and especially the actions of the Campaign for Labour Party Democracy. It was set up twenty-four days after the Wembley conference in February 1981 as the result and recognition of the failure of the moderates to organise against the adoption of the 40:30:30 formula for the electoral college. Its objective was to challenge the dominance of the left within the party and constituencies, and also to convince those on the right of the party and tempted by the SDP breakaway that they still had a home within the Labour movement. The NEC, the party's ruling body, was dominated by the left and sympathetic to Benn, and Militant was well placed to take over weakly organised constituency Labour parties. Before becoming co-chair, Shore had lamented the state of the party, noting that 'public attention is riveted upon the Roman spectacle of a great party tearing itself to pieces – to the amazement and horror of its own supporters and to the open delight of its Conservative enemies ... The splitters and the wreckers have had a field day.'[42] The 'splitters' was a term given to those who had joined the SDP from the Labour Party, and the 'wreckers' were the hard left who had infiltrated constituency Labour parties.

Shore wanted to reach out to grassroots members who shared his concern that the Benn insurgency would be fatal for the party's electoral prospects. At the first recorded meeting of the Solidarity Steering Committee, Roy Hattersley welcomed Shore's attendance and invited him to become joint chairman. Denis Howell had pressed on Hattersley the need for a second figurehead – and another 'aspirant for leadership' of the party – so that the organisation did not look like an embryo 'Hattersley for leader' campaign. Shore accepted, stressing that the 'only people not organised in the Labour Party are the great majority'.[43] Clearly, with Shore as co-chair, Solidarity wouldn't be outwardly pro-European, though it attracted many Europhiles. Neither did it take a position on one of the most divisive issues for Labour: that of nuclear weapons. Solidarity's lack of clarity on policy was a deliberate attempt to avoid divisions within the group, which would have hampered its objectives.

Shore's speeches reflected the dual objectives of Solidarity, highlighting the incompatibility of Militant with the values of the

Labour Party, and damning the beliefs, or lack thereof, of the SDP. Shore outlined that the party's constitution had been carefully balanced to represent party democracy (with a strong emphasis on conference) with the considerations of electoral and parliamentary democracy. He deemed this to be a good balance, as the party had to win a parliamentary majority and, in the process, reconcile the views of the electorate with the views of the party. Moreover, it was the PLP that had the responsibility of implementing the party's manifesto and had an important role in electing the party leader, not the NEC. To give that power to the NEC would be a case of separating power from responsibility. As a party of democratic socialism, it would be unwise to assert the authority of party over Parliament, and, after all, the Labour Party was not a 'Vanguard' or 'Cadre' party where the electorate is by definition excluded. In a democracy such as Britain, Shore felt that 'the politics of socialism are essentially the politics of persuasion. If the Labour Party was ever to take the view that it did not need to persuade the electorate and all it needed was to demonstrate its own ideological purity, it would wither and shrink to an insignificant political force.'[44] Tinkering with the party's constitution was not going to resolve the nation's difficulties.

Dianne Hayter writes that a notable fringe meeting took place in Ely in June 1981. The MP Ken Weetch had found that the room that had been booked was

a long way from the Eastern regional conference. He asked Shore how he felt about outdoor meetings and, receiving an enthusiastic reply, set up a massively successful rally on the Green which, despite 'heckling from the Trots', gave real energy to the large, loyalist membership that existed in East Anglia.[45]

Shore outlined the problem with the 'ultra-left', and compared it to Labour's ideology, which had greater flexibility but the same commitment to socialist values. For Shore, the ultra-left had a historical comparison, namely to the First World War generals of the Maginot line. In this instance, the ultra-left were the

> socialists of the Maginot line, generals of the rule book, who are again and again outflanked and encircled by events, doomed to failure – and certain in the end to surrender. The democratic left understands, respects but is not trapped by ideology. It is guided by Socialist principles. It does seek equality; its purpose is to counter powerful and hostile forces; it knows that the main goal is freedom – freedom from the tyranny of circumstance and from the command of men.[46]

Shore also attacked Benn for his role in encouraging the Militant Tendency and for challenging Denis Healey for the deputy leadership of the party. While Shore deliberately attacked Benn with historical references, including those from the English Civil War, a period of English history that interested both men, he also never openly endorsed Healey. As Hayter writes, 'it was not the person that Shore feared, but a deputy leader being imposed on the PLP contrary to its own preference.'[47] Benn was the 'cuckoo in the nest', determined to create a 'New Model Party' not based on policy but based on a different doctrine of party democracy. The New Model Party was necessary, he thought, because elected members 'are, through the corruption of power and the dominance of the Prime Minister, the principal enemies of the Party and all its aspirations'.[48] Shore considered that Benn, 'like the Calvinists of the sixteenth century, believed that Labour Members and supporters are divided into the Elect and the non-Elect – and that he uniquely represents the former'. The elect was the elect not because of their work, but because of their zealous faith and ideology; 'intolerant, fanatical and authoritarian … They are, in Benn's New Model Party, the Ironsides, drilled and trained, anxious and ready for war: for civil war. And if they win, they will be just as ready to execute the elected monarch as to crush the Levellers.'[49]

Shore continued, emphasising that the Labour Party and the causes it represents were more significant than any individual, an apparent rebuff to Benn. 'We have never believed that salvation lies with any political messiah – but only through the collective effort and resolve of men and women determined to achieve a better life for all,' he said.[50] Benn had propagated the belief that the last Labour government, of which he had been a part, had let down socialism, and that all future Labour governments would do the same. Only the election of himself as deputy leader would prevent the betrayal of socialism, he suggested.

Shore, in contrast, wanted the Labour Party to reflect on its achievements and remember that it is a crusading party: 'its goal is the transformation of society', its quest is for 'Jerusalem in England's Green and Pleasant Land'. However, Shore also urged people to recall the history of the Crusades, deeming that the most pathetic and absurd of all was the Children's Crusade, in which, according to the story, thousands of children embark on a crusade to peacefully convert Muslims in the Holy Land to Christianity. However, they reached only as far as the Mediterranean Sea before being tricked and sold into slavery by merchants. While the party was on a crusade, it was 'not a Children's Crusade. It has to think as well as feel; it has to persuade as well as to inspire; it has to plan as well as proclaim.'[51] Shore returned to this point in the aftermath of the 1983 general election defeat. He rejected the view that 'the truth of socialism' was revealed to a small minority within the party: 'It's a theory, a view of the electorate which has contempt for the electorate, and I haven't that.' Yet, respecting the electorate did not entail being pushed around, but rather a dialogue, convincing them 'of the relevance of your principles, the relevance of democratic socialism to their own lives and to the future of their country'.[52]

Shore was no less scathing towards the SDP. While he faced a battle in his constituency in Bethnal Green & Stepney against Militant, he was not prepared to leave Labour, as it was the party that 'held the title deeds to Democratic Socialism in Britain'. He came under pressure to join the party as it recognised that he was not on the left and was opposed to unilateral nuclear disarmament. While Shore liked and respected party founders Shirley Williams and Bill Rodgers, he had little in common with Roy Jenkins, 'the true standard-bearer of their cause'. Jenkins was known in the Shore family home as 'Mr Smooth Chops',[53] and Shore referred back to Jenkins's 1972 statement that 'a Social Democratic Party without deep roots in the working-class movement will quickly fade away into an unrepresentative intellectual sect'. The SDP was a party of the press and media, its allies were the Conservatives and it therefore had considerable potential to damage the Labour Party. The one strong binding commitment of 'this otherwise rudderless and disparate group [was] Euro-fanaticism, the transfer of ambitions and allegiances from Westminster to Brussels'.[54]

In addition, the SDP obsessed over proportional representation (PR) and the restructuring of British politics, something Shore wholeheartedly opposed. It was a nonsense, he thought, to claim that the major issues facing Britain could be resolved by breaking the two-party system, as these problems were rooted in other causes. Shore believed that only the opposition can form an alternative government and that PR produced instability, as even in a stable democracy like West Germany, a minority party effectively decides who is or is not to form a government. The SDP's espousal of PR was based on self-interest according to Shore, as he reflected on 'the poverty of their thinking about the real problems of the country'.[55] Shore's opposition to the Common Market was in stark contrast to the pro-Europeanism of those who went over to the SDP; he was a defender of the traditional Westminster model of politics, as well as first-past-the-post. According to Lord Rodgers, there was 'no possibility that Peter would join the SDP. Peter was a Wilsonite, the heir of Bevan ... If you would have asked the parliamentary party, he would have been in the last fifth who might have joined the SDP. His political ideology was quite separate.'[56]

THE FALKLANDS WAR

Shore's position as shadow Chancellor saw him play an important role within the shadow Cabinet, the PLP and wider country during the Falklands crisis. As shadow Foreign Secretary in 1980, shortly before he moved to his economic brief, he asked the government to clarify its position on the 'conflicting and unsettling reports about statements' made by Nicholas Ridley, the then Foreign and Commonwealth Office Minister, in response to the 'lease-back' proposals of the government.[57] The proposals would have given Argentina nominal sovereignty over the islands, but the British would continue to rule the Falklands for ninety-nine years before a final handover. The previous Labour government had received representations in 1975 from Vignes, the Argentine Foreign Minister, advancing lease-back proposals, and had come to see an arrangement along those lines as 'the most realistic solution'.[58] Despite similarities between the previous Labour government's solution and the Conservative government's lease-back proposals, on 2 December Ridley was confronted by Shore and Jay, who would go on to play a leading role between April and May 1982. Shore, in Churchillian tones, defined Ridley's words as a 'worrying statement', directly attacking the idea of abandoning 'people of British descent' to the mercy of the Argentines. He reiterated that British sovereignty over the islands was indisputable and that, as such, the wishes of the Falklanders had to be 'of paramount importance' and 'not just "guidance" to the British Government', as Ridley had affirmed. Instead of discussing a lease-back, the government had to 'make it clear that we shall uphold the rights of the islanders to continue to make a genuinely free choice about their future, that we shall not abandon them and that, in spite of all the logistical difficulties, we shall continue to support and sustain them'.[59] Shore set the conceptual boundaries of the debate: the principle of sovereignty; the Britishness of the Falklanders; and their right to self-determination.

Following the invasion of the Falklands by Argentina at the be-ginning of April 1982, Shore would take up the same position he had adopted in the parliamentary debates in 1980, namely that the Falkland Islands were sovereign British territory and the islanders considered themselves to be British. Socialist politician Eric Heffer's concerns that Labour might appear 'jingoistic and more nationalistic than the Tories', an idea that would behove Labour to adhere to the government's decision to send a task force, were played down by Foot,

THE SHADOW CABINET AND THE 1980 LEADERSHIP CONTEST 135

Shore and Silkin. Shore also expressed doubts about the likelihood of obtaining the Argentines' retreat without resorting to force, as well as about the effective possibility of postponing the question of sovereignty.[60] At the end of April, when the Prime Minister had invited the leaders of the opposition parties to meetings, updating them on the evolution of the crisis, Shore was the only shadow Cabinet minister to oppose Foot's decision not to attend.[61] By May, at which point military operations had escalated, Shore supported the absolute correctness of the British position, both regarding the controversial sinking of the *Belgrano* outside of the Argentine naval exclusion zone, and on the Falklands issue as a whole. In a speech given to the American Chamber of Commerce, Shore lectured his audience on the necessity of British military action, on what he considered was a simple matter:

> An island territory … self-governing in all important respects and entirely peaceful, offering no threat or offence to any neighbouring power, wholly British in population in culture and sentiment, has been brutally assaulted and overpowered in a disgraceful act of force and deception by those with whom we foolishly imagined we were holding discussions in good faith only six weeks ago.

Shore continued, arguing that British colonialism was not at stake, but Argentinian colonialism and expansion was. The Labour Party had a long tradition of challenging oppression and aggression, and it detested fascist and militarist regimes; the Argentinians had to leave the Falklands and Labour's preference was for an agreed evacuation of their troops. However, in a line that he crossed out on the hard copy of his speech and replaced with a statement on the importance of UN Resolution 502, Shore noted, 'our reluctant but clear alternative, if agreement cannot be reached, is to take such measures as will ensure the surrender of their garrison'.[62] Yet, converse to his updated statement, in the shadow Cabinet Shore confirmed his suspicions about the capability of the UN to play a productive and positive role in the developing conflict. While Heffer argued in favour of a truce and negotiation, even if the Argentinians remained on the islands, Shore declared a different suggestion, arguing for the necessity of linking a truce with the retreat of the invaders.[63]

Shore remained convinced that there had been no change in the sovereignty of the Falklands. Indeed, he thought the sovereignty of the islands should remain unaltered until the islanders had been convinced that it was in their interests to become Argentinian. He told *Weekend World* that it had never occurred to him that the UK should cede the sovereignty of the islands to Argentina: 'As far as I'm concerned the crux of the matter is what the people of the Falkland Islands freely wish for their own future.'[64] However, Shore wrote in the *Daily Telegraph* that this option was 'closed as far ahead as we can see by Argentina itself when the Junta invaded the islands. For Britain to accept or acquiesce now in an Argentine future, against the will of the Islanders, will be a disgrace and a betrayal.' While the Falklanders could choose from three options over the future of their islands – remain a British territory, become an independent mini-state, or become a special self-administrating Trust Territory of the UN – the long-term security of the islands against Argentinian assault would only be guaranteed by the installation and maintenance of effective British sea and air power. That was the best method of protecting the independence and freedom of the Falklands Islands, it was decided.[65]

CONCLUSION

In the early 1980s Shore was a leading figure, playing a key role in the debates that defined the period addressed in this chapter. Although Shore doubted whether he would have gained the necessary support to win the 1980 leadership contest, there is a strong case that, had Foot not stood, Shore would have beaten Healey. In public, he was gracious towards Foot, both at the time and later in *Leading the Left*. However, it can be argued that Shore's qualities would have made him a much more effective leader of the party than Foot. Indeed, Vernon Bogdanor wrote that Shore would have better served the party as a 'compromise candidate', and was therefore better placed to unite it.[66] While any leader would have struggled to win in the face of dominant Conservative statecraft, Shore could have avoided the catastrophe that the Labour Party endured in the 1983 general election campaign. It is possible, for example, that his natural patriotism would not have allowed the Conservatives to so easily play the 'patriotic card' and label Labour as unpatriotic. In fact, the patriotism Shore displayed during the Falklands conflict and in his position on Europe would have appealed to Labour's traditional vote base, as would his empha- sis on state involvement in the economy and reviving British industry. In addition, given his broad centrism, it is fair to say that he would have been a more unifying leader than Foot, particularly in relation to the SDP. For some who defected, their unhappiness with Labour predated the events of the early 1980s and they therefore would have left regardless of who was leader. However, Shore was better placed firstly to respond to the concerns of the right of the party and, sec- ondly, to hold the party together. Therefore, he would have been able to limit the SDP breakaway, although, in return, he would have had to tone down his Euroscepticism.

Shore should be given recognition for countering the arguments of the New Right and putting forward a radical Keynesian response. He should also take credit for his role as co-leader of Solidarity and the way in which he attacked Benn – using phrases such as 'a Roman Spectacle', 'New Model Party' and 'Children's Crusade' – an act that, given their longstanding friendship, came at some personal cost. His speeches emphasised that the Labour Party was a broad-based, tolerant party of democratic socialism, having nothing in common with the 'entryists' who subscribed to Marxist–Leninism, while simultaneously damned the SDP 'splitters' for being a party of the media, bound together through an obsession with the Common Market and proportional representation. During this challenging period for the Labour Party, Shore rejected the advances made to him by those in the SDP and remained committed to his principles and the values of the Labour Party.

7

THE 1983 LABOUR LEADERSHIP CONTEST

JOCKEYING FOR POSITION

THE 1983 LABOUR LEADERSHIP contest was Shore's final chance at becoming party leader and, as McSmith writes, 'Shore had imagined that he was Michael Foot's right-hand man and natural successor.'[1] According to *The Times*, Shore had begun to plan his leadership bid soon after the 1981 conference. He started an initiative to instigate private talks with union leaders, which was handled by Will Camp, a veteran political lobbyist and former head of information at the British Steel Corporation. Camp emphasised the virtues of Shore's centrist values as those of someone who could command the backing of all groups within the party.[2] Rumours about Shore's leadership ambitions continued to circulate following suggestions in the late summer of 1982 that senior party and union figures were mustering support for Shore to replace Foot as leader. However, Kinnock called for 'the guessing and kite flying to stop. If it continues, it will cripple us politically ... There is no justification for anyone who diverts attention from the pursuit and presentation of policies by a formal or informal campaign to replace Michael Foot as leader of the Labour Party.'[3] Kinnock's comments strengthened Foot's position and ensured that he would be the man to lead the Labour Party into the 1983 general election, despite doubts over his suitability as leader and the Conservatives' revival in the polls after the Falklands War. The comments also benefited Kinnock, whose relationship with Foot was reinforced, and he could claim that he had displayed loyalty to the leadership. Kinnock had also been steadily improving his position within the party. In 1982 he won 131 votes in the shadow Cabinet elections, leaping from seventh place to second and outstripping Shore and Hattersley, two men who had each long been spoken of as possible leaders of the party.

The crushing general election defeat of '83 was quickly followed by the news of Foot's resignation. Shore was giving a live television interview on *Weekend World* when journalist Brian Walden broke the news to him. Walden asked him whether he intended to stand; Shore said he did and went on to criticise the 1983 electoral strategy of the Labour Party, deeming that it adopted the theory of the American Democratic Party, concerned with constructing majorities by mobilising minorities. It was not possible, he said, to build a majority 'based upon the principles of solidarity and community consciousness which we need in the Labour Movement, if you try to enlist the single issue, egotism and selfishness of particular groups'.[4] Instead, he suggested that the Labour Party needed to develop a broad appeal to the majority of people. Hattersley followed suit, on the same day appearing on Channel 4's *Face the Press* to announce his candidacy.

Kinnock had already announced that he would be standing on the Radio 4 news programme *The World This Weekend*.

SHORE'S CAMPAIGN

The 1983 Labour leadership contest was the first to be held under the new electoral college rules. While garnering the support of MPs was still important, it was necessary to build a following in the country and among the trade unions, too. Unfortunately for Shore, as in 1980 he lacked a powerbase in the PLP, had few supporters in the trade union movement, and was perhaps less suited to the constituency campaign compared to other candidates, particularly Kinnock. Shore's supporters included notable Eurosceptics such as Gwyneth Dunwoody, Jack Straw, Bryan Gould, Austin Mitchell, Bob Sheldon and Harry Ewing, and what support Shore did enjoy came mainly from the Labour Common Market Safeguards Committee. However, his supporters were under no illusions about his prospects: 'by that stage, it was quite clear he was going to lose. By 1983 Shore's time had passed,' Jack Straw said.[5]

Indeed, according to Robert Harris in his biography of Kinnock, Foot's resignation and the announcements of Shore, Hattersley and Kinnock caused confusion among the right-wing trade unions: Terry Duffy, president of the engineers' union, publicly came out for Shore, while his general secretary, Gavin Laird, simultaneously declared for Hattersley. 'I phoned the big unions,' recalls Duffy, 'but I couldn't get the rest of the guys to go with me. And if you've not got the big votes, then it's no use.'[6] As a result of this private carve-up, Shore's chances of becoming leader were effectively finished by the end of the first afternoon.[7]

According to Nick Butler, 'Shore's idea of standing was to make intellectual speeches', believing 'that was politics'. He travelled widely throughout the campaign, speaking on the values and issues facing the Labour Party. He also made a trip to Stockholm to give a lecture on the New Right but, regrettably, 'they received no coverage at all'.[8] Shore positioned himself as a 'socialist and strategist', based on clear thinking, foresight and courage, looking back at his time as head of the party's research department and the role he played in turning the party around after 1959. The same was needed now, based not on watering down the policy but making it understandable and relevant to the new generation of voters, as well as old. Shore considered that the direction Labour had to take was clear, including the development of new and existing industries to provide employment and improve living standards, and the pursuit of a society based on socialist principles of liberty, equality, community and cooperation. Moreover, he emphasised the maintenance of a strong and independent socialist Britain making its decisions in London, not Brussels, as well as the protection and extension of individual freedom, the rebuilding of a spirit of community in place of greed and selfishness, and the promotion of international cooperation through the United Nations.[9]

Shore fleshed out his vision of the Labour Party and the type of society he wished to implement as he travelled around the country. In his first speech of the campaign, Shore outlined the magnitude of the 1983 general election defeat. He dismissed those who declared that 'we won a famous victory for socialism on 9 June' – a claim made by some on the party's left – and condemned the 'torpor and escapism that is already settling over the Labour movement ... which contains too many Field Marshal Earl Haigs', ready to continue with the same policies without entertaining a change of direction. Labour had lost because it had indulged in a 'cultural revolution', a campaign to cleanse and purify the party to prevent any further alleged betrayals by the leadership. Furthermore, Labour lost, he thought,

> because we lost contact with and lost the confidence of the mainstream of our traditional support. Because we seem no longer to relate to and to articulate their anxieties, their hopes and their interests, because we ceased in the minds and hearts of millions to be the Party which they knew, respected and trusted. Because the energies of our Party were turned year in and year out, not against the Tory enemy but against ourselves.[10]

He told the Central London Fabian Society that the 'cultural revolution', along with other factors, had widened the gap between the party and the electorate. The decline in membership and the party's preoccupation with pressure groups and minorities meant that 'the great majority of our supporters find their interests overlooked and ignored: and then switch off'. The party was now out of touch with majority opinion, due to the infiltration of groups and revolutionaries that did not believe in democracy, and the narrow definition of 'working people' that ignores 'the occupational shifts and the class shifts of the past quarter of a century'. Shore put forward six remedies, including standing for 'the majority of the people who have to earn their own living and whom we seek constantly to represent'; a reappraisal of how the party makes its policies and runs its organisation; tackling the 'enemy presence' within the party, the Leninist/ Trotskyist doctrine of the inevitability and desirability of revolution, and their belief in the doctrine of the dictatorship of the proletariat;

the restoration and maintenance of the 'historic compromise' between the NEC and the shadow Cabinet on the party manifesto; the
implementation of a one-person, one-vote system for the selection of
parliamentary candidates and the election of the leader; and the NEC
comprising a majority of people 'in sympathy with the broad outlook
of the Labour movement and the voter'.[11]

Shore also focused on social and economic change and Labour's
response. Despite Labour dedicating itself to 'the political, social
and economic emancipation of the people and, more particularly of
those who depend directly upon their own exertions by hand or by
brain for the means of life', people were still moving away from the
party. There was nothing inevitable about this, and while Labour's
policy was already geared towards the concerns of the new 'earning
classes' – housing, pensions, public transport, taxation – more had to
be done to recognise the new needs and interests of emerging social
groups.[12] Labour's values had not changed with the passage of time,
but the application of those values through specific policies had to
be adapted to changing circumstances. Socialists had to carry a picture of modern Britain, not a picture of a society that had ceased to
exist, and therefore appeal to both the traditional working class and
the non-industrial workers. Moreover, 'owning a house or flat with
a garden or a garage does not transform a socialist into a capitalist.
It should not be allowed to transform a Labour voter into a Tory
voter.'[13] Labour had to understand the distinction between 'enlarged
personal property ownership ... which the Labour Party had and
should always welcome and which help to enlarge personal security, personal freedom and individual choice – and the very different
ownership of productive property, social property, from which profit,
interest and rent are obtained'.[14]

Shore proceeded to tackle one of those most divisive issues within the Labour Party: defence policy and nuclear weapons. This was an issue that has caused controversy for much of the party's history and, while it was important that Labour strived for peace and disarmament, Shore made an intellectual case for the increase of conventional forces and the maintenance of nuclear weapons – a position that he realised was unpopular within the party. Yet, he was willing to campaign in favour of Britain maintaining a nuclear deterrent as if he was elected leader; he wanted the country to know that he was not willing to send his Foreign Secretary 'naked into the conference chamber', and nor was he prepared to leave Britain without adequate defences. It is worth quoting his reasoning at length:

> We do not have armed forces and weapons of war simply for their own sake. They exist for a purpose – a purpose of defending something which we value, something which we value sufficiently to pay the cost in terms of resources, of manpower and, if need be, of lives. I believe that what they exist to defend is our independence as a country, and it is that independence which should be the starting point of any debate on foreign and defence policies.
>
> Independence is the first of all freedoms: freedom not to be occupied, not to be colonised, not to be coerced by the power of another state. Independence gives us – and others – the power to choose, to make our own decisions democratically, to join or not join with others in the pursuit of wider goals but to be free from external authority.

Shore distinguished between positive and negative unilateralism. Positive unilateralism was, he said, a creative and proactive policy that, not without risks, would allow Britain to set an example of refusing to increase its existing nuclear arsenal. It would not leave Britain defenceless, and it had the added benefit of providing room to manoeuvre depending on how it was received. On the other hand, negative unilateralism would result in a 'neutralist and powerless Britain, dependent neither on itself nor its Allies for its defence but upon the uncertain and contemptuous goodwill of its adversaries. It is a doctrine for those who may love peace and hate war: but not for those who value independence and freedom as well.' What mattered to Shore was refusing to place the future of the country in the hands of another power, as well as the history and the abiding sentiment of the British people.

> What is unique to Britain; what separates us from every other European country, indeed from every country in the world, is our centuries-long experience of independence and freedom. What we are as a people – the way we relate to each other, the humour and the tolerance which have become ingrained, how we see the world outside – owes most to this than to any other single factor. Those who try to persuade our people that what they have is not worth having; that surrender is preferable to resistance, whatever the cost, will never succeed. Nor do they deserve to do so.[15]

Shore then shifted his attention to international economic affairs and the Common Market. The monetarist policies adopted by the major powers of the West had led to a restriction on credit, control of the money supply and high interest rates, with a deflationary impact on developing countries. A future Labour government would have to support the cause of national independence, including freedom from the coercion of external economic powers, from the constraints of poverty and from the rule of generals and juntas. This would be possible through cutting interest rates, pursuing economic expansion, reducing world debt, promoting lending, and reinforcing a less US-dominated version of the IMF and World Bank.[16] The Common Market had resulted in significant British job losses, as EEC exports had eaten into the domestic market; the idea that two and a half million British jobs would be lost if Britain left the Common Market was, Shore posited, a myth and an absurdity, presupposing that we would cease to trade with the EEC.[17]

In his seventh campaign speech, Shore addressed the present and future prospects of the British economy. The missing component in Labour's economic programme in 1983 had been a convincing policy on inflation: a consequence of uncertainty and division within the trade union movement over the role of collective bargaining, the need for an incomes strategy, and its relationship to the primary goal of job creation. While Thatcher supported free collective bargaining in the private sector, this was possible due to 3 million unemployed, and Shore noted that 'without a firm agreement on incomes, we shall not be able to achieve our goals of rapid economic expansion and a rapid reduction in unemployment'. He advocated for a National Enterprise Board and a National Investment Bank to establish new public enterprises, public purchasing and import control to protect new and surviving industries, and a counter-inflation policy to reduce interest rates.[18] What Labour had to do, according to Shore, was reject the Victorian values of Thatcherism and reiterate that the party's concern was with human dignity, personal freedom, equality and respect. Moreover, it was essential to reinforce a strong sense of community and moral obligation as opposed to the individualism and greed of Thatcherism; promote freedom from tyranny and poverty and the pressure of want; and create a society in which needs, not profit, cooperation, not competition, were the principal values.[19]

REACTION AND RESULT

Baston, writing in 2002, affirmed that 'Shore's manifesto was the most modernising on offer in 1983, arguing that aspirations to higher education and home ownership should not be denied and drawing attention to the changing class structure'.[20] However, Shore's spirited campaign and thorough intellectual analysis of the Labour Party, the state of British politics and the policies required to reverse Thatcherism failed to cut through against the appeal of Kinnock. Shore's position on defence, the economy and blaming his party's own follies and incompetence for the disastrous 1983 general election defeat was a message that was unlikely to play well and garner support.

Shore received a much more positive reception from outside the Labour movement. In August, he had received the backing of *The Times* and the *Daily Telegraph*, and the columnist Paul Johnson in a conversation with Shore considered 'everyone outside the Labour Party – whether they're Liberal or Social Democrat or Conservative or just neutral, the press, the media and so on – they all think you are by far the best candidate'.[21] Anne Sofer thought that Shore spoke with 'passion and conviction' and was the only candidate who gave 'any impression at all of being able to run the country',[22] while the *Sunday Standard* perceptively considered that 'it's an irony, but perhaps no more than we should have learned to expect, that the man who has taken the necessary analysis furthest, Peter Shore, is struggling many metres adrift as the front-runners in the leadership race stride towards the inevitable conclusion'.[23]

Shore received no nominations from the CLPs, including his own, which supported Heffer by thirty-two votes to twenty-nine,[24] and none from the trade unions. Instead, his support came from one Socialist Society – Poale Zion – and twenty-two fellow MPs.[25] The final figures were:

- Kinnock – 71.3 per cent
- Hattersley – 19.3 per cent
- Heffer – 6.3 per cent
- Shore – 3.1 per cent

Knowing that the party wanted to move on to a new generation, and that there was a clamour to elect someone on the left, begs the question of why Shore desired to stand. He was aware of the challenge he faced from the outset, based on the early declarations of the trade union leaders, but he decided to stay in the contest for a variety of reasons.

> Number one, when I start something I go on. That's a kind of, if you like, a personal stubbornness. And I wouldn't dream of withdrawing. Secondly, because I actually believe that in the course of an election campaign of this kind you have an opportunity of saying things; of major issues and affairs and if you are sensible you might even contribute something to that discussion.
>
> The crucial thing that the Party leader has to do … is not only inspire the faithful; he's got to actually win the majority of opinion in

the country and in my view that is a task that I believe I could do....
And I believe that it is that broader appeal beyond just the Party itself,
that I actually have. I think that my standing in the country is probably
a great deal higher than the actual votes that I'm going to get from
particular parts of the Labour movement... I often feel that I have a
more instinctive understanding of what people in this country want
and believe in.[26]

While Shore had his motivations for continuing, despite the unlike-
liness of success, other reasons can be put forward. Margaret Beckett
identified that there was a different approach towards contesting
internal party elections in previous decades: 'If you had standing
and ability, there was the view that why shouldn't you put your name
forward?' This would change by the late 1980s and early 1990s, when
a candidate would stand only when they thought that they would
win.[27] Shore's distinct position within the party and his unwillingness
to 'wave the white flag' prompted him to stand, and David Cowling
thought that 'he represented a voice and a tradition that's flag had to
be in the battlefield', and that the contest 'needed some intellectual
rigour'.[28] Moreover, at that point, there was not another candidate of
the same standing and politics as Shore, with Butler stating, 'If he did
not put the arguments up no one else would.'[29]

There is every possibility that Shore, as Harris notes, 'might
have won had the election been held a couple of years before', yet
the scale of defeat meant that he was 'humiliated'.[30] He had been
overtaken as the centre candidate by Hattersley, and Kinnock's rise
through the party as a 'man of the left' resulted in Shore's position
and potential support being squeezed. Jim Callaghan wrote to Shore

during the campaign and encapsulated the problem facing him; despite Callaghan's view that Shore 'would make a splendid leader' his candidature was irrelevant 'for no reasons connected with your own personal qualities. It is Kinnock or Hattersley.' This did not undermine Shore's 'courage, integrity and ability', Callaghan said, but instead showed 'the unpleasant truth about this contest', that it had 'come at the wrong time for you'. Callaghan predicted that Shore would get only a 'small vote, but that will be in no sense a reflection of the respect in which the Party holds you'.[31] Combined with the heavy defeat in the 1980 Labour leadership contest, it spelt the end of Shore's leadership ambitions.

CONCLUSION

Despite being a well-respected Labour figure and enjoying significant Cabinet experience, Shore fared badly in the 1980 and 1983 leadership elections, with both, though to a lesser extent the 1980 contest, coming at the wrong time. In 1980, the party wanted to move to the left, and while Shore could have appealed to this group, as he was to the left of Healey, he was outflanked by Foot. Comparatively, in 1983, the party wanted to move to a new generation, while Shore, as shadow Chancellor, had been heavily involved in the disastrous 1983 general election and was therefore tainted. One observer aptly thought that Shore had the air of a 'Battle of Britain pilot gallantly risking all, knowing he is unlikely to survive, but hoping that his efforts, even at the eleventh hour, will save the party'. Unlike the servicemen whom Shore celebrated, the commentator correctly asserted that 'he will get no thanks for it'.[32] Defeat marked the beginning of the end of his frontline career in politics, and he was viewed by this time as 'yesterday's man'.

Yet, 'the wrong time' argument only goes so far, as politics is often said to be about making the most out of events as they present themselves. Therefore, other reasons must be put forward. The *Observer* political columnist Alan Watkins believed that Shore suffered in the 1980 and 1983 leadership contests from the inability of people to categorise him as on the right or on the left, and noted that British political parties are 'uneasy with people who cannot be put into boxes, tied up neatly and labelled'.[33] This view is supported by Beckett, who considered that 'the inability to pigeonhole Shore made a lot of people suspicious, and that's never a good place to be. He was very bright but something of a loner. I don't know how just that is, but that's an impression people had.'[34] Towards the end of his life, Shore reflected on how others perceived him, stating,

> I've always been a somewhat ambivalent figure in terms of left, right and centre in Labour politics ... A lot of people see me as an establishment man, a kind of headquarters man, a chap at the centre and they're right. But they also see me as being really a rather dangerous radical, and maybe they're right about that too.[35]

Therefore, when MPs and later the electoral college had to judge his candidature, he lacked some of the necessary characteristics and components to be successful. Unlike some of his contemporaries, he never had a set of policies or a clearly articulated vision that allowed him to gather a following within the PLP, the trade union movement and the constituencies. Indeed, while he was well-known for his stance on Europe, on other matters his views were not so pronounced, and his ministerial achievements were less notable than others'. The thorough analysis he offered in 1983 failed to cut through and he paid the price for his candid criticisms of his own party.

In the days following the 1983 leadership contest Shore wrote a review of Philip Williams's *The Diary of Hugh Gaitskell*. Although he focused on the tensions between Gaitskell and Bevan, he also considered the following on the complexity of leading the Labour Party:

> The Labour Party cannot be led successfully either by those who are immersed in the dream or by those who have never glimpsed Jerusalem. It is that which makes the Labour Party so particularly difficult to lead – and it is also what makes leadership so essential in the Labour Party.[36]

Judged by his own criteria, Shore had 'glimpsed Jerusalem'; he believed in creating a more equal and prosperous Britain and, importantly, his socialism was not merely 'immersed in the dream' but rooted in 'the practical', reaching the deepest instincts of the British people. He had many admirable qualities, alongside a considerable intellect, but he was in the unenviable position of being 'everyone's second choice'; while few objected to him, few wholeheartedly supported him, and, unfortunately for Shore, the party to which he had given so much failed to acknowledge the contribution he could make as party leader.

8

THE MILITANT TENDENCY AND
THE BATTLE FOR STEPNEY

IN THE EARLY 1980S Peter Shore and his supporters became aware of organised attempts to push for his deselection. The first serious efforts followed the 1983 general election defeat and Shore's bid for the Labour leadership after the departure of Michael Foot. Following a two-year battle, Shore won out, but the left lingered to organise again for his deselection in 1986 and yet again in 1992. Shore held the Militant Tendency responsible for these attempts, though in reality there appeared to be myriad far-left groups, all with differing agendas, who wanted Shore's seat.

The Militant Tendency's growth and success came during a period of ideological weakness within the Labour Party leadership. Harold Wilson had promised much but delivered little in the eyes of a broad spectrum of Labour members and supporters, and this was crystallised in his unexpected defeat to Ted Heath's Conservative Party in the 1970 general election. As Labour lost active members through disillusionment, the small number of Militant supporters were able to fill the void and take positions in CLPs. The tactics of 'deep entryism' were serving Militant well and the group won a majority on the national leadership of the Labour Party Young Socialists in 1970, while a groundswell of radicalism began to permeate through the party's grassroots as Heath tried to introduce unpopular anti-trade union laws.

There was a dramatic shift to the left in the leadership of Britain's trade unions as moderate leaders retired. This radicalisation spread throughout the Labour movement and into the Labour Party, which itself shifted to the left as the record of the Wilson and Callaghan governments drew a sense of an opportunity lost by a generation of members. There was significant vitriol and condemnation of the 1974–79 Labour governments, epitomised by Tony Benn's 1979 conference speech, which marked former Cabinet members as obstructionists to socialism who also failed to listen to party members. The defeat of the Callaghan government in 1979 itself resulted in a sharp radicalisation, reflecting the unhappiness with Labour's supposed pro-capitalist policies, and took the form of the rise of Bennism within the Labour Party. The split of Labour's social democratic right to form the SDP cemented the leftward trajectory of the Labour Party in this period.

There was a significant drive for new members after the general election defeat in 1979, and particularly in the early 1980s: by 1982 Stepney & Poplar had a membership of 635. However, this new activism in Shore's CLP brought with it logistical problems. The sheer scale of resolutions being passed by wards to be presented and voted on at General Meetings far outstripped the time available for such meetings. In fact, by the end of 1982, there were fifty-two resolutions still waiting to be discussed at the constituency level, and there was a plea from the General Management Committee that fewer motions be sent forward, as well as that some be rescinded in the hope to get through the backlog. Militant's membership tended to be young and/or politically inexperienced, and the initial attraction for these members were policies that were put into simple terms or 'transitional demands' in the manner of Leon Trotsky's approach. These basic demands included the nationalisation of major British businesses, the banks, the introduction of a 35-hour working week, the abolition of the monarchy and the reversal of all spending cuts. This was not a political programme but a set of demands with which to attract a broad section of the working class to Militant's banner.

However, the group's success was limited to areas where Labour was without strong traditions. The actual size and influence of Militant was overplayed both by Labour's right and its Conservative opposition, though its success in some individual CLPs saw it wield power enough to remove a sitting MP, like Reg Prentice in Newham North East. Only in one city, Liverpool, did Militant manage to take effective control of local government apparatus, and then only with a minority of councillors. John Callaghan, writing in *Marxism Today* in August 1982, argued that 'the extraordinary hysteria that has been generated ... is to be understood not in terms of the actual size and influence of the Militant Tendency but in connection with the extraordinary crisis in Labourism'.[1] Indeed, Labour's right saw the ratcheting up of the campaign against Militant in the early 1980s as the spearhead of a general assault on the gains made by the Labour left since the 1970 general election defeat. The secrecy under which Militant operated gave further ammunition to Labour's right and encouraged inaccurate and malicious reporting in the media, and there is no denying that Militant's ideology was not in line with the spirit of democratic socialism and reformism generally practiced by the Labour Party. That said, though, there was no prospect of Militant coming to power in the Labour Party, let alone in Britain, and at its high point it enjoyed just three Labour MPs and, as the authors calculate, less than 100 councillors.

SHORE BATTLES AGAINST DESELECTION

The targeting of Shore by the 'hard left' throughout the 1980s and into the early 1990s makes for an interesting case study of how the Militant Tendency and other left groups operated. Also, it raises the question of why they sought to deselect an MP who was a committed Keynesian and anti-European and who was not, as we have argued, on the right of the party. As for Shore, his temperament, intellectualism and political outlook were less suited to the 'rough and tumble' that was needed for such a fight. In fact, according to Christine Sibley, a local party worker in Tower Hamlets, Shore 'refused to open a local constituency office like other MPs despite local members pleading with him to do so. Shore said he would not claim expenses to pay for an office for his own self-promotion.'[2] John Spellar, now Labour MP for Warley but then national political officer for the Electrical, Electronic, Telecommunications and Plumbing Union (EETPU), 'which saw itself as the Praetorian Guard of the Labour Right',[3] said, 'Peter only partially understood the politics of this type. It just was not his world or his mindset. We had to get a grip on the situation, take control and get people in. We saved him.'[4] In order to get through this long and draining process, Shore also relied on the support of Nick Butler and his wife Rosaleen, David Cowling, David Bean, John Rentoul, Michael Crick and, later, Stephen Pollard. John Biggs, a London Labour activist, recalls that Shore enjoyed much support from the trade unions, particularly the postal workers, and for Butler it was Shore's closeness to the right-wing unions, who, at this stage, gave their support to any Labour figure who opposed the Bennite left, that helped him to survive.[5]

According to Biggs, the left in Shore's CLP was centred around Phil Maxwell, Jill Cove, Robbie MacDuff and Lesley Pavitt. Biggs, on the other hand, belonged to the 'pragmatic centre' and was very protective of Shore.[6] At local meetings, some people gave the impression of attending merely to pick a fight with Shore, while Butler viewed Shore's opponents to be poorly organised, assuming that 'Shore would just roll over or that he could not get the sufficient people behind him from the area or the unions'. The left-wingers belonged to a mixture of groups, 'SWP, Militant, IMG, Socialist Organiser', according to Butler, but Shore's supporters 'succeeded in dividing them as they wanted different people to get the seat'.[7] Cove was the constituency chair and won re-election to that post in March 1984 ahead of a Shore loyalist. Biggs, himself currently Mayor of Tower Hamlets, remembers Shore as a maverick who was suspicious of incomers to the party, and who suffered from a paranoia then common among MPs concerned about deselection.[8]

In particular, Shore became suspicious of young members whom he believed had been influenced by Trotskyist groups to enter the party and deselect him. He believed they had an unrealistic belief that socialism could be achieved almost overnight if only Labour were to put forward a radical enough agenda. *London Labour Briefing*, a monthly magazine regarded as Trotskyist in outlook and which led the 1983–85 deselection campaign, admitted that Shore, along with several other Labour MPs, had cause for concern. *Briefing* suggested that Shore was an 'anachronism utterly incapable of speaking the language or voicing the anger of the communities from which our strength now derives'.[9] Elsewhere, *Briefing* lambasted Shore for 'using the anti-Labour capitalist media to damage the left and reject socialist policies', and for being 'British capitalism's main ally in the Labour Party today', part of an 'apologist Tory remnant failing to represent or fight for working-class interests'.[10] One of those young members of whom Shore was suspicious was John Rentoul, then a Labour activist sympathetic to many of *Briefing*'s left policies, who was also 'pretty suspicious' of Shore. However, Rentoul felt that those seeking to deselect Shore had failed to find a sufficiently good candidate to replace him: 'I came to the conclusion', he said, 'that the deselection of Peter Shore would be a media disaster for the Labour Party. So I decided to grit my teeth and, for the good of the party, organise for Shore's reselection.'[11]

Shore was very much an old-school MP. He had been elected at a time when MPs were rarely seen in their constituencies; he would do some casework but spend most of his time in Parliament. However, things had begun to change radically, and by the 1980s a new generation of Labour MPs and a more enthusiastic and radical membership had changed the role of an MP to be that of an extension of their community activism. The rise of the new left in Tower Hamlets mirrored a similar movement in other inner-city areas, particularly in London, gaining control of two constituency parties: those of Shore and Ian Mikardo. Robert Kilroy-Silk, who was an active supporter of Shore in this period, nominated him in shadow Cabinet elections. However, he wondered how Shore would be able to do an effective job as Leader of the House if his constituency battles became ever more drawn out:

> Reselection is, indeed, the dominant and often the sole topic of conversation amongst my colleagues in the Tea Room, at dinner and in the bars, at the House of Commons. No one seems capable of talking about anything else ... They have sleepless nights. They are constantly looking over their shoulders, spend more time in their constituencies on party politics and have to devote more time and energy to organising their supporters when they should be in Parliament. As they have all reiterated dozens of times, we will not be able to run a Labour Government in these circumstances.[12]

Throughout the 1980s Holy Trinity Ward Labour Party was one of two militantly anti-Shore wards in the constituency, and during Shore's 1980 leadership campaign those in the ward distributed a leaflet across the constituency membership titled *Why Shore Must Not Succeed*.[13] The leaflet was short, to the point, and clear in its antipathy:

> Bethnal Green and Stepney have reluctantly returned Mr Shore as their MP for another term on the cosy leather benches at the Palace of Westminster.
>
> His election in this part of East London reflected the rather re-signed character of support which most remaining members of the Wilson/Callaghan government received at the polls.
>
> Working class electors, with sharp memories of that government's

reactionary handling of their unions' pay demands do not want a re-run of those Keynesian years which bring austerity, hardship and conflict for the poorly paid.

In Shore we have the prospect of blatantly anti-working class 'wage restraint' and the absurd plan to devalue Sterling by 30 per cent which will mean a massive increase in food prices for working class people. For Shore, unemployment is not caused by the crisis-prone nature of capitalism but merely by silly economic policies of monetarism.

If Shore was to be elected as leader, therefore, the Socialist desire of changing society in the direction of working-class people would be suppressed by the right-wing commitment to support capital.

SHORE MUST GO!!!!

The authors of the leaflet presumably preferred Michael Foot as Labour leader, but Foot was also guilty of some of the supposed crimes committed by Shore. For example, Foot, like Shore, was a Keynesian who had served in the Wilson and Callaghan governments. Shore had expected to gain support from the left of the party and thought he was in with a chance of beating Denis Healey to the leadership in 1980 with their votes, had Foot not changed his mind. As we have noted, placing Shore on the left–right spectrum is problematic, and while Shore viewed himself more towards the left of the party, this was not a unanimous view. It was not only some in Shore's local party who questioned his left credentials, but also his neighbouring MP Ian Mikardo. According to Kinnock, the two men 'detested each other', a view corroborated by some of Shore's former party workers and John Spellar, who remembered Mikardo as 'an old leftist warrior who knew how to handle these things. He was a cunning, devious manipulator and I don't say that disparagingly.'[14] Mikardo wrote in his memoirs that Shore was, 'a right-winger who had acquired a false reputation as a leftist merely because he was anti-EEC'.[15] However, Neil Kinnock has recalled that, although Shore and Mikardo detested each other, Mikardo did send some of Labour's 'old guard' to bolster support for Shore in his constituency.[16]

The striking thing about the anti-Shore leaflet, and the accompanying deselection campaign, was its lack of clear ideology. It is not a Militant leaflet, nor from appearance the work of any other Trotskyist group like the SWP, for it contains none of the jargon or branding that would be associated with such a group. It would appear, then, to be the work of a group of disaffected members of Labour's left wing, unhappy with Labour's approach in its 1964–70 and 1974–79 governments and their failure to implement radical change in the cause of socialism. As Solidarity co-chairman, Shore had voted for Healey in the deputy leadership contest but never publicly endorsed him, though this may have been due to some lingering respect for Benn after their long friendship or his dislike of Healey, more than any attempt to keep more left elements of his CLP onside. At the General Meeting of 10 December 1982, a resolution was put forward by Holy Trinity Ward calling for the rejection of attacks on the Labour Party Young Socialists (LPYS):

This meeting believes that any expulsion organised by the right wing/ SDP elements in the PLP and its secret and ultra-right wing organisation in the Labour Party called 'Solidarity', would require in return the immediate expulsion of all supporters and members of SOLIDARITY from the Tower Hamlets Labour Party.

The change of tone and language from the anti-Shore leaflet produced by the Holy Trinity Ward and this motion is striking. There is a clear line of attack on Solidarity, a regular target for Militant, and a call for their immediate expulsion just as Militant's editorial board was facing a similar fate. Millwall Ward called the setting up of a new proscribed register 'an attempt by sections of the Labour Party to limit democratic debate' and called for the membership to 'fight against the proposed expulsion of Militant supporters and other socialists who may be expelled on the basis of their ideas'. Correspondence had also been received directly from Militant itself, stating its support for the Labour Against the Witchhunt group. The agenda notices were distributed with a flyer for *Tribune* magazine, which had supported Foot's leadership bid over Shore's, with the offer of a free copy of Alan Freeman's *The Benn Heresy,* a hagiography which cast Benn as a heroic figure.

Constituency changes added to Shore's worries and did not help him feel any more secure. His Stepney & Poplar constituency was abolished and would cease to exist at the end of the 1979–83 parliament, with the Boundary Commission rotating the seats so that Shore's constituency became Bethnal Green & Stepney and neighbouring MP Ian Mikardo's constituency became Bow & Poplar. The left were happy with the old firebrand Mikardo to continue as an MP and put forward no objection, but the same could not be said for Shore. One of the left's gripes was that Shore lived in Putney, which they used to create a sense that he had been 'imposed from the outside'. The NEC had decided that after the boundary changes any MP who still represented a majority of their old constituents in the newly created seats would be automatically reselected. Any less than that and an open selection would be held. Shore's new constituency of Bethnal Green & Stepney included just under 50 per cent of his former constituents, meaning there would be a full parliamentary selection, and, in this atmosphere, Shore was in danger of losing. Shore's friends were quick to jump to his aid and Solidarity activist David Bean, now a High Court judge, drafted a get-out clause to be sent to the NEC. It read:

Where the boundaries of two or more constituencies adjacent to each other with endorsed candidates are altered, but where the number of seats remains the same and no other constituency is involved, then each of the endorsed candidates shall be treated as having a majority claim in any of the new constituencies which includes a part of his or her old constituency.[17]

The moderate majority in the NEC adopted the clause as Tony Benn, Shore's old friend, muttered menacingly, 'I know what you're doing.'[18] The moderates and the 'traditional right' saw it as a victory that Shore did not have to face reselection, as the seat would have been in danger of falling to the left, while the Tower Hamlets Labour Party (THLP) Executive Committee received a letter from the St Katharine's Ward Labour Party accusing the THLP of being undemocratic and questioning the legitimacy of Shore's reselection. The Executive Committee rejected the allegations. John Spellar, behind moves to keep Shore, had long campaigned against Benn and his followers, and noted that 'Peter was a very capable, thoughtful man, and you need people like that in government. I believed it was the duty of the party to protect these people.'[19]

Shore and his committed team continued to push back, and Christine Sibley paired Shore up with local Labour councillors and members to do regular constituency walkarounds. However, his canvassing never really improved due to his shyness, and he was known to 'cling to one doorstep for forty-five minutes'. Strangely, though, Shore was renowned for his oratory in Parliament, despite seeming unable to replicate this skill at local party meetings.[20] Still, there were notices posted through doors in advance stating Shore's visit to the area, as well as a membership form and flyer on how to join the Labour Party. On the days themselves, Shore's team would knock on doors telling residents that their MP was there if they wanted to meet him, and posting cards to houses with no response, informing them that Shore had visited. Regular surgeries were set up on the second and fourth Fridays of the month from 7 p.m., usually with another councillor, John Brannigan. This now reads like standard fare for any MP, but for many of Shore's vintage it was quite different to how they had previously perceived their role.

The older generation in the constituency had considerable time for Shore, as did the Bangladeshi community.[21] He had been one of the first MPs to stand up publicly for the independence struggle of Bangladesh and he never pandered to racism, unlike the local Liberals, who thought they had a chance of winning the constituency but were accused of attempting to exploit racism in order to win local support. Shore was seen on anti-racism demonstrations and was, therefore, popular with the Bangladeshi community, which comprised 24 per cent of the constituency population.[22] Shore was also active in speeding up the processing of passport and asylum applications for members of the community and their families. Philip Webster, writing in *The Times*, considered that

the biggest irony is that Shore is a highly respected and popular MP;

the 1983 general election showed that. He inherited five wards from Mikardo, four of which – Weaver's, St Peter's, St James's and Holy Trinity – are controlled by the Liberals. The seat was effectively a marginal, but he got in with 51 per cent of the vote.[23]

Shore survived what he considered to be another coordinated attempt to deselect him led by the new left, who wanted CLP chair Jill Cove, winning by forty-six votes to Cove's thirty-eight in the first round in January 1986. Shore had learned tough lessons from the likes of John Spellar, and through his supporters managed to get enough people into the selection meeting to back him.

The issue of Shore's selection would return to the fore for the 1992 general election. Two prominent councillors in the Bethnal Green & Stepney constituency party opposed Shore: Rajan Uddin Jalal, a Bangladeshi councillor in the St Katharine's Ward, and Phil Maxwell, leader of the Labour opposition on Tower Hamlets council. The left wished to remove him as an MP because of his strong support for the British troops in the Gulf War. According to his critics, who were advocating a ceasefire on a 'stop-the-war' ticket, Shore's hard-line approach towards Iraq had offended his Bangladeshi constituents. However, he was aided by the actions of the NEC, who managed to delay the re-selection process by ousting thirteen suspected Militant Tendency supporters from the Tower Hamlets party, which was partly formed by Shore's constituency. Also, if Maxwell had defeated Shore, the NEC would have vetoed him becoming the candidate, as he had broken party policy by refusing to pay his poll tax. Regardless, Shore was reselected with 57 per cent of the vote on the first ballot, despite a gaffe, described here by John Rentoul:

He was giving a good old-fashioned tub-thumping left-wing speech, when his false teeth started to fall out, so he had to spin round with his back to the audience, shove them back in and then carry on. It was a bit embarrassing, although it didn't really matter because the votes were already committed one way or the other and he had a comforta-ble majority.[24]

CONCLUSION

Militant was active in Tower Hamlets but, despite the popular nar-rative, the group was not central to seeking Shore's deselection. The left was very anti-European at the time, and Derek Gadd got the impression that having Shore as a target sat ill with Militant, who regarded his eloquent anti-Europeanism as important. Militant rarely confronted its opponents outside of articles in its newspapers and pamphlets. It shared with its left detractors a cast-iron belief in the Marxism of Lenin and Trotsky and that all current political prob-lems could be solved with its correct implementation. Militant also felt the same disdain for the non-Militant Labour left, and referred to Tony Benn, perhaps its leading tacit supporter, as the Kerensky to its Lenin. It was a mostly non-aligned left grouping that supported Cove as an alternative candidate in the early 1980s and, according to Gadd, the nerve centre of the operation to deselect Shore was a shared flat in a Spitalfields tower block. Robbie MacDuff, who was a research as-sistant to Labour MP Allan Roberts and who was 'left' – but not Mil-itant – sold critical papers outside of the meetings, although he was not a principal conspirator.[25] This did, however, reflect the distrust in CLPs at the time of the right-wing 'establishment' Labour Party that Shore seemed to represent. He was still respected throughout the 1980s in his constituency as an intellectual with a sharp mind, even by many of his detractors, who saw deficiencies in some of his policy positions and his association with the Wilson and Callaghan years, rather than in his intellectual ability. The only real criticism of Shore was that he was a part of the Labour governments that activists felt had failed to implement enough socialist change; the attempts for his deselection were not down to his politics, therefore, but what he supposedly represented.

9

THE BACK BENCHES, EUROPE
AND THE LORDS

THE WILDERNESS YEARS

DEFEAT IN THE 1983 Labour leadership contest marked the end of Shore's career as a frontline politician, and although he would remain in Kinnock's shadow Cabinet until 1987, he was demoted once Kinnock became leader. While the October 1983 shadow Cabinet election results saw Shore elected, along with his running mate Gwyneth Dunwoody, Kinnock possessed discretion in the allocation of posts, and his major change was to move Shore from shadow Chancellor to shadow Secretary of State for Trade and Industry and shadow Leader of the House of Commons. For Kinnock, Shore was too involved with the economic policies that had been rejected in 1983 and was, therefore, unable to 'drag our economic policy towards reality'.[1] According to Andy McSmith, three candidates had been considered for the Trade and Industry post (Shore,

John Smith and Robin Cook), of which Shore was the one Kinnock least wanted.[2] Kinnock recalls:

> Peter Shore played hell. In fact, he was so uncooperative that I de-
> cided to pile him with gifts – if he did well with two jobs, so much
> the better. If he didn't shine, politics would take its course, and he'd
> be voted off the Shadow Cabinet. That's what happened – and that's
> why I gave him two portfolios.[3]

It was during the mid-1980s that Shore struggled both personally and politically. Personally, he suffered from a deep depression and politically, his career as a frontline politician was ending. Labour was planning an ambitious campaign to promote itself as the party that could revive industry and effect a dramatic drop in the unemployment figures. Even Shore's former allies in the Solidarity group could not fail to see a problem with having the campaign fronted by an old anti-Marketeer who did not believe that economic regeneration was possible while the rules of the Community tied Britain and, in 1984, Shore was dropped from his economic portfolio. Shore had fallen to sixth place in that year's shadow Cabinet election, giving Kinnock the excuse he needed to sack him from his economic job. He would remain in his post as shadow Leader of the House until 1987 – criticising the NUM's decision not to hold a ballot immediately prior to the miners' strike as a 'disaster' – but was voted off the shadow Cabinet in July 1987, in part because he had remained critical of Labour's non-nuclear defence posture. *The Times* wrote,

> The chief sadness here must be the defeat of Mr Peter Shore, whose

career has been blighted partly by sheer bad luck and partly by his attachment to unfashionable principles. Had he chosen his principles more expediently, or stuck to them less resolutely, he would certainly have held higher office in the party. Indeed, he might possibly have ended his career on the front bench as the leader himself... That the new parliamentary party feels it can dispense with his services on the front bench is not an encouraging sign.[4]

Shore and Kinnock shared no personal warmth or relationship. Shore blamed him for ending his own frontline political career and considered him ill-suited and ill-equipped to be the leader of the Labour Party, lacking in intellect and experience. Indeed, Shore wrote in *Leading the Left* that Kinnock's

utterances reflected lightly-rooted, rather than settled beliefs ... Not one of the major policy positions that Kinnock enthusiastically embraced at the time of his election as leader in 1983 ... survived to the end of his leadership. Moreover, he made no public attempt to explain why he had changed his mind on so many crucial issues.[5]

Indeed, of all the Labour leaders since George Lansbury in the 1930s, Shore was the most critical of Kinnock, accusing him of travelling a long way before he came to his political Journey's End:

as a candidate for the Brussels Commission: dedicated to a Federal Europe, based upon a clutch of treaties that enshrined the goals of the free market; free movement of labour, capital and enterprises; non-intervention in the economy by the governments of member states; the control of currency, interest rates and exchange rates by a European Central Bank with an overriding commitment to price stability and zero inflation.[6]

From the back benches, Shore criticised Kinnock's position on unilateral disarmament, as Kinnock had throughout the mid-1980s remained in favour of unilateralism. In comparison, Shore openly wanted to remove unilateralism from Labour's programme. He demanded that the party reconsider its attitude towards unilateralism and left sectarianism, as these policies had hurt Labour's electoral chances in the 1987 general election. Labour's poor showing was also, he thought, because

> our socialism is not democratic and libertarian but violent and coercive, that we seek not to change and unify the nation but ... to wage class war against the rest of society, that our concerns are so exclusively with the 'rainbow coalition' of the poor, the underprivileged and the disadvantaged that we have little understanding or interest in the problems of the majority of ordinary people.

Shore also issued a public warning that Kinnock would have to achieve 'moral, intellectual supremacy' over Thatcher, or go.[7] He returned to the themes he had outlined in the 1983 leadership contest: the adoption of unilateralism in 1981 had, as far as Shore was concerned in 1987, 'done great and demonstrable damage to the Labour Party ... It is a policy that is at best irrelevant to the search for peace and disarmament.'[8] There was no issue on which the electorate trusted the Tories more and Labour less than that of defence, and the majority of

British people remained convinced that Britain should retain a nuclear capability. While Labour had been right, Shore believed, to emphasise the primacy of conventional armaments and persuade NATO allies to abandon reliance on nuclear weapons progressively, the argument that US bases be withdrawn and that the decommissioning of Polaris, a nuclear programme, should begin was unconvincing. As a member of NATO, there was no neutrality for the UK, falling as it did under the protection of the American strategic nuclear deterrent.[9]

Shore would return to the issue of unilateralism in 1988, condemning Kinnock's promise to decommission Trident and Polaris as 'Black Tuesday'. He elaborated on his opposition to total UK unilateral nuclear disarmament, saying the policy was a 'cop-out ... [a] postured placebo to relieve and express the feelings of its sponsors'. As Britain had so few of the world's nuclear weapons, 'no one in their sense can believe that by renouncing them, Britain would make either the world or itself a safer place'. The arithmetic did not add up, he thought; it was right that 'Britain should retain her own nuclear weapons as long as other nuclear powers retain theirs', as it was necessary to have leverage in future NATO strategy and in future East/West negotiations for reducing and abolishing nuclear weapons. Shore also questioned whether the United States, in a crisis, would come to the aid of Europe if it was subject to a Soviet attack.[10] Shore's well-articulated and intellectual case for multilateralism deserves credit, as it opened the political space for Kinnock to drop Labour's unilateral stance in 1989.

Further to this, during the first Gulf War (August 1990–February 1991), Shore continued to take a harder line than Kinnock on defence and foreign affairs, calling for early military action after the expiry of the United Nations deadline for Iraq to leave Kuwait. He strongly backed war to oust Iraq from Kuwait and as a method of erasing aggression and upholding the authority of the UN. Indeed, he thought that the credibility of the UN was at stake

> if we do not accept that the meaning of collective security – above all in this post-cold war age – means the willingness to use international force, economic or, if need be, military, to achieve the goals of international security and justice which many of us came out of the second world war determined to achieve.[11]

Shore called it 'the first time since 1945 that an aggressor state has sought to change not just the Government of another country or rectify its borders or impose penalties but to destroy and annex the victim nation'. If war proved unavoidable it would be a war not for oil and American imperialism, but for the purpose that the UN was founded, rescuing the 'damaged, ravaged and abused' people of Kuwait.[12]

From Labour's back benches Shore also challenged the increasingly pro-European leadership, firstly under Kinnock, then Smith and finally Blair. While Labour had dropped its commitment to withdraw in February 1988, there had been a softening of attitudes towards the EEC after the 1983 general election defeat and the failure of the Mitterrand experiment in France. Consequently, the focus shifted towards what membership entailed for unemployment and the real economy. Under Kinnock, Shore raised the unwelcome topic of Labour conditions for European Exchange Rate Mechanism (ERM) membership and the tougher conditions agreed by the 1989 Labour

Party conference. Hattersley, as shadow Chancellor, had initially set the conditions for ERM membership, namely entry at a sustainable level that would encourage British exports, with European policy co-ordination to promote expansion and reduce unemployment, and an increase in monetary cooperation rather than a reliance on high interest rates in less competitive countries. After Britain had joined the ERM, Kinnock and Smith compromised, agreeing to a commitment in principle to join the single currency if there was real economic convergence, including low employment.[13] Shore pointed out that none of the conditions that Labour had set out a year earlier in *Meet the Challenge, Make the Change*, which was positive about European integration but unenthusiastic about joining the ERM, had been met. As McSmith notes, those, of course, were Bryan Gould's conclusions. Gould shared Shore's attitude towards Europe, rather than John Smith's, though it is notable that Smith's conditions had not been met either.[14] *Looking to the Future*, published in 1990, dropped the objections to ERM membership and advocated entry, arguing that the ERM would 'provide a stable framework for long-term investment and steady growth'.[15] Shore found it difficult to fathom why the Labour Party and the trade union movement had failed to recognise what was entailed in the ERM/Economic and Monetary Union (EMU), including the question of employment and the prioritising of the interests of bankers and financiers above jobs and industry. Either the party did not understand, or it had underestimated the impact of handing over the powers of economic self-government. It seemed to Shore that the party was depressed about the prospects of Britain and had concluded that the UK was no longer capable of sustaining an independent economic life, or, alternatively, it had fallen into the trap of subscribing to Euro-rhetoric in the belief that nothing would happen.[16]

In June 1990, Shore was congratulated by Thatcher for 'beginning to sound more and more like me' after he attacked the 'Gadarene rush towards economic, monetary and political union in Europe'.[17] This hurt Shore, as he had nothing in common with the economic policies of Thatcherism and had spent the 1980s critiquing the New Right. However, on the issue of Europe he was prepared to campaign with those from across the political spectrum, and in July 1990 he gave a speech at the Conservative-dominated Bruges Group. He did so because, while he represented a different political tradition, he shared with his Conservative opponents a belief in self-government, the rejection of a European super-state, and the view that the boundaries of the Community should expand to Eastern and Central European countries. His concluding comments are especially prescient in light of the portrayal and treatment of Eurosceptics from across the political spectrum by the most ardent pro-Europeans since Britain voted 'Leave' in June 2016:

> We shall be subjected to a barrage of insults about our insularity and threat about the terrible consequences that await us if we dare to say No. We shall withstand it. More, we must be ready to explain and inform, to argue and to expose. Above all, those of us in Parliament, regardless of party, must be resolute in the defence of our people, our nation and our democracy.[18]

The drive towards the creation of a European Union was, in Shore's opinion, the position of West Germany. In economic terms, West Germany dominated the economies of Europe through a trading surplus and the formation of the European Monetary System, while the EMS allowed the Bundesbank, the central bank of the Federal Republic of Germany, to control the interest and exchange rates of Western Europe. To contain West Germany's economic power and to bring the Bundesbank under collective control, the other nations of Western Europe 'have persuaded themselves that they have no alternative but to abandon all the crucial elements of National economic sovereignty'.[19] This was particularly true of France, which had come to believe that the only method of containing German power was through enmeshing the German state in a European Union. The objective of economic, monetary and political union was 'reviving the "Europe of Charlemagne" … the creation of a new and powerful European state'.[20] While the drive towards Economic and Monetary Union was primarily political, Shore also objected to the EMU because it would threaten the living standards of the less competitive countries. The variations in productivity, uninhibited by free competition and fixed exchange rates, would undermine the industry in those less competitive countries, therefore leading to unemployment. On this basis, a united Germany was more than willing to go along with these developments, in effect becoming the 'Prussia within the EC Zollverein'.[21]

Shore attacked the Labour front bench over the rate at which the pound was tied to the Deutschmark and the Maastricht Treaty, urging the party to remember the historical dangers of supporting fixed exchange rates. Labour needed, he thought, to learn from the experience of 1931 and 1967, but instead it had become wedded to anything 'European', and its position was closer to that of 'see no evil, hear no evil'.[22] George Robertson bore the brunt of one of Shore's attacks for not opposing Maastricht, a treaty that 'handed over great chunks of British power to decision making in the European institutions, adding: "if my hon. Friend [Robertson] cannot understand that, he is not fit to speak for my party"'.[23] Shore felt that the issue was about 'the future of our country' because control over monetary policy was being given to the European Central Bank (ECB). He rubbished Smith's argument that the French and British socialist model of a more democratically accountable ECB had prevailed at Maastricht. Shore claimed that the Franco-British position was not 'worth a damn, if it ever existed' and concluded that 'the Frontbench hasn't got the guts to stand up for Britain, and if this amendment is carried it will go down as a day of infamy in the history of the Labour Party'.[24]

Elsewhere in his time on the back benches, Shore published *Leading the Left* in 1993, an account of the post-MacDonald leaders of the Labour Party. Rather than a simple historical account, Shore wrote a personalised assessment of successive Labour leaders' relationships with the institutions of the Labour movement – the party conference, the trade unions and the PLP – assessing how each leader had managed to reconcile the competing interests. The unique problem facing all Labour leaders (as opposed to Tory or Liberal leaders) stemmed directly from the importance of the conference as Labour's policy-making body, and the overwhelming weight given to the unions in their decisions. As a result, he noted, Labour leaders continuously face the possibility that they may have policies foisted on them that they do not support. Shore argued that a change in the constitution and power structure of the party was the necessary pre-condition to its ultimate electoral success.

It was also in *Leading the Left* that Shore disparaged Smith's Scottishness, deeming that under Smith the party was dominated by Scots and was, therefore, unable to connect with voters in the south of England.[25] Smith rejected that the Scottish domination of the leadership made it difficult for the party to win the hearts and minds of English voters. Indeed, he was 'always amused that Scots are not supposed to understand the South-East, yet the South-East is always supposed to understand Scotland', as the issues are not that different.[26] Shore identified that the rationale underpinning Smith's commitment to Scotland and Europe was an attempt to replace the nation state with a new and dynamic framework of government in which decisions affecting the UK would be made at different levels.[27]

In Parliament, Shore's concern with the effect of 'interests' on political parties had long been a component of his very English radicalism, and his membership of the Nolan (and Neill) committees, set up in 1994 to advise the Prime Minister on ethical standards in public life, was an obvious and much-deserved recognition of his strong sense of parliamentary duty and personal probity. Given his intellect and respect for Parliament, Shore was a good appointment to these committees, as he was someone who would look at the evidence and issues seriously, and not play political games. Indeed, he pressed John Major to include party funding in the remit for the committee on standards in public life; however, the parlous state of Tory election funds meant that Conservative Central Office ruled out any investigation into party finances.

CRITICAL OF NEW LABOUR

Shore's vocal opposition to 'ever closer union' was by the 1990s matched by his criticisms of the Labour leadership. The increasingly Europhile leadership was moving towards supply-side socialism and, therefore, away from Shore's Keynesian approach. Shore accused the last years of Kinnock's leadership and the first year of Smith's as 'intellectual timidity and conformity',[28] and such criticisms continued once Blair became party leader in 1994. Indeed, Shore's son recalls that he was fascinated by Blair, keeping a large box of press cuttings, speeches and interviews, and attempting to get a sense of who he was as a person.

> We sat together listening to one of his party conference speeches and we appreciated that Blair was charismatic, but afterwards, Peter turned to me and said, 'He is not a socialist, he has got no ideology at all.' What he came to realise was that Blair had no clear political philosophy beyond a vague desire to do 'good works' and be a 'good man' in a general Christian sense.[29]

Interestingly, Shore had campaigned for Blair in the Beaconsfield by-election of 1982. As shadow Chancellor, Shore went on the economic attack from the stage and denounced the advocates of monetarism in Margaret Thatcher's Cabinet. He asked, 'What is the one thing these people have in common? – they're all lawyers', while Blair, the young barrister, sat stiffly next to him.[30] When Blair later lost his deposit, Shore told the BBC television audience that 'he really is a most entertaining, attractive and obviously first-rate candidate, and we'd very much like to have him in the Parliamentary Labour Party'.[31] Also, Shore thought he was right to want to distance the party and the unions;[32] after all, the dominant theme in *Leading the Left* is the belief that the power and influence of the trade unions within the Labour movement needed to be curtailed.

However, Shore, along with Hattersley, was critical of the policies and style of New Labour. The Labour Party was a radical party of change, committed to making Britain more equal, and it would be denying its heritage 'if it was to play safe for too long'.[33] Mullin records Shore as saying that he was 'offended by New Labour's constant repudiation of our past ... It used to be the role of politicians to offer leadership. Now we just follow public opinion.'[34] While it was pleasing that the political and intellectual hegemony of Thatcherism – that poverty can be solved by income 'trickling down' through the operation of the 'free' market – had been challenged, Shore believed that the party's instincts were for higher taxes, more public spending, redistributing wealth, and incomes controls. Speaking on BBC One's *Breakfast with Frost*, Shore added, 'it is no good pretending that we are a party which is no longer interested in redistributing income in favour of those who are less advantaged than us in our society'.[35]

Moreover, Shore believed that Thatcherism had to be challenged at a macroeconomic level, dispelling the belief that price stability is the primary objective of economic policy. The Labour Party had to reassert that demand management was the key to job creation and growth, and there were two options available: either stimulating domestic expenditure or stimulating export sales. However, Shore deemed that Labour was coy about doing so, as it would involve a discussion about incomes policy. His case, comparatively, was that those expansionist policies needed to deliver full employment would inevitably generate inflationary pressures that, in turn, could only be controlled by some form of pay restraint, or by strangling the expansion with higher interest rates. The latter involved the abandonment of full employment as a viable goal and an incomes policy was therefore necessary.

Shore believed that underpinning Labour's coyness on the use of demand management to maintain full employment was the idea that it directly contradicted the major provisions in the Maastricht Treaty.[36] According to Shore, the greatest danger of all to demand-side policies in Britain was the introduction of the European single currency, the regime of the ECB, and the government borrowing limits laid down in the Maastricht Treaty.[37] It would also have implications for democracy and the electorate, as, while under the British system it is possible to get rid of governments that have done wrong, it is not possible to get rid of the European Commission and ECB bankers.[38] To abandon the pound and the Bank of England would be an act of abandoning self-government, Shore thought, and this had implications for Europe's social chapter and the 48-hour working week directive. While this was a welcome, though small, contribution to welfare at work, Shore noted, 'we are an independent, self-governing democracy, not a colony and the laws of our land should reflect the will of our people as expressed in Parliament, not the decisions of alien authorities. Improving welfare and working conditions is a job for the next Labour government – and no one else!'[39]

Shore had decided to stand down as an MP in 1995 and duly left the Commons in 1997, receiving his life peerage in John Major's dissolution honours list in April 1997. He had by this time become a detached figure, but membership of the Lords provided a platform from which he could focus on the British national interests and the principle of parliamentary independence. He continued to attack his party, opposing New Labour's decision to change the European Parliament electoral system from first-past-the-post to the closed-list system, in which voters can only vote for parties, rather than for specific people, and have no influence on the order in which party candidates are elected. While Shore had a strong dislike of PR in general (as it would make coalition government the norm in British politics), the closed-list system was 'an affront to democracy', as MEPs under that system would not be accountable to the electors, but to the party group that selected them.[40]

While PR and constitutional reform had been discussed by Labour in detail since the late 1980s, the policy contained political benefits for the party. The Liberal Democrats had long argued in favour of reform, and Labour's renewed interest moved it closer to the Lib Dems. Therefore, it was thought that, in the event of a hung parliament, it could form the basis of an agreement between the two parties. The landslide victory in 1997 effectively ended the 'project', however, as the political imperative was lacking. Shore condemned both the scheme to realign the British left and New Labour's Euro-peanism, stating that, 'apart from its basic strategy for winning and holding political power through coalition with the Lib Dems, the very purpose of New Labour is the immersion of Britain into the EU; that is the "project". Without Europe, it is nothing.'[41]

He lamented the lack of thought given by MPs and trade unionists over Gordon Brown's decision to allow the Bank of England to set interest rates, with the overriding importance given to keep infla-tion down, thus forcing interest rates to rise. Shore supposed that those who were bemoaning the rise in interest rates were the same people arguing for the adoption of the single currency: 'The failure to make the connection between making the Bank of England inde-pendent of the Chancellor and making the Bank of England itself a branch of the European Central Bank is an intellectual failure almost without equal in my experience of politics,' he said.[42]

Shore also slammed the class-conscious cultural preferences and elitism of New Labour, its Europeanism and its sneering attitude towards patriotism and nationalism. Shore's objection to what he perceived as the unpatriotic left intelligentsia was his belief in the nation state – something that, for New Labour, had a reduced capacity to act in a globalised world. Indeed, it was globalisation that encouraged thoughts that only by pooling sovereignty and acting with like-minded European partners at a supranational level was it possible to tackle the excesses of global capitalism. Such a view stemmed from the 'deepest philosophical beliefs and world outlook of Gordon Brown and Tony Blair ... that globalisation of markets, capital communications and information have rendered the nation state – even ours, with the fourth or fifth largest economy in the world – virtually impotent in the management of its own affairs'.[43]

The dislike and distrust of the Blair government was not merely due to its view that the nation state was powerless in a globalised economy, but also to its contempt for patriotism and national allegiance. Shore deemed that New Labour considered the nation state 'to be responsible for most of the horrors – war, tyranny and perse-cution – of the century that has just ended'. With its anthem, flag, exclusiveness and frontiers, it represented 'all those conservative and historical things that awaken memories of a guilt-laden national past ... which the Prime Minister so ardently wishes to abjure'. The weakness of the nation state and its chequered past reinforced each other, especially for those who 'either misread or never read modern history', as what 'objection can there be among rational and progres-sive men and women to the surrender of state power and "the pooling of sovereignty"?'[44]

While New Labour's constitutional reform programme was part

of the 'modernisation' of the British constitution, Shore considered it to be distinct from the European issue. Writing in an article titled 'Traitors to their nation', Shore considered that Blair and Cook 'cannot make the dismantling of the British state and democracy a patriotic activity'.[45] He understood that there were arguments in favour of devolution and the decentralisation of decision-making in the UK, 'but New Labour cannot recognise that the downside is fragmentation and a weakening of the nation as a whole'.[46] Moreover, they would probably lead to a weakening of British democracy, and the devolved assemblies would be targets for the power brokers in the European Commission who foster separatist, regional and ethnic identities within the European nation states.[47] Shore had long considered that the abiding ambition of the European federalists had been the dismantling of the nation states of Europe, resulting in a 'Europe of Regions'.[48] He had written in the 1970s about the dangers of the EEC threatening the integrity of the UK, prophetically warning that the 'troubles of tomorrow' could include the Scottish and Welsh nationalists arguing that if Denmark, Belgium and Luxembourg could be full members, so too could they: 'It is not too much to say that, lacking consent, the price of unwilling union of the UK with the EEC could be the disintegration of the United Kingdom itself.'[49]

He echoed Attlee's belief that patriotism was the 'natural feeling of every Briton', but it now caused unease and was the object of left-wing satire and scorn.

> The problem arises when we have to deal not with racists and xenophobes, but with normal, average citizens: those who simply have a decent affection for their own country, a normally unspoken pride in its history and respect for its institutions: people who entertain no

aggressive, hostile or contemptuous feelings towards the peoples of other states.

What does the intellectual left say to those who evince a feeling of affection towards their country and fellow citizens which is far stronger than the friendly but cooler feelings they have for those outside their political community: a feeling for their country so strong – as we recalled recently on Armistice Day – that people are ready to sacrifice their wealth, even their lives to defend it?[50]

Whereas in the 1930s the attraction of Marxism and the Soviet Union had resulted in 'fellow travelling' with Moscow, according to Shore the intellectual left now engaged in 'Euro travelling' and 'Anglo-scepticism'. 'Among the intelligentsia and the establishment, there has taken place an emotional and intellectual transfer of loyalty from London to Brussels,' he said. The intellectual left had been wrong in the 1930s and they were equally wrong at the start of the twentieth century, Shore argued, asking: 'Where does Europeanism end – and something like treason begin?'[51] Shore amended George Orwell's thoughts on the English intelligentsia: 'In intention, at any rate, the English intelligentsia are Europeanised. They take their cookery from Paris, their holidays in Tuscany and their opinions from Brussels. In the general patriotism of the country, they form a sort of island of dissident thought.'[52]

CONCLUSION

From his defeat in the 1983 Labour leadership contest until his death in 2001, Shore stuck firmly to his principles. He became increasingly disillusioned by the direction of the Labour Party, despite the party coming around to his views on multilateralism. Greater stress was placed on his Euroscepticism, his sense of Britishness and identity and, in part, this was heightened by the Labour Party moving in the other direction. However, Europe brought a looking glass onto Shore's view of the nation state, nationhood, democracy and political economy. Powers were moving upwards to the supranational level and he was concerned with how it operated, how it was controlled and by whom, and whether they were answerable to Parliament. His conclusion that there had been an erosion of national sovereignty that had come at a significant cost to Britain was different to the prevailing view within the Labour Party, which had come to accept supranational institutions and the forces of globalisation.

From the Lords, Shore also wrote *Separate Ways: Britain and Europe*. This account stressed that there was no 'manifest destiny' about 'ever closer union' and, due to Britain's global links, alternative relationships with Europe were readily available. He recommended a two-speed Europe, in which Britain would be in the slow lane, leaving those countries committed to a Federal Europe free to pursue a United States of Europe. Given that it was written at a time when New Labour was considering the merits of the euro currency and there was virtually no possibility of Britain leaving the EU, Shore's two-speed conclusion is understandable. Consequently, rather than viewing the book as Shore watering down his anti-Europeanism, it should be read as a principled but pragmatic piece emphasising that Britain still had the opportunity to pursue a different course compared to its continental allies. In the book, Shore identified seven major findings about Britain's relationship with Europe: the British people do not share their European counterparts' enthusiasm for 'ever closer union'; there is a conspicuous lack of a 'European identity' in Britain; European aspirations do not match British realities and, as such, British politicians fall into doubletalk, dishonesty and self-deception; there is no limit to European encroachment; a new treaty is needed that recognises the UK's separate history and purpose; the nation state and the desire for self-government continue to be a major driving force across the world; and, lastly, only global solutions, not regional, can tackle major issues.[53] In the context of Brexit, these findings remain highly relevant.

Shore's health began to fail after he moved to the Lords, but he never allowed his respiratory and heart conditions to sap his intellectual energy, or to deter him from regular attendance in the Lords and making himself available for conferences, public meetings and broadcasts. Remarkably, in the week that he suffered his first heart attack, he managed to attend a conference in Paris on the Monday, write a speech on the Tuesday and deliver a blistering critique of government economic policy on the Wednesday. Shore collapsed while speaking in the House of Lords and died two months later, on 24 September 2001 at St Thomas's Hospital, of chronic obstructive pulmonary disease and coronary heart disease. He was survived by his wife, two daughters and a son.

Blazoned on Shore's gravestone are the words 'Democrat, Socialist and Champion of British Independence', as, from the first to the last, he stood for the national interest.

CONCLUSION

MAKING AN OVERALL ASSESSMENT of Shore's contribution and legacy is made more complicated by the fact
that he did not write his memoirs and no full-length biography has
been written on him previously. We must therefore turn, in the first
instance, to his obituary writers. Here, opinion is strongly divided.

In terms reminiscent of Michael Foot's ridiculing of David Steel in
his summing up of the 1979 vote of no confidence in which the Liberal
Party sided with the Conservatives, that Steel had passed from 'rising
hope to elder statesman without any intervening period whatsoever',
Edward Pearce wrote that 'Shore's political life involved a long dwin-
dling, without there ever having quite been a solid achievement to
dwindle from'. The obituary went on to state that Shore was a man
of many contradictions who had brought about his own career failures as a politician, and references the pithy phrase of Harold Wilson
(as recorded by Richard Crossman): 'He's no good.' According to
Pearce, Shore lacked charisma, he lacked media presence and he
lacked the cunning that was necessary to make it in frontline politics. He was a rebel with the cloak of a drab ministerialist, but one

without any meaningful ministerial achievement. Over-promoted by his patron, Wilson, he was to enter a long decline, and his lack of support was clearly evidenced by his poor showing in the 1980 leadership contest.[1]

Pearce's judgement is harsh. It was a product of his own mindset; known for his polemical and ruthless journalistic style, Pearce sometimes went too far, not least in his immediate coverage of the Hillsborough disaster in 1989 when he said that Liverpool was 'the world capital of self-pity', and excused the police all blame, apart from perhaps the failure to recognise that 'a good and sufficient minority' of the Liverpool fans 'behave like animals'. His judgement of Shore was also based on his own political approach. A Labour man, Pearce had stood twice to be an MP, though he was never successful. Firmly on the right of the party and a realist in international politics, he wrote a very sympathetic biography of Denis Healey and perhaps adopted a negative attitude towards all those who opposed him, including Shore, who was, for a while, the left's preferred candidate against him. Pearce himself made peculiar career moves, becoming a Thatcherite when his then newspaper editor, Bill Deedes, was a critic, before once again becoming more critical of Thatcher when the editor had changed to the more Thatcherite Max Hastings, leading him to part company with the *Daily Telegraph*.

Some of Pearce's specific assertions are also suspect. For example, blaming the internal opposition to Shore in his constituency party on Asians playing the race card led a group of people closer to Shore, including Gwyneth Dunwoody and David Lipsey, to write that it was in fact the predominantly white, middle-class, left-wing activists who had sought to dislodge him. They wrote that the obituary was 'carping and mean-spirited', while, conversely his 'shining personal integrity' had 'won Peter many admirers, even among those who did not share his views on Europe. So did his personal charm and diffidence, and his resolute refusal to follow transient political fashions.'[2] As an MP he was influenced by the priorities of his working-class constituents in the East End of London and, in turn, he was greatly admired by them, including by the large Bangladeshi community. Tam Dalyell's abiding memory of Shore was witnessing him after a branch meeting having an earnest conversation with a greatly upset elderly Bangladeshi constituent. A large compliment was paid to Peter by one of his constituency party officers, who noted that 'Peter takes Akbar's problem as seriously as he takes the Treaty of Rome'.[3] Indeed, those who worked for Shore spoke of his commitment to local residents – an old-fashioned relationship of an MP and his constituents – in one of the poorest constituencies in the country.[4]

If such a harsh judgement should come from someone with Labour leanings, then the much more sympathetic obituary by veteran Conservative commentator Patrick Cosgrave (who predeceased Shore) is also remarkable. Cosgrave claimed that 'between Harold Wilson and Tony Blair, Peter Shore was the only possible Labour Party leader of whom a Conservative leader had cause to walk in fear. His party, alas for them and for him, never appreciated that fact.' Shore was, according to Cosgrave, so dangerous because he was (like Enoch Powell and Margaret Thatcher, of whom Cosgrave wrote biographies) a patriot. As Cosgrave emphasises – and as he apparently tried to explain to his wife when she asked why Shore was not a Conservative after hearing his nationalism at first hand – there had been a patriotic tradition in the Labour Party which 'had come to be viewed by old and new left alike as unacceptable; and this [had] happened by the middle of the 1980s'. Moreover, he was an intellectual force and a stellar public speaker, as Cosgrave notes: 'Shore was, with Enoch Powell, the most captivating rhetorician of the age.'[5]

Writing ten years later, Neil Clark argued that Shore was by now very much a neglected prophet on both Europe and the economy: 'with the eurozone facing an ever-deepening crisis and the outrageous iniquities of the free-market neoliberal economic system clear for all to see, it's surely time for the democratic socialist policies that he espoused to be put back on the political agenda'.[6] As this biography has shown, Shore warned of the issues with the single currency and the dominance of the German economy within the EU's economic framework. As he feared for the UK, the economies of southern Europe have faced considerable problems with unemployment and industrial competitiveness, in part due to the euro, which has prevented domestic governments from devaluing their currency. Shore thought that the diverse economies that make up the Eurozone require different economic policies and, while the ECB may set interest rates that favour German manufacturing, this may not be in the best interests of other economies. As for the response of the British Labour movement, the imposition of austerity on Greece and the introduction of technocratic governments in some southern European states prompted little criticism. As Shore understood, they either underestimated the impact of the EU's policies, misunderstood what was at stake, or remained silent for fear, no doubt, of being seen as anti-European. It is very much in this spirit that the authors of this biography began their endeavour. Indeed, it is notable that Clark was writing this in 2011; the failure of politicians to grasp this essential message in the meantime makes it still relevant almost ten years later.

In our view Shore had numerous achievements. His politics was shaped at an early age by the profound effect of the financial crisis that his family experienced, and his move from Norfolk to Liverpool which this brought about. Shore had experienced poverty both at first hand and in his local community, seeing children his own age having to walk to school without shoes. It was something that would remain with him even after his academic successes, becoming a scholarship student at Cambridge and a member of the elitist and secretive Apostles; compared to many around him at this time he came from lower down the social order. He was also imbued with an innate sense of Englishness (or Britishness, as these things were synonymous at that time), not least through seeing active military service in the RAF between 1943 and 1946. He distinguished himself in the Labour Party Research Department and in writing the manifestos for 1964, 1966 and 1970. His ministerial achievements may have been slight in those governments, but it is possible that this had more to do with the positions he was given, notably in the Department of Economic Affairs when it was being wound down. Whether he was right to have come out in Cabinet against the 'In Place of Strife' proposals in 1969 is still open to debate. Economically, there was little justification for the proposals. By this time politicians were increasingly concerned with 'relative economic decline', and there was much searching to find the cause, as there was little evidence to say that the trade unions were the source of the phenomenon. However, politically, Wilson and Barbara Castle were on firmer ground. The trade unions were becoming more unpopular and Labour's alliance with them was a potential cause of electoral unpopularity, with Edward Heath's Conservatives pledging to restrict their powers. Moreover, reform at this stage would have been in the long-term interests of the trade unions themselves, as it may well have avoided the much more draconian attacks on the 'enemy within' by Margaret Thatcher later on.

During the troubled Labour governments of 1974–79, Shore was arguably on the right side of the debate against Healey in the 1976 IMF Crisis. The cuts demanded by the IMF in return for financial support were, in economic terms, unnecessary, as the measures already taken by the government had started to work. The figures that showed a larger public sector borrowing requirement were false, as the Treasury later admitted, and in his memoirs Healey accepts that the numbers were wrong. Shore's proposals for limited import restraint, together with fiscal stimulation along Keynesian lines, were valid. Unfortunately, he was unable to form an alliance with Tony Crosland, who also opposed cuts but was slow to accept protection, and the initial weight of Cabinet opinion shifted in Healey's favour. The short-term effects of the IMF Crisis may have been limited as the economy quickly recovered, but in the longer term this was to add to that body of opinion – strong by the 1990s – that the ability of the nation state to determine its own economic policy relatively unimpeded by outside forces had significantly and irreversibly declined. The more immediate consequence was that the cause of protectionism was taken over by the radical left in the form of the Alternative Economic Strategy (AES), under which what could have been sensible and selective measures became an article of faith every bit as dogmatic as adherents to free trade. This also made the case for sensible protectionism all the harder to make, as it would henceforth be labelled as wishing to return to 1983.

Another Shore achievement at this time ought to have been his proposals for inner-city regeneration. Recognising that there was an urban problem and seeking to use the state to remedy it would most probably have avoided the inner-city riots of the early 1980s. But after 1979 the regeneration project was consigned to a corporatist past, which was to be overthrown in favour of economic liberalism. Shore also sought to develop ways in which home ownership could be extended, including through the sale of council houses. After the 1979 general election defeat the Labour left opposed such measures and they became, by default, an initial flagship policy of Thatcherism, allowing the Conservatives to gain a new electoral base among the working class.

Shore was always fascinated by the leadership of the Labour Party, on which he was later to write *Leading the Left*. However, when his turn at leadership came he fared badly, later confiding in his diary, 'I could not, on major issues, say what I do not believe in', and he could not understand those who put promotion before principle.[7] Such intellectual honesty, alongside his more reserved character and dislike of political manoeuvring, hampered his leadership ambitions. Had he been prepared to compromise and do the necessary conspiring, he may well have fared better. As it was, however, in the 1980 leadership contest he obtained the support of just thirty-two MPs and was eliminated in the first ballot. He had been tipped to be the successor to James Callaghan and had, it would seem, won the support of Michael Foot, standard-bearer for the Tribunite (at this stage soft) left. He may then have gone on to defeat the right-wing candidate Healey and, had he stood, the radical left challenger Tony Benn, given the balance of opinion in the Parliamentary Labour Party (this was to be the last election fought under the old rules where only the PLP voted). However, none of this would come to pass. Foot was persuaded, not least by his wife, to stand, and went on to win. Whatever Foot's other qualities, he was ill-equipped to be leader, and the party continued to shift radically leftwards, while some of the right-wing MPs broke away to form the Social Democratic Party. The Labour Party struggled to mount an effective opposition to Thatcher's Conservatives and one of the saving graces at this time was Labour's decision to support the Falklands War, for which Shore takes a good deal of credit. Had the party followed the decision of those on its hard left to oppose the war, it could well have gone down to even greater defeat in 1983.

At this time, Shore served as shadow Chancellor, and Labour's economic policies became more radical. However, this did not save him from attempted deselection in the run-up to the 1983 general election, due to his association with the right. He served as joint chair of Labour Solidarity with Roy Hattersley in an effort to see off the challenge of the Militant Tendency, as he recognised the dangers of this far-left entryist organisation seeking to take over the party. However, his stances on the Falklands War and Militant were in stark contrast to those on the New Left of the Labour Party.

Shore stood again in 1983, with Dunwoody as his running mate for deputy. They occupied a distinctive position, being firmly Eurosceptic but also distancing themselves starkly from the hard left of the party. However, this position was squeezed, with Shore and Dunwoody coming last in the race. Shore was not personally close to the new leader, and when the party became more pro-European from the late 1980s he became even more marginalised. He also found himself in opposition to the Policy Review findings. The review had been established by Kinnock after the 1987 general election defeat. Shore's viewpoint was similar to that of Bryan Gould, who wanted a more overtly Keynesian approach to economic policy to be maintained instead of the 'supply-side' ideas then being promoted by

John Smith and Gordon Brown. If the party was still committed to redistribution and elements of economic interventionism in the 1992 general election, this was to have all but disappeared by 1997 under Brown and Tony Blair, as the party became strongly pro-European and much more comfortable with the free-market reforms of the preceding eighteen-year Conservative administration. Shore was to see out the final years of his life from the House of Lords, as someone who had little in common with the government he had long campaigned for.

Two further achievements deserve credit. Firstly, Shore, having served on the Indian sub-continent, retained an interest in that part of the world, particularly the state and affairs of Bangladesh. Throughout his parliamentary career he was attentive to the political and economic developments in Bangladesh, flying with the Bishop of Stepney to Bengal in August 1971 to call for Bangladeshi independence, and he later chaired the all-party parliamentary group on Bangladesh. He warned against dealing with the repressive and undemocratic President Ershad in 1989, as he wished to see a flourishing and democratic state emerge.

Secondly, from a very early stage Shore was a supporter of the Solidaność (Solidarity), the Polish trade union established in 1980 by Lech Wałęsa, which was at that time the only trade union not under Soviet control. Indeed, he was 'the most senior Labour politician to publicly and consistently support the Solidarity Movement in Poland'.[8] On 13 December 1981 the union was outlawed when martial law was imposed, and three days later Shore made his first speech in support of the organisation. In 1983, he criticised Arthur Scargill for supporting the Communist government of Poland, stating that he did not speak on behalf of the Labour Party. Shore remained a supporter of it until the end of his life, and a year before his death he spoke at a twentieth anniversary celebration of the formation of Solidaność. Blick recalls: 'Though frail, Shore addressed a packed audience with passion and conviction, giving a broad account of Solidaność's role in the world's progress to a more free and just society, and his pride in taking some part in that journey.'[9] Underpinning his commitment to both Bangladesh and Solidaność was the belief that 'the principal driving and liberating force in the world today is precisely the demand of peoples for self-government, for freedom and for democracy'.[10]

History doesn't ever quite repeat itself, as the circumstances and certainly the individuals are different at any given moment. However, we can say that it would have been extremely likely that Shore would have been a supporter of the Leave campaign in the 2016 referendum on continued membership of the European Union. Shortly before his death, Shore wrote that 'by process of deception and stealth, much of the birthright of the British people has been surrendered and what is still left is dangerously at risk'. Moreover, 'the fact is that our Constitution, our democracy, our independence and our rights as British citizens and electors have been violated and diminished in a truly disgraceful way'.[11]

Indeed, had he been alive in 2016, it is likely that he would have argued that events had proved him right. The charge that those campaigning for renegotiation and withdrawal have made is that, over time, membership has resulted in much greater and tighter control by the EU. The direction of travel within the EU would eventually lead to a federal Europe, and consequently Britain would be no more than a mere province in northern Europe. While the 'In' side would deny and dismiss the encroachment of the EU as a form of insular paranoia, Shore would have argued that the level of control exercised by the EU was much greater – a European parliament, laws passed by that parliament binding on our own, a European civil service, head of state, central bank, and single currency – and that this was acting against the domestic and international interests of Britain, the British working class and the implementation of a democratic socialist policy agenda.

Shore had been a lifelong opponent of the European project, seeing it from the outset as federalist in nature. However, he would refer to himself as a Euro-realist rather than a Eurosceptic. His opposition was not to 'Europe' or 'European culture' but to the political, constitutional and economic aspects of membership. It was easier for the continental Europeans to pursue 'ever closer union', he thought; after all, they shared the same land mass, the history of Charlemagne, the Holy Roman Empire, the trauma of defeat and occupation by fascism followed by liberation by the Allies, and the Treaty of Rome was a continuation of that history. The Franco-German political core was based on the determination of France never to face again the prospect of attack by a more powerful and aggressive Germany as it had experienced in 1870, 1914 and 1939. For Shore, it was antithetical to British history. The UK had not been defeated and occupied, 'even if, at times, some of our more demented Europhiles seem almost to regret it', and therefore, with its distinctive and happier history, a different assessment of Britain's domestic and world role is readily available.[12]

Indeed, Shore was perhaps one of the few in politics to have read in detail the Treaty of Rome, apparently reading it in bed from cover to cover. He told his son that he considered himself 'a secular protestant', not belonging to the Church of England or the Protestant faith, but culturally he had been brought up in the Protestant ways of seeing – anti-authority, with the tradition of dissent as free-born Englishmen who are not beholden to a priest or an intermediary.[13] As such, he was not prepared to submit himself or his country to an external authority. He had been a seminal influence on Hugh Gaitskell's 1962 party conference speech, in which he memorably stated that entering the EEC would be the 'end of a thousand years of [British] history'. Shore went on to oppose membership, in 1967 under Wilson and again in the early 1970s under Heath. Having voted for a referendum on continued membership, he became one of the leading 'No' campaigners, and his speech at the Oxford Union just before the vote remains, according to several people interviewed in the course of writing this book, the greatest speech of its kind. He began by debunking the idea that membership was necessary and that it had brought economic benefits, before going on to state:

> ... Now what do they say? What is the message that comes now? No longer to tell the British people about the goodies that lie there. No longer that. That won't wash, will it? Because the evidence will no longer support it. So the message, the message that comes out is fear, fear, fear. Fear because you won't have any food. Fear of unemployment. Fear that we have somehow been so reduced as a country that we can no longer, as it were, totter about in the world independent as a nation. And a constant attrition of our morale. A constant attempt to tell us that what we have – and what we had is not only our own achievements but what generations of Englishmen have helped us to achieve – is not worth a damn.[14]

Moreover, although the referendum result was an emphatic 'Yes' in 1975, Shore continued to oppose further integration. He believed, firmly, that the project had always been federalist in nature but that there had been a persistent attempt by those in favour of such a project, realising its unpopularity, to disguise it as something else.

I am quite prepared to debate the merits, or lack of them, of European federation. There is not necessarily a dishonourable case for those who advocate it, arising to a great extent out of the history of which we are all familiar, just as our different view arises from our own history. But what is intolerable is that we should be lied to. It is not deception, and it is not self-deception. It is lying! The sooner we face this, and expose those who treat us in this disgraceful way, the better.

Our reason for quoting Shore at length here is that his words are strikingly relevant to the 2016 referendum and the debate that has flowed from it in the run-up to leaving the EU. Few, and certainly no senior politician on the Remain side of the referendum, argued for federalism, presumably because they either failed to recognise the ultimate destination the founding fathers of European integration wished to reach, or because they did understand this but realised its unpopularity. Instead, it has been argued that they rested on an essentially negative case, designed to frighten people into voting to remain in the EU. For Leavers, if Shore had stated in 1975 how so few benefits had arisen from membership by that stage, how much truer after forty years. Leavers would argue that, in a sustained attempt at attrition, this fear-mongering has remained a consistent feature for pro-EU politicians and commentators in the UK since the referendum result.

Shore's legacy is wider still. In policy terms it would be foolish to point to specific and detailed measures designed in the 1960s and 1970s and say they are still relevant today. Instead, we must draw on the distinction between means and ends made by revisionists such as Gaitskell and Crosland, and also in more recent times by New Labour. If the means relate to policies, the ends relate to the underlying values, and it is at the level of values that we can perhaps identify Shore's relevance to contemporary politics, especially the politics of the left.

Labour has long struggled with the concept of the nation state. For many postwar politicians this was not so, as many had seen active military service in the Second World War and were proud patriots. This was true of those who were on the left, centre or right of the party, as seen in the debate over atomic weapons in the 1950s, with the leading left figure Bevan eventually endorsing the multilateralist policy of Gaitskell on the basis that you cannot send a future Foreign Secretary 'naked into the conference chamber'. It was Old Labour's faith in the nation state to which Cosgrave referred in his obituary of Shore and on which other independent-minded rightists have commented favourably.

The postwar politicians also recognised the importance of the state in managing the economy and providing welfare, confident in its belief in the beneficial role of the state as an agent of social and economic progress. The post-1945 reforms included a significant extension of the powers of the state in terms of economic management and as a provider of welfare. The intellectual inspiration for this settlement – Beveridge and Keynes – were liberals, not socialists, and politicians from all three parties came to accept this framework. Shore, influenced by the postwar generation of thinkers and Labour politicians, understood the domestic and international importance of the nation state; as far as he was concerned, the world was made up of nation states and the nation is the level at which you can construct a coherent sense of a political community. Moreover, through a parliamentary majority at Westminster you could get your hands on the levers of power, utilising the state to effectively counter the tendency of capitalism towards greater inequality in the interests of the whole nation.

However, the left subsequently developed a more hostile attitude towards the nation. It believed that patriotism was an enemy of class solidarity and that the UK had done more harm than good, especially in terms of the Empire. Although the Labour Party moved a long way in opposition before it was to return to power in 1997, it remained dismissive of almost any espousal of patriotism. In its place both the left and the right of the party adopted forms of cosmopolitanism in place of patriotism. The metropolitan liberal 'citizen of the world' position became increasingly pervasive and, at its core, it was replete with apology for British history and an overwhelming sense of guilt. In contrast, Shore had a strong sense of national history. Britain's past was far from perfect, but there were also good things and in aggregate this past is what made Britain. To Shore, Britain had 'within living memory, and again and again in its history, successfully withstood some all-conquering European tyranny'.[15] Shore understood that British history stretched back thousands of years, good, bad or indifferent in a reality rather than an artificial narrative designed to serve a contemporary progressive cause. During the 1980 Labour leadership contest, Shore fleshed out his patriotism and the importance of English history:

I think Britain is a very special and unique country. Democracy means something here, far more than current cynicism would have us believe. It means the rectification of grievance, that *habeas corpus* works, that we don't live in fear of anyone. It's the relaxation that comes to a country which has known 800 years of total independence; not a conquering step has been heard anywhere in this country.

I think we are a remarkable country and people, and ... our institutions should [not] be over-ridden and tampered with by those who subscribe to a written constitution that we had no part in writing... So [is] the awfulness of those British in the past twenty-five years who have come to the conclusion that nothing they inherited is worth a damn. That, too, fills me with anger. It really does, and if that's patriotism, I plead guilty.[16]

Shore concluded by echoing John of Gaunt, from Shakespeare's *Richard II*: "'England hath made a shameful conquest of itself'" – that's it. That's what we've done.'[17] His knowledge and love of English history offers a stark contrast to the self-styled progressives, for whom Europe offers a more enlightened alternative to the backward ways of Englishness. Patricia Hewitt rejected Shore's Euroscepticism, horrified by what she perceived as the 'chauvinism, protectionism and sheer little Englandism of it all'.[18] While the national identities of Wales, Scotland and Irish nationalists could be tolerated, if not celebrated because they were often defined in terms of throwing off their subjection by the English, the left considered that England was conservative, prejudiced and inward-looking. Accordingly, the constitutional reform agenda and social liberalism of New Labour was an attempt to 'modernise' what they perceived as the 'small-c conservatism' of Britain in favour of a more sophisticated 'Europeanism'.

Internationally in the postwar era, despite the world dividing between the USA and the USSR, there remained a confidence in the British state that it still had a world role to play through institutions such as the Commonwealth. Shore adhered to this view, believing passionately in what Britain could do, not just for itself but for its friends and allies across the world. While the vision of Britain bestriding the world stage became increasingly unfashionable among 'progressive' opinion as an overinflated and romantic vision of Britain, Shore remained steadfast in his pride in what Britain had done, what Britain could do, and what Britain was doing in the Commonwealth and in other international institutions. For Shore, you could be both a nationalist and internationalist, and he passionately lived his life expressing that truth. His concern was that a 'totally paralysed, lacking in self-confidence, self-flagellating Britain would be no use to anyone'.[19]

However, by the time Labour returned to power in 1997 after its long period of opposition, it had greatly lost confidence in the capacity of the state to deliver social and economic gains. Instead, it sought to redistribute by stealth, believing it was inherently unpopular and grafting it on top of an essentially free-market economic model. According to Vernon Bogdanor, the reason it was so committed to constitutional reform by the time of its return to power in 1997 was that it had lost faith in social and economic reform.[20] Shore would adopt a similar criticism, deeming that New Labour's adoption of supply-side economics, the pro-Europeanism of the leadership, the far-reaching constitutional reform and the courting of the Liberal Democrats were all part of the 'project' with which he had little in common.

The banking crisis and subsequent recession exposed the limits of this model, and although Blairites continued to advocate it, it appeared increasingly irrelevant to contemporary conditions that were much changed since the mid-1990s, when it was created. The principal intellectual response within the party was Blue Labour. Although much stronger on the nation than the party had been for many years, it accused New Labour of being too statist, when in fact the opposite was true. Labour had emerged from a tradition of trade unionism that was decentralist, according to its chief exponent Maurice Glasman.[21] Over the course of the twentieth century the party had become statist, but such statism had undermined its old voluntarist tradition. The high watermark of the Labour movement had not therefore been the creation of the National Health Service, but rather the 1889 London dock workers' strike, which was a clear example of local, bottom-up social organisation. While recognising the importance of localised collective action, such an argument fails to take account of the fact that only the central state can deliver certain social goods and services, such as the NHS, to all, and only the central state can regulate national economic activity.

The 2015 general election defeat provided new impetus for change. The leadership of Ed Miliband had often appeared tentative in challenging the government's austerity agenda and many of Labour's own activists had grown frustrated with this, seeing it as 'austerity lite'. In this context they supported the leadership candidate least associated with the preceding years of government and opposition, and most likely to move the party in a more radical direction. Jeremy Corbyn had no such reservations about the power of the state to do good. Since then, the Labour Party's policy agenda has become more overtly statist. However, Corbyn is profoundly uncomfortable with patriotism. He sees the world divided between oppressors and oppressed, with Britain being guilty of oppression either in its past colonialism or its present association with Israel and America.

The contemporary Labour Party has much to learn from Shore and the wider tradition of Euroscepticism on the left/centre left, though the Parliamentary Labour Party was, and still is, strongly Remain. Seemingly against his instincts, Jeremy Corbyn was pressured into backing a second referendum and this became Labour's manifesto commitment in the December 2019 general election. Consequently, Labour lost a swathe of seats in Leave-voting areas, experiencing its worst defeat since 1935. Pro-Remain MPs feature prominently among the leadership contenders to replace Corbyn. Indeed, if anything, the comments made by Labour MPs during the passing of the withdrawal legislation in January 2020 show that the Remain position is now even stronger within the parliamentary party, with only one Leaver remaining in the leadership race. But in order to win back at least some of the lost seats next time, Labour must rediscover its Eurosceptic tradition, and unearthing the arguments of Peter Shore is an essential part of that task.

ACKNOWLEDGEMENTS

T HIS BOOK STEMS FROM our involvement in the Labour
Leave campaign in 2016 and our observation of the ensuing,
and, at the time of writing, still unfinished, debate over what form the
UK's relationship with the EU should take. In studying the historical
evolution of Britain's relationship with Europe, one figure stood out.
However, the absence of a political biography of Peter Shore was a
clear omission within the literature: hence the rationale for this book.

The authors would like to thank all those who assisted in the
production of the book. Special thanks must go to Bryan Gould
for writing the foreword and to those who kindly endorsed the
biography. We would also like to thank those who gave their time
to be interviewed and/or responded in writing to our numerous
requests. We would also like to thank the archivists responsible for
the collected papers we consulted, especially at the LSE, where the
Shore papers are housed. The Shore family also cooperated with our
requests while allowing us complete autonomy over what we wrote.

We would like to thank our publisher, Biteback, and especially
our commissioning editor Olivia Beattie and her assistant editor

Lucy Stewardson, for their faith in this project despite numerous delays in the writing of the book.

Above all we would like to thank our families for their love, encouragement and patience while we pursued what no doubt to any dispassionate observer would seem our idiosyncratic interests in the minutiae of contemporary British political history.

Kevin Hickson, Jasper Miles and Harry Taylor
Wistaston, Ealing and Shrewsbury
January 2020

BIBLIOGRAPHY

A. INTERVIEWS

Peter Shore	London	30 January 2001
Liz Shore	Cornwall	15 December 2016
Cris Shore	London	18 January 2017
Lord Kinnock	London	4 September 2018
John Mills	London	5 September 2018
Christine Sibley	London	30 September 2018
Lord Owen	London	2 October 2018
John Biggs	London	2 October 2018
David Cowling	London	2 October 2018
Lord Rodgers	London	3 October 2018
Lord Clinton-Davis	London	3 October 2018
Derek Gadd	London	4 October 2018
Stephen Pollard	London	16 October 2018
Lord Lipsey	London	16 October 2018
Dame Margaret Beckett MP	London	17 October 2018
Lord Morris	London	17 October 2018
Eric Deakins	London	23 October 2018
Nick Butler	London	20 November 2018

Sylvia Padwick	London	10 December 2018
John Spellar MP	West Bromwich	3 January 2019

B. ARCHIVES

Peter Shore papers, London School of Economics

The National Archives, Kew

Tower Hamlets Labour Party papers, Tower Hamlets Local History
  Library and Archives

C. WORKS BY PETER SHORE

'Britons deceived: We can vote out Tony Blair when we get fed up with
  him but not the president of the European Bank', *The Guardian*,
  6 January 1999

'Capitalism and Equality: Ends and Means', *New Statesman and
  Nation*, 1 October 1955

'Capitalism and Equality: The Real Case for Public Ownership',
  New Statesman and Nation, 8 October 1955

'Dream Ticket', *London Review of Books*, vol. 5, no. 18 (1983)

'Europe's shadow over Blackpool', *The Times*, 2 October 1972

'European Union Takeover of UK' in K. Sutherland (ed.), *The Rape
  of the Constitution?* (Thorverton: Imprint Academic, 2000)

'Foreword' in Gould, B., Mills, J. and Stewart, S., *Monetarism or
  Prosperity* (London: Macmillan, 1981)

'Hands up if you voted for Europe', *The Ecologist*, vol. 31 (2001)

'Ignore the scare stories: it's time to get out', *The Times*, 4 January 1983

'In the Room at the Top' in N. MacKenzie (ed.), *Conviction* (London: MacGibbon & Kee, 1958)

'Into the French Trap', *New Statesman*, 11 June 1971

'Justifiable optimism in Bangladesh', *The Times*, 10 February 1973

'Labour as a Human Factor', *The Twentieth Century*, vol. 163 (1958)

'Labour, Europe and the World', *The Round Table*, vol. 63 (1973)

'Never underestimate New Labour's determination to take us into the euro', *The Times*, 16 November 2000

'Stand up for the nation state', *Fabian Review*, 16 November 1993

'The Brussels Treaty Sell-Out', *New Statesman*, 11 February 1972

'The Case Against', *New Statesman*, 15 January 1971

'The deadly gap left by Labour', *Tribune*, 8 July 1994

'The Labour Party and the European Question', *The European Journal*, vol. 4 (1997)

'The Principles of State Intervention, A Socialist View', *Public Law* (autumn 1957)

'Traitors to their nation', *The Guardian*, 28 November 2000

'Whatever happened to the opposition?', *London Evening Standard*, 27 August 1992

'Who are you kidding, Mr Blair?', *The Times*, 8 March 1999

'Why as a democrat I had to vote against my own party', *Independent on Sunday*, 22 November 1998

'Why Blair must oppose the euro', *Sunday Times*, 27 December 1998

Entitled to Know (London: MacGibbon & Kee, 1966)

Europe: The Way Back (London: Fabian Society, 1973)

(with Hattersley, Roy, Heffer, Eric and Kinnock, Neil), *Labour's Choices* (London: Fabian Society, 1983)

Leading the Left (London: Weidenfeld & Nicolson, 1993)

Separate Ways: The Heart of Europe (London: Duckworth, 2000)

The Real Nature of Conservatism (London: Labour Party, 1952)

D. BIOGRAPHIES, MEMOIRS AND DIARIES

Baston, L., 'Roy Hattersley' in K. Jefferys, *Labour Forces: From Ernest Bevin to Gordon Brown* (London: I. B. Tauris, 2002)

Benn, T., *Years of Hope: Diaries, Papers and Letters, 1940–62* (London: Arrow, 1995)

— —, *Out of the Wilderness: Dairies, 1963–67* (London: Arrow, 1988)

— —, *Office Without Power: Dairies, 1968–72* (London: Arrow, 1989)

— —, *Against the Tide: Diaries, 1973–76* (London: Arrow, 1990)

— —, *Conflicts of Interest: Diaries, 1977–80* (London: Arrow, 1991)

— —, *The End of an Era: Diaries, 1980–90* (London: Arrow, 1994)

Brivati, B., *Hugh Gaitskell: A Biography* (London: Richard Cohen, 1997)

Callaghan, J., *Time and Chance* (London: Collins, 1987)

Campbell, J., *Roy Jenkins: A Well-Rounded Life* (London: Vintage, 2015)

Castle, B., *Fighting All the Way* (London: Macmillan, 1993)

Crick, M., 'Peter Shore, 1924–2001', *Dictionary of National Biography* (Oxford: Oxford University Press, 2004)

Crosland, S., *Tony Crosland* (London: Coronet, 1983)

Crossman, R., *The Diaries of a Cabinet Minister, Volume One: Minister of Housing, 1964–66* (London: Book Club Associates, 1976)

— —, *The Diaries of a Cabinet Minister, Volume Two: Lord President of the Council and Leader of the House of Commons, 1966–68* (London: Hamish Hamilton/Jonathan Cape, 1977)

— —, *The Diaries of a Cabinet Minister, Volume Three: Secretary of State for Social Services, 1968–1970* (London: Book Club Associates, 1978)

Donoughue, B., *Prime Minister: The Conduct of Policy under Harold Wilson and James Callaghan* (London: Cape, 1987)

— —, *The Heat of the Kitchen: An Autobiography* (London: Politicos, 2003)

— —, *Downing Street Diary: With Harold Wilson in No. 10* (London: Jonathan Cape, 2005)

— —, *Downing Street Diary: With James Callaghan in No. 10* (London: Jonathan Cape, 2008)

Driberg, T., *Guy Burgess: A Portrait with Background* (London: Weidenfeld & Nicolson, 1956)

Foot, M., *Another Heart and Other Pulses* (London: Collins, 1984)

Golding, J., *Hammer of the Left* (London: Biteback, 2016)

Gould, B., *Goodbye to All That* (London: Macmillan, 1995)

Harris, R., *The Making of Neil Kinnock* (London: Faber & Faber, 1984)

Healey, D., *The Time of My Life* (London: Penguin, 1990)

Howard, A. (ed.), *The Crossman Diaries, 1964–70* (London: Book Club Associates, 1979)

Jay, D., *Change and Fortune: A Political Record* (London: Hutchinson, 1980)

Jenkins, R., *A Life at the Centre* (London: Macmillan, 1991)

Jones, M., *Michael Foot* (London: Victor Gollancz, 1994)

Kilroy-Silk, R., *Hard Labour: Political Diary of Robert Kilroy-Silk* (London: Chatto & Windus, 1986)

Lipsey, D., *In the Corridors of Power: An Autobiography* (London: Biteback, 2012)

McSmith, A., *John Smith: A Life, 1938–1994* (London: Verso, 1993)

Mikardo, I., *Back-bencher* (London: Weidenfeld & Nicolson, 1988)

Mitchell, A., *Confessions of a Political Maverick* (London: Biteback, 2018)

Moore, C., *Margaret Thatcher: The Authorised Biography, Volume One: Not For Turning* (London: Allen Lane, 2013)

Morgan, J. (ed.), *Backbench Diaries of Richard Crossman* (London: Hamish Hamilton and Jonathan Cape, 1981)

Morgan, K. O., *Callaghan: A Life* (Oxford: Oxford University Press, 1997)

— —, *Michael Foot: A Life* (London: HarperCollins, 2007)

Mullin, C., *A Walk-On Part* (London: Profile Books, 2012)

Owen, D., *Time to Declare* (London: Michael Joseph, 1991)

Pearce, E., 'Denis Healey' in K. Jefferys, *Labour Forces: From Ernest Bevin to Gordon Brown* (London: I. B. Tauris, 2002)

— —, *Denis Healey* (London: Little, Brown, 2002)

Pimlott, B., *Harold Wilson* (London: HarperCollins, 1992)

Rentoul, J., *Tony Blair: Prime Minister* (London: Faber & Faber, 2013)

Rodgers, B., *Fourth Among Equals: The Autobiography of Bill Rodgers* (London: Politicos, 2000)

Seldon, A., 'In Conversation with Peter Shore', *Contemporary Record*, vol. 1, no. 2 (1987), pp. 38–42

Sheard, S., *The Passionate Economist: How Brian Abel-Smith Shaped Global Health and Social Welfare* (Bristol: Policy Press, 2014)

Straw, J., *Last Man Standing* (London: Pan Books, 2013)

Stuart, M., *John Smith: A Life* (London: Politico's, 2005)

Tebbit, N., *Upwardly Mobile* (London: Weidenfeld & Nicolson, 1988)

Westlake, M., *Kinnock: The Biography* (London: Little, Brown, 2001)

Williams, P., *Hugh Gaitskell: A Political Biography* (London: Jonathan Cape, 1979)

Wilson, H., *The Labour Government, 1964–70: A Personal Record* (London: Weidenfeld & Nicolson and Michael Joseph, 1971)

Ziegler, P., *Wilson* (London: Weidenfeld & Nicolson, 1993)

E. OTHER PUBLICATIONS

Aitken, I., 'The incredible journey', *New Statesman & Society*, 1 October 1993

Annan, N., *Our Age: Portrait of a Generation* (London: Weidenfeld & Nicolson, 1990)

Bacon, R. and Eltis, W., *Britain's Economic Problem: Too Few Producers* (London: Macmillan, 1978)

Beck, P. J., 'The Future of the Falkland Islands: A Solution Made in Hong Kong?', *International Affairs*, vol. 61, no. 4 (1985)

Beech, M., Hickson, K. and Plant, R. (eds.), *The Struggle for Labour's Soul: Understanding Labour's Political Thought Since 1945*, 2nd edn (London: Routledge, 2018)

Benn, T., *Arguments for Socialism* (London: Penguin, 1980)

Bogdanor, V., *Politics and the Constitution: Essays on British Government* (Aldershot: Dartmouth, 1996)

— —, 'Constitutional Reform' in A. Seldon (ed.), *The Blair Effect* (London: Little, Brown, 2001)

Bruni, D. M., *The British Political Parties and the Falklands War* (London: Palgrave Macmillan, 2018)

Butler, D. and Kitzinger, U., *The 1975 Referendum* (London: The Macmillan Press Ltd, 1976)

Crick, M., *Militant* (London: Biteback, 2016)

Crines, A. and Hickson, K. (eds), *Harold Wilson: The Unprincipled Prime Minister?: Reappraising Harold Wilson* (London: Biteback, 2016)

Crosland, C. A. R., *The Future of Socialism* (London: Jonathan Cape, 1956)

— —, 'Socialism Now' in D. Leonard (ed.), *Socialism Now and Other Essays* (London: Jonathan Cape, 1974)

Davies, A. J., *To Build a New Jerusalem: The Labour Movement from the 1880s to the 1990s* (London: Michael Joseph, 1992)

Eglin, R. and Ritchie, B., *Fly Me I'm Freddie* (London: Weidenfeld & Nicolson, 1980)

Gaffney, J., *Leadership and the Labour Party: Narrative and Performance* (Basingstoke: Palgrave, 2017)

Galbraith, J. K., *The Affluent Society* (Boston, Mass.: Harcourt, 1958)

Glasman, M., Rutherford, J., Stears, M. and White, S. (eds), *The Labour Tradition and the Politics of Paradox* (London: Soundings, 2011)

Godley, W. and Cripps, F., *Macroeconomics* (London: Fontana, 1983)

Goodhart, D., *The Road to Somewhere: The New Tribes Shaping British Politics* (London: Penguin, 2017)

Hatfield, M., *The House the Left Built: Inside Labour Policy Making, 1970–75* (London: Gollancz, 1978)

Hayter, D., *Fightback!: Labour's Traditional Right in the 1970s and 1980s* (Manchester: Manchester University Press, 2005)

Hennessy, P., *Cabinet* (Oxford: Basil Blackwell, 1986)

— —, *Muddling Through* (London: Victor Gollancz, 1996)

— —, *The Prime Minister: The Office and Its Holders Since 1945* (London: Allen Lane, 2000)

Hickson, K., *The IMF Crisis of 1976 and British Politics* (London: I. B. Tauris, 2005)

Hill, R., *The Labour Party's Economic Strategy, 1979–1997: The Long Road Back* (Hampshire: Palgrave, 2001)

Holland, S., *The Socialist Challenge* (London: Quartet, 1976)

Holmes, M., *The Labour Government, 1974–79: Political Aims and Economic Reality* (Basingstoke: Macmillan, 1985)

Jay, D., *The Socialist Case* (London: Faber & Faber, 1937)

Jefferys, K. (ed.), *Labour Forces: From Ernest Bevin to Gordon Brown* (London: I. B. Tauris, 2002)

Kaufman, G., *Renewal: Labour's Britain in the 1980s* (Harmondsworth: Penguin Books, 1983)

King, A., *Britain Says Yes: The 1975 Referendum on the Common Market* (Washington: American Enterprise Institute for Public Policy Research, 1977)

Labour Party, *Looking to the Future* (London: Labour Party, 1990)

Michie, A. and Hoggart, S., *The Pact: The Inside Story of the Lib–Lab Government, 1977–78* (London: Quartet, 1978)

Mills, J., *Why is the UK Economy Growing at Less Than Half the World Average Rate?* (London: John Mills, 2018)

Minkin, L., *The Contentious Alliance: Trade Unions and the Labour Party* (Edinburgh: Edinburgh University Press, 1991)

Mitchell, A., *Four Years in the Death of the Labour Party* (Methuen, London, 1983)

— — and Wienir, D. (eds), *Last Time: Labour's Lessons from the Sixties* (London: Bellew, 1997)

Plant, R., Beech, M. and Hickson, K. (eds), *The Struggle for Labour's Soul: Understanding Labour's Political Thought Since 1945* (London: Routledge, 2004)

Pearce, E., *Hummingbirds and Hyenas* (London: Faber & Faber, 1985)

Pliatzky, L., *Getting and Spending* (Oxford: Blackwell, 1982)

Pugh, M., 'Long March', *London Review of Books*, vol. 5, no. 10 (1983)

Pugh, M., *Speak for Britain!: A New History of the Labour Party* (London: Vintage, 2011)

Rosen, G., *Old Labour to New: The Dreams That Inspired, the Battles That Divided* (London: Politico's, 2005)

Saunders, R., *Yes to Europe!: The 1975 Referendum and Seventies Britain* (Cambridge: Cambridge University Press, 2018)

Schumpeter, J., *Capitalism, Socialism and Democracy* (London: Harper, 1942)

Seale, P., *Philby: The Long Road to Moscow* (London: Hamish Hamilton, 1973)

Seldon, A. and Hickson, K. (eds), *New Labour, Old Labour: The Wilson and Callaghan Governments, 1974–79* (London: Routledge, 2004)

Shipley, P., *Militant Tendency: Trotskyism in the Labour Party* (London: Foreign Affairs Publishing Company Ltd, 1983)

Sofer, A., 'Diary', *London Review of Books*, vol. 5, no. 16 (1983)

Taaffe, P., *Rise of Militant: Thirty Years of Militant* (London: Militant Publications, 1995)

Thorpe, A., *A History of the British Labour Party* (Basingstoke: Palgrave, 2008)

Turner, A. W., *A Classless Society: Britain in the 1990s* (London: Aurum Press, 2013)

Wainwright, H., *Labour: A Tale of Two Parties* (London: Hogarth Press, 1987)

Wall, S., *The Official History of Britain and the European Community, Volume II: From Rejection to Referendum, 1963–1975* (London: Routledge, 2013)

Watkins, A., *The Road to Number 10: From Bonar Law to Tony Blair* (London: Duckworth, 1998)

Wickham-Jones, M., *Economic Strategy and the Labour Party: Politics and Policy-Making, 1970–83* (Basingstoke: Palgrave, 1996)

Widgery, D., *Some Lives: A GP's East End* (London: Simon & Schuster, 1993)

F. NEWSPAPERS AND PERIODICALS

Daily Mail

Evening News

Financial Times

The Guardian

The Independent

London Evening Standard

New Statesman

New Statesman and Society

The Observer

The Scotsman

The Spectator

Sunday Standard

Sunday Times

The Times

G. TELEVISION

How We Fell for Europe, BBC 2, 4 June 2005

The Pursuit of Power, BBC 2, 18 December 1995

NOTES

INTRODUCTION

1   Interview with Lord Morris, London, 17 October 2018

2   J. Golding, *Hammer of the Left: The Battle for the Soul of the Labour Party* (London: Biteback, 2016), pp. 304, 335

3   E. Pearce, *Denis Healey* (London: Little, Brown, 2002), p. 539

4   E. Pearce, 'Denis Healey' in K. Jefferys, *Labour Forces: From Ernest Bevin to Gordon Brown* (London: I. B. Tauris, 2002), p. 142

5   E. Pearce, *Hummingbirds and Hyenas* (London: Faber & Faber, 1985), p. 81

6   Ibid., p. 89

7   I. Aitken, 'The incredible journey', *New Statesman & Society*, 1 October 1993, p. 9

8   Interview with the Rt Hon. Dame Margaret Beckett MP, London, 17 October 2018

9   Interview with Stephen Pollard, London, 16 October 2018

10 M. Crick, 'Peter Shore, 1924–2001', *Dictionary of National Biography* (Oxford: Oxford University Press, 2004)

11 R. Plant, M. Beech and K. Hickson (eds), *The Struggle for Labour's Soul: Understanding Labour's Political Thought Since 1945* (London: Routledge, 2004) and M. Beech, K. Hickson and R. Plant (eds), *The Struggle for Labour's Soul: Understanding Labour's Political Thought since 1945*, 2nd edn (London: Routledge, 2018)

12 Interview with Dr Cris Shore, London, 18 January 2017

13 Shore papers, Labour Solidarity meeting, Glasgow, 13 September 1981, SHORE/2/18, LSE

14 Quoted in the *Sunday Times*, 'Everyone's second choice', 19 October 1980

15 Ibid.

16 'Shore: A patriot in rough waters', *The Observer*, 19 October 1980

17 Quoted in A. Roth, *Parliamentary Profile, 1992–1997* (1967), p. 1360

18 Ibid.

19 D. Goodhart, *The Road to Somewhere: The New Tribes Shaping British Politics* (London: Penguin, 2017)

20 I. Aitken, 'The incredible journey', *New Statesman & Society*, 1 October 1993, p. 9

21 Shore papers, 'Government and the Governed', The Reith Lectures Discussion, British Broadcasting Company, Talks and Documentaries Department, Radio 4, 25 January 1984, SHORE/14/5, LSE

22 *Sunday Times*, 17 October 1993

23 'The haunting refrains of Banquo's ghost', *The Guardian*, 2 July 1990

24 R. Hattersley, 'Shore, arch Eurosceptic, dies at 77', *Daily Mail*, 25 September 2001

25 Shore papers, 'Face the Press' Transcript, Channel 4, 25 September 1983, SHORE/13/170, LSE

1: EARLY LIFE

1 A. Seldon, 'In Conversation with Peter Shore', *Contemporary Record*, vol. 1, no. 2 (1987), pp. 38–42

2 Interview with Neil Kinnock, 4 September 2018

3 Quoted in 'A patriot in rough waters', *The Observer*, 19 October 1980

4 B. Rodgers, *Fourth Among Equals: The Autobiography of Bill Rodgers* (London: Politico's, 2000), p. 13

5 Ibid., p. 39

6 Seldon, 'In Conversation with Peter Shore'

7 Ibid.

8 Ibid.

9 Ibid.

10 N. Annan, *Our Age: Portrait of a Generation* (London: Weidenfeld & Nicolson, 1990), p. 411

11 T. Driberg, *Guy Burgess: A Portrait with Background* (London: Weidenfeld & Nicolson, 1956), pp. 21–2

12 P. Seale, *Philby: The Long Road to Moscow* (London: Hamish Hamilton, 1973), p. 19

13 Interview with Neil Kinnock, 4 September 2018

14 Interview with Liz Shore, 15 December 2016

15 Ibid.

16 Seldon, 'In Conversation with Peter Shore', p. 38

17 Ibid.

18 A. Thorpe, *A History of the British Labour Party* (Basingstoke: Palgrave, 2008), p. 142

19 P. Shore, *The Real Nature of Conservatism* (London: Labour Party, 1952), pp. 25–6

20 Ibid., p. 41

21 Rodgers, *Fourth Among Equals*, p. 39

22 Ibid.

23 Ibid.

24 P. Shore, *Leading the Left* (London: Weidenfeld & Nicolson, 1993), p. 69

25 T. Benn, *Years of Hope: Diaries, Papers and Letters, 1940–62* (London: Arrow, 1995), p. 263

26 One of their discussions reportedly questioned the union sponsorship of Labour candidates, though this seems to have been quickly discarded.

27 Benn, *Years of Hope*, p. 294

28 C. A. R. Crosland, *The Future of Socialism* (London: Jonathan Cape, 1956)

29 A. A. Rogow and P. Shore, *The Labour Government and British Industry, 1945–51* (Westport: Greenwood, 1955)

30 Ibid., p. 186

31 Ibid., p. 187

32 Ibid.

33 P. Shore, 'Capitalism and Equality: Ends and Means', *New Statesman*, 1 October 1955

34 P. Shore, 'Capitalism and Equality: The Real Case for Public Ownership', *New Statesman*, 8 October 1955

35 P. Shore, 'The Principles of State Intervention: A Socialist View', *Public Law* (autumn 1957), p. 223

36 Ibid., p. 229

37 Shore, *Leading the Left*, p. 66

38 B. Brivati, *Hugh Gaitskell: A Biography* (London: Richard Cohen, 1997), p. 303

39 P. Williams, *Hugh Gaitskell: A Political Biography* (London: Jonathan Cape, 1979), p. 447

40 Brivati, *Hugh Gaitskell*, p. 303

41 Ibid.

42 Ibid., p. 304

43 J. Morgan (ed.), *Backbench Diaries of Richard Crossman* (London: Hamish Hamilton and Jonathan Cape, 1981), p. 600

44 Ibid.

45 Shore, *Leading the Left*, p. 69

46 Ibid., pp. 60–61. Peter's wife Liz remembers him weeping after watching *Kathy Come Home*. 'It hit him hard,' she recalled. Interview with Liz Shore.

47 Shore, *Leading the Left*, p. 61

48 Crosland, *The Future of Socialism*

49 N. MacKenzie, 'After the Stalemate State' in N. MacKenzie (ed.), *Conviction* (London: MacGibbon & Kee, 1958)

50 P. Shore, 'In the Room at the Top' in MacKenzie (ed.), *Conviction*, p. 34

51 Ibid., p. 53

52 Benn, *Years of Hope*, p. 311

53 Ibid., p. 319

54 http://www.labourcounts.com/oldclausefour.htm, accessed 17 June 2019

55 Seldon, 'In Conversation with Peter Shore'

56 Ibid.

57 J. Gaffney, *Leadership and the Labour Party: Narrative and Performance* (Basingstoke: Palgrave, 2017), p. 37

58 Shore, *Leading the Left*, p. 59

59 Seldon, 'In Conversation with Peter Shore'

60 B. Pimlott, *Harold Wilson* (London: HarperCollins, 1993), p. 177

61 P. Shore, *Separate Ways: The Heart of Europe* (London: Duckworth, 2000), p. 2

62 Interview with Liz Shore

63 Shore, *Separate Ways*, pp. 2–3

64 Labour Party, *Britain and the Common Market* (London: Labour Party, 1962)

65 Quoted in G. Rosen, *Old Labour to New* (London: Politico's, 2005), p. 239

66 D. Healey, *The Time of My Life* (London: Penguin, 1990), p. 211

67 P. Shore, 'Dream Ticket', *London Review of Books*, vol. 5, no. 18 (1983), pp. 3–4

68 Shore, *Leading the Left*, p. 87

69 Ibid., p. 88

70 Ibid., p. 87

71 T. Benn, *Out of the Wilderness: Diaries, 1963–1967* (London: Arrow, 1988), p. 33

72 Ibid., p. 66

73 Ibid., p. 67

74 Ibid., p. 92

75 Ibid., p. 134

76 Ibid., p. 134

77 Ibid., p. 136

78 Ibid., p. 140

79 Ibid., p. 142

2: WILSON'S LAPDOG?

1   E. Pearce, 'Lord Shore of Stepney', *The Guardian*, 26 September 2001, https://www.the-guardian.com/news/2001/sep/26/guardianobituaries.obituaries, accessed on 17 June 2019

2   Healey, *The Time of My Life*, p. 331

3   Pimlott, *Harold Wilson*, p. 265

4   A. Mitchell and D. Wienir (eds.) *Last Time: Labour's Lessons from the Sixties* (London: Bellew, 1997), p. 95

5   Pimlott, *Harold Wilson*, p. 347

6   Crosland, *The Future of Socialism*

7   Shore, *Leading the Left*, p. 89

8   Pimlott, *Harold Wilson*, p. 278

9   H. Wilson, *The Labour Government, 1964–1970: A Personal Record* (London: Weidenfeld & Nicolson and Michael Joseph, 1971), p. 201

10 J. K. Galbraith, *The Affluent Society* (Boston, Harcourt, 1958)

11 Mitchell and Wienir (eds), *Last Time*, p. 44

12 Ibid. See comments by Peter Shore, p. 35

13 Ibid., p. 96

14 Ibid., p. 150

15 C. A. R. Crosland, 'Socialism Now' in D. Leonard (ed.), *Socialism Now and Other Essays* (London: Jonathan Cape, 1974)

16 D. Jay, *The Socialist Case* (London: Faber & Faber, 1937)

17 D. Jay, *Change and Fortune: A Political Record* (London: Hutchinson, 1980), p. 346

18 Ibid. p. 347

19 Mitchell and Wiener (eds), *Last Time*, p. 150

20 Jay, *Change and Fortune*, p. 346

21 R. Crossman, *The Crossman Diaries, 1964–1970* (Mandarin, 1991), p. 131

22 Pimlott, *Harold Wilson*, p. 397

23 Ibid., p. 403

24 Crossman, *The Crossman Diaries, 1964–1970*, p. 210

25 Wilson, *The Labour Government, 1964–1970*, p. 220

26 Crossman, *The Crossman Diaries, 1964–1970*, p. 265

27 Benn, *Out of the Wilderness: Diaries, 1963–1967*, p. 456

28 Mitchell and Wienir (eds), *Last Time*, p. 198

29 Pimlott, *Harold Wilson*, pp. 413–14

30 Wilson denies that this was the reason. Wilson, *The Labour Government, 1964–1970*, p. 427

31 Crossman, *The Crossman Diaries, 1964–1970*, p. 325

32 R. Crossman, *The Diaries of a Cabinet Minister, Volume Two: Lord President of the Council and Leader of the House of Commons* (London: Hamish Hamilton/Jonathan Cape, 1976), p. 463

33 Quoted in P. Hennessy, *The Prime Minister: The Office and its Holders Since 1945* (London: Allen Lane, 2000), pp. 302–3

34 K. O. Morgan, *Callaghan: A Life* (Oxford: Oxford University Press, 1997), p. 266

35 Wilson, *The Labour Government, 1964–1970*, p. 669

36 L. Pliatzky, *Getting and Spending: Public Expenditure, Employment and Inflation* (Oxford: Blackwell, 1982), p. 85

37 Shore, *Leading the Left*, p. 93

38 Hennessy, *The Prime Minister*, pp. 316–17

39 S. Crosland, *Tony Crosland* (London: Coronet, 1982), p. 186

40 Crossman, *The Crossman Diaries, 1964–70*, p. 365

41 Ibid., p. 368

42 Mitchell and Wienir (eds), *Last Time*, p. 154

43 Shore, *Leading the Left*, p. 93

44 For instance, J. Tomlinson, 'Economic Policy' in A. Crines and K. Hickson (eds), *Harold Wilson: The Unprincipled Prime Minister?: Reappraising Harold Wilson* (London: Biteback, 2016)

45 Shore papers, Letter to Rosalind Caine, 25 June 1965, SHORE/6/21, LSE

46 Ibid.

47 Shore papers, 8/8, LSE

48 Shore papers, Letter dated 1st March 1966, SHORE/8/8, LSE

49 Shore papers, 6/31, LSE

50 S. Sheard, *The Passionate Economist: How Brian Abel-Smith Shaped Global Health and Social Welfare* (Bristol: Policy, 2014), pp. 145–6

51 Shore papers, 5/64, LSE

52 *Comprehensive Education*, Issue 1 (autumn 1965) in Shore papers, 5/64, LSE

53 Crosland, *Tony Crosland*, p. 195

54 J. Schumpeter, *Capitalism, Socialism and Democracy* (London: Harper, 1942)

55 Crossman, *The Crossman Diaries, 1964–1970*, p. 343

56 Shore, *Leading the Left*, p. 96

57 Ibid., p. 97

58 Ibid., p. 99

59 Shore, *Separate Ways*, p. 72

60 Shore, *Leading the Left*, pp. 94–5

61 Pimlott, *Harold Wilson*, p. 388

62 Quoted in ibid., pp. 388–9

63 Healey, *The Time of My Life*, p. 336

64 Morgan, *Callaghan*, p. 332

65 J. Callaghan, *Time and Chance* (London: Collins, 1987), p. 273

66 Ibid., p. 274

67 Morgan, *Callaghan*, p. 337; Pimlott, *Harold Wilson*, p. 540

68 Pimlott, *Harold Wilson*, p. 545

69 Crossman, *The Crossman Diaries, 1964–1970*, p. 557

70 T. Benn, *Office Without Power: Diaries, 1968–72* (London: Arrow, 1989), p. 193

71 Ibid.

72 Crossman, *The Crossman Diaries, 1964–1970*, p. 565

73 Ibid., p. 568

74 Ibid., p. 582

75 Mitchell and Wienir (eds), *Last Time*, p. 215

76 Shore, *Leading the Left*, p. 102

77 Morgan, *Callaghan*, p. 365

78 Crosland, 'Socialism Now' in Leonard (ed.), *Socialism Now and Other Essays*

79 Morgan, *Callaghan*, p. 371

80 Mitchell and Wienir (eds), *Last Time*, p. 230

81 See in Crines and Hickson (eds), *Harold Wilson: The Unprincipled Prime Minister?* for a recent reappraisal

3: THE CHARGE INTO EUROPE AND THE 1975 REFERENDUM

1   Labour Party General Election Manifesto, 1970, p. 28

2   'Big Labour vote to let the electors decide on EEC membership', *The Times*, 5 October 1973

3 Shore, *Separate Ways*, pp. 70–71

4 Ibid., p. 72

5 Jay, *Change and Fortune*, p. 460

6 P. Shore, *Entitled to Know* (London: MacGibbon & Kee, 1966), p. 23

7 'British Minister casts doubts on entry to EEC', *The Times*, 26 March 1970

8 Benn, *Office Without Power: Diaries, 1968–72*, p. 222, diary entry for 6 April 1970

9 Cabinet of 26 March 1970, CC (70) 14 Conclusions, CAB 128/45 TNA, Quoted in S. Wall, *The Official History of Britain and the European Community: Volume II: From Rejection to Referendum, 1963–1975* (London: Routledge, 2013), p. 357

10 Press release of speech by Shore on 6 May 1970, PREM 13/3201, TNA, quoted in ibid., p. 357

11 'From Shore to shining Shore', *The Spectator*, 6 October 1973, p. 440

12 Jay, *Change and Fortune*, pp. 443, 444

13 Quoted in *The Times*, 'Mr Shore calls Brussels talks unmitigated defeat in face of hard French national interests', 17 May 1971

14 Jay, *Change and Fortune*, p. 451

15 House of Commons debate, vol. 819, col. 1626, 24 June 1971

16 P. Shore, 'Labour and the Common Market', Report of a special conference of the Labour Party, Central Hall, Westminster, 17 July (London: Labour Party, 1971), pp. 18–19

17 Ibid.

18 'From Shore to shining Shore', *The Spectator*, 6 October 1973, p. 440

19 P. Shore, 'The Case Against', *New Statesman*, 15 January 1971, p. 72

20 Ibid.

21 Ibid., p. 73

22 P. Shore, 'Labour, Europe and the World', *The Round Table*, vol. 63, no. 253 (1973), p. 427

23 Ibid., pp. 432–4

24 Labour Party, *Report of the Seventy-First Annual Conference of the Labour Party* (London: Labour Party, 1972)

25 P. Shore, *Europe: The Way Back* (London: Fabian Society, 1973), pp. 1–3, 18

26 Ibid., p. 17

27 Ibid., p. 20

28 Ibid., p. 19

29 Ibid.

30 Ibid., pp. 20–21

31 Ibid., pp. 22–3

32 Ibid., pp. 23–4

33 Ibid., p. 24

34 *Daily Telegraph*, 15 June 1973, quoted in S. Heffer, *Like the Roman* (London: Weidenfeld & Nicolson, 1998), pp. 671–2

35 Jay, *Change and Fortune*, pp. 476–7, 479

36 Quoted in Wall, *From Rejection to Referendum, 1963–1975*, p. 512

37 Callaghan, *Time and Chance*, p. 303

38 A. King, *Britain Says Yes: The 1975 Referendum on the Common Market* (Washington: American Enterprise Institute for Public Policy Research, 1977), p. 78

39 Wall, *The Official History of Britain and the European Community, Volume II: From Rejection to Referendum, 1963–1975*, p. 543

40 Minute from Shore to Wilson and other Ministers of 15 August 1974, PREM 16/210, TNA, quoted in ibid., p. 544

41 Minute from Shore to Wilson and other Ministers of 1 November 1974, PREM 16/76, TNA, quoted in ibid., p. 553

42 B. Donoughue, *Downing Street Diary: With Harold Wilson in No. 10* (London: Jonathan Cape, 2005), p. 252

43 Cabinet of 17 and 18 March 1975 CC (75) 14 Conclusions, CAB 128/56, TNA, quoted in Wall, *The Official History of Britain and the European Community, Volume II: From Rejection to Referendum, 1963–1975*, p. 579

44 R. Saunders, *Yes to Europe!: The 1975 Referendum and Seventies Britain* (Cambridge: Cambridge University Press, 2018), p. 140

45 Ibid., p. 141

46 'Shore: A patriot in rough water', *The Observer*, 19 October 1980

47 'The case for the committed politician', *The Guardian*, 3 July 1980

48 'How We Fell for Europe', BBC 2, 4 June 2005

49 B. Castle, *The Castle Diaries, 1974–76* (London: Weidenfeld & Nicolson, 1980), p. 333

50 Ibid., p. 383

51 Quoted in Crick, 'Peter Shore, 1924–2001', *Dictionary of National Biography*

52 Shore papers, Oxford Union Debate, 3 June 1975, SHORE/16/173, LSE

53 Shore papers, St John's College, York, 9 May 1975, SHORE/12/96, LSE

54 'The case for the committed politician', *The Guardian*, 3 July 1980

55 *Financial Times*, 2 June 1975

56 Shore papers, St John's College, York, 9 May 1975, SHORE/12/96, LSE. William Pitt – 'England has saved herself by her exertions, and will, as I trust, save Europe by her example'

57 Shore papers, Labour Party meeting in the Brangwyn Hall, Swansea, 27 May 1975, SHORE/12/96, LSE

58 *The Director*, May 1975, p. 202, quoted in Saunders, *Yes to Europe!*, p. 174

59 Shore papers, Brangwyn Hall, Swansea, 27 May 1975, SHORE/12/96, LSE

60 Ibid.

61 D. Butler, and U. Kitzinger, *The 1975 Referendum* (London: The Macmillan Press Ltd, 1976), p. 280

62 *The Guardian*, 7 June 1975

63 'From Shore to shining Shore', *The Spectator*, 6 October 1973, p. 440

64 Butler and Kitzinger, *The 1975 Referendum*, p. 256

65 'Shore: A patriot in rough water', *The Observer*, 19 October 1980

66 Shore, *Separate Ways*, p. 73

67 Shore, 'Labour, Europe and the World', p. 425

68 Quoted in A. W. Turner, *A Classless Society: Britain in the 1990s* (London: Aurum Press, 2013), p. 567

69 T. Heath, 'Speech for Trafalgar Square Rally', 4 May 1975, BIE 19/49(b), quoted in Saunders, *Yes to Europe!*, p. 124

70 King, *Britain Says Yes*, p. 38

71 Butler and Kitzinger, *The 1975 Referendum*, p. 280

4: TERMS OF TRADE 1974-76

1 B. Donoughue, *Prime Minister: The Conduct of Policy under Harold Wilson and James Callaghan* (London: Cape, 1987), p. 48

2 Ibid., p. 50

3 See M. Wickham-Jones, *Economic Strategy and the Labour Party: Politics and Policy-Making, 1970–83* (Basingstoke: Palgrave, 1996) and M. Hatfield, *The House the Left Built: Inside Labour Policy Making, 1970–75* (London: Gollancz, 1978)

4 S. Holland, *The Socialist Challenge* (London: Quartet, 1976)

5 W. Godley and F. Cripps, *Macroeconomics* (London: Fontana, 1983)

6 *Labour's Programme 1973* (London: Labour Party, 1973)

7 Crosland, 'Socialism Now' in Leonard (ed.), *Socialism Now and Other Essays*

8 R. Eglin and B. Ritchie, *Fly Me I'm Freddie* (London: Weidenfeld & Nicolson, 1980)

9 N. Tebbit, *Upwardly Mobile* (London: Weidenfeld & Nicolson, 1988), p. 167

10 Ibid., p. 168

11 The following discussion draws on K. Hickson, *The IMF Crisis of 1976 and British Politics* (London: I. B. Tauris, 2005)

12 T. Benn, *Against the Tide: Diaries 1973–76* (London: Arrow, 1989)

13 Hickson, *The IMF Crisis of 1976 and British Politics*, p. 57

14 R. Bacon and W. Eltis, *Britain's Economic Problem: Too Few Producers* (London: Macmillan, 1978)

15 B. Gould, J. Mills and S. Stewart, *Monetarism or Prosperity?* (London: Macmillan, 1981)

16 Crosland, *Tony Crosland*, pp. 294–5

17 J. Mills, *Why is the UK Economy Growing at Less than Half the World Average Rate?* (London: John Mills, 2018)

18 Hickson, *The IMF Crisis of 1976 and British Politics*, p. 75

19 Ibid., p. 78

20 B. Donoughue, *The Heat of the Kitchen: An Autobiography* (London: Politico's, 2003), p. 211

21 Healey, *The Time of My Life*, p. 388

22 Benn, *Against the Tide: Diaries, 1973–76*, p. 540

23 Morgan, *Callaghan*, p. 477

24 Callaghan, *Time and Chance*, p. 303

25 Morgan, *Callaghan*, p. 479

26 Healey, *The Time of My Life*, p. 428

27 Crosland, *Tony Crosland*, p. 353

28 Benn, *Against the Tide: Diaries, 1973–76*, p. 637

29 Ibid., p. 654

30 Interview with Peter Shore, 30 January 2001

31 Crosland, *Tony Crosland*, p. 239

32 Healey, *The Time of My Life*, p. 431

33 Cabinet papers, Limited Circulation Annex, 1st December 1976, CAB128/60, TNA

34 Ibid., p. 2

35 Ibid., p. 4

36 Cabinet papers, Limited Circulation Annex, 2 December 1976, CAB128/60, TNA

37 Benn, *Against the Tide: Diaries, 1973–76*, p. 676

38 Hickson, *The IMF Crisis of 1976 and British Politics*, p. 142

39 Ibid., p. 144

40 Callaghan, *Time and Chance*, p. 441

41 Cabinet papers, Limited Circulation Annex, 6 December 1976, CAB128/60, TNA

42 Benn, *Against the Tide: Diaries, 1973–76*, p. 682

43 K. O. Morgan, *Michael Foot: A Life* (London: HarperCollins, 2008), p. 346

44 Ibid.

45 Cabinet papers, Conclusions of a Meeting of the Cabinet, 14th December 1976, CAB128/60, TNA

46 Healey, *The Time of My Life*, p. 432

5: THE DEATH OF DEMOCRATIC SOCIALISM? 1976-79

1   M. Holmes, *The Labour Government, 1974–79: Political Aims and Economic Reality* (Basingstoke: Macmillan, 1985)

2   Benn, *Arguments for Socialism*

3   See A. Seldon and K. Hickson (eds), *New Labour, Old Labour: The Wilson and Callaghan Governments, 1974–79* (London: Routledge, 2004) as an example of the 'revisionist' historiography

4   Benn, *Conflicts of Interest: Diaries, 1977–80*, pp. 213, 215

5   D. Lipsey, *In the Corridors of Power: An Autobiography* (London: Biteback, 2012), p. 63. Interview with Lord Lipsey, London, 16 October 2018

6   Interview with David Cowling, London, 2 October 2019

7   S. Sheard, *The Passionate Economist* (Bristol: Policy Press, 2013), pp. 348–54

8   B. Gould, *Goodbye to All That* (London: Macmillan, 1995), pp. 112–14

9   Morgan, *Callaghan*, p. 489

10 Donoughue, *Prime Minister*, p. 36

11 Ibid., p. 90

12 Interview with Lord Morris

13 Interview with Lord Rodgers, London, 3 October 2018

14 Lipsey, *In the Corridors of Power*, pp. 72–3. Interview with Lord Lipsey

15 Shore papers, Ministers' meeting 2 November 1976, SHORE/11/26, LSE

16 Shore papers, Ministers' meeting 23 November 1977, SHORE/11/26, LSE

17 Donoughue, *Prime Minister*, p. 105

18 Shore papers, Speech to Institute of Housing, 23 June 1978, SHORE/11/2, LSE

19 Shore papers, Ministers' meeting 22 February 1977, SHORE/11/26, LSE

20 Shore papers, Press release, 14 December 1976, SHORE/11/18, LSE

21 Shore papers, Ministers' meeting 17 May 1977, SHORE/11/26, LSE

22 Shore papers, Ministers' meeting 16 June 1976, SHORE/11/26, LSE

23 Shore papers, Press release, 7 September 1976, SHORE/11/18, LSE

24 Donoughue, *Prime Minister*, pp. 108–9

25 Ibid., p. 108

26 Morgan, *Callaghan*, p. 502

27 Interview with Lord Lipsey

28 C. Moore, *Margaret Thatcher: The Authorized Biography, Volume One: Not For Turning* (London: Allen Lane, 2013)

29 R. Hattersley, E. Heffer, N. Kinnock and P. Shore, *Labour's Choices* (London: Fabian Society, 1983), p. 17

30 Quoted in Donoughue, *The Heat of the Kitchen*, p. 201

31 Donoughue, *Prime Minister*, p. 105

32 Shore papers, Press release, 3 February 1977, SHORE/11/42, LSE

33 Shore papers, Press release, 9 February 1977, SHORE/11/42, LSE

34 Shore papers, Press release, 15 June 1977, SHORE/11/42, LSE

35 https://api.parliament.uk/historic-hansard/commons/1978/feb/09/inner-urban-areas-bill

36 Shore papers, SHORE/11/42, LSE

37 Shore papers, Press release, 4 August 1977, SHORE/11/42, LSE

38 Interview with Dr Cris Shore, London, 18 January 2017

39 Healey, *The Time of My Life*, p. 409

40 Shore papers, Ministers' meeting 29 June 1976, SHORE/11/26, LSE

41 Shore papers, Press release, 31 March 1977, SHORE/11/42, LSE

42 Interview with David Cowling

43 https://api.parliament.uk/historic-hansard/commons/1978/mar/22/windscale-inquiry-report

44 Shore papers, Press release, 6 April 1977, SHORE/11/42, LSE

45 A. Michie and S. Hoggart, *The Pact: The Inside Story of the Lib–Lab Government, 1977–78* (London: Quartet, 1978)

46 Benn, *Conflicts of Interest: Diaries, 1977–80*, pp. 86–9

47 Ibid.

48 Ibid., p. 154

49 Interview with Stephen Pollard

50 Benn, *Conflicts of Interest: Diaries, 1977–80*, p. 88

51 Shore, *Leading the Left*, p. 116

52 Healey, *The Time of My Life*, p. 403

53 Interview with Stephen Pollard

54 Ibid.

55 Interview with Lord Lipsey

56 Shore, *Leading the Left*, p. 117

57 Shore papers, Nye Bevan Memorial Lecture, Bromsgrove, 5 December 1976, SHORE/11/22, LSE

58 Interview with Nick Butler, London, 20 November 2018

59 Shore papers, Ministers' meeting 30 November 1976, SHORE/11/26, LSE

60 Benn, *Conflicts of Interest: Diaries, 1977–80*, p. 473

61 Donoughue, *Prime Minister*, p. 122

62 Ibid., p. 123

63 Benn, *Conflicts of Interest: Diaries, 1977–80*, p. 487

64 Gould, *Goodbye to All That*, pp. 123–4

65 Benn, *Conflicts of Interest: Diaries, 1977–80*, p. 457

66 Healey, *The Time of My Life*, p. 449

67 Benn, *Against the Tide: Diaries, 1973–76*, p. 473

68 Ibid., p. 579

69 Benn, *Conflicts of Interest: Diaries, 1977–80*, pp. 365, 380

70 Ibid., p. 256

71 Interview with Lord Lipsey

72 Shore papers, Ministers' meeting 2 March 1977, SHORE/11/26, LSE

73 Ibid., p. 326

74 Callaghan, *Time and Chance*, p. 533

75 Donoughue, *Prime Minister*, p. 177

76 Ibid., p. 179

77 Donoughue, *The Heat of the Kitchen*, p. 311

78 Ibid., p. 304

79 Benn, *Conflicts of Interest: Diaries, 1977–80*, p. 438

80 'Lord Shore', *The Scotsman*, 25 September 2001, https://www.scotsman.com/news-2-15012/lord-shore-1-577284, accessed 12 June 2019

81 Quoted in D. Sandbrook, *Seasons in the Sun: The Battle for Britain, 1974–79* (London: Penguin, 2013), p. 753

82 Callaghan, *Time and Chance*, p. 538

83 Shore, *Leading the Left*, p. 118

84 P. Worsthorne, 'Too Much Freedom' in M. Cowling (ed.), *Conservative Essays* (London: Cassell, 1978)

85 Shore, *Leading the Left*, pp. 118–19

86 Morgan, *Callaghan*, p. 667

87 Moore, *Margaret Thatcher: The Authorized Biography, Volume One: Not For Turning*, pp. 374–5
88 Morgan, *Callaghan*, p. 640
89 Ibid., p. 697

6: THE SHADOW CABINET AND THE 1980 LEADERSHIP CONTEST

1 'The case for the committed politician', *The Guardian*, 3 July 1980
2 D. Owen, *Time to Declare* (London: Michael Joseph, 1991), p. 421
3 'MPs vote for boycott of Olympics by majority of 168', *The Times*, 18 March 1980; 'Moscow should not be allowed an Olympics spectacle', *The Times*, 18 March 1980
4 T. Dalyell, 'Obituary: Lord Shore of Stepney', *The Independent*, 26 September 2001
5 Shore papers, 'The inaugural H.G. Wells Memorial Lecture', 22 September 1980, SHORE/2/17, LSE
6 'Candidates for the Labour leadership', *The Times*, 3 November 1980
7 'The shrewd socialist of inspiring practical idealism', *The Times*, 29 September 1980
8 Gould, *Goodbye to All That*, p. 139
9 J. Straw, *Last Man Standing* (London: Pan Books, 2013), p. 138
10 Quoted in 'Enter the Third Man', *Evening News*, 16 October 1980
11 Interview with Nick Butler
12 P. Shore, 'Unite to fight the politics of despair', *The Guardian*, 31 October 1980
13 'Candidates for the Labour leadership', *The Times*, 3 November 1980
14 'The case for the committed politician', *The Guardian*, 3 July 1980
15 Shore papers, Interview given on BBC Radio 4, Transcript, 17 October 1980, SHORE/13/66, LSE
16 Straw, *Last Man Standing*, p. 138
17 Stuart Holland to Michael Foot, 17 October 1980 (Foot Papers (PHM) L1), quoted in Morgan, *Michael Foot*, p. 377
18 Quoted in M. Jones, *Michael Foot* (London: Victor Gollancz, 1994), p. 492
19 Shore papers, 'Face the Press' Transcript, Channel 4, 25 September 1983, SHORE/13/170, LSE
20 Ibid., p. 139
21 Gould, *Goodbye to All That*, p. 139
22 Crick, 'Peter Shore, 1924–2001', *Dictionary of National Biography*
23 Interview with Stanley Clinton-Davis, London, 3 October 2018
24 Gould, *Goodbye to All That*, p. 139
25 Shore, *Leading the Left*, pp. 139, 151–2
26 Straw, *Last Man Standing*, p. 139
27 P. Shore, 'Foreword', in Gould, Mills and Stewart, *Monetarism or Prosperity?*, p. ix
28 Ibid., p. x
29 Shore papers, Annual Conference of the National Association of Colliery Overmen, Deputies and Shotfirers, 27 June 1981, SHORE/2/18, LSE

30 Shore papers, Annual Dinner of the Labour Economic Finance and Taxation Association, 16 July 1981, SHORE/2/18, LSE

31 Shore papers, Colliery Overmen, Deputies and Shotfirers, 27 June 1981, SHORE/2/18, LSE

32 Straw, *Last Man Standing*, p. 140

33 P. Shore et al., *Programme for Recovery: A Statement by the Shadow Chancellor and the Treasury Team* (1982) quoted in Wickham-Jones, *Economic Strategy and the Labour Party: Politics and Policy-Making, 1970–83*

34 Ibid., p. 109

35 A. Mitchell, *Four Years in the Death of the Labour Party* (Methuen, London, 1983), pp. 62–3

36 Straw, *Last Man Standing*, p. 140

37 P. Shore, 'The Purpose of Labour's Economic Programme' in G. Kaufman, *Renewal: Labour's Britain in the 1980s* (Harmondsworth: Penguin Books, 1983)

38 M. Pugh, 'Long March', *London Review of Books*, vol. 5, no. 10 (2 June 1983), pp. 4–5

39 PC minutes, 4 May 1983 and 10 May 1983, quoted in Wickham-Jones, *Economic Strategy and the Labour Party*, p. 111

40 *The Times*, 12 May 1983; M. Foot, *Another Heart and Other Pulses* (London: Collins, 1984), pp. 30–36

41 Golding, *Hammer of the Left*, p. 310

42 Shore papers, Labour/Trade Union Rally in Canning Town Public Hall, 29 January 1981, SHORE/2/18, LSE

43 Steering Committee Minutes, 24 February 1981, quoted in D. Hayter, *Fightback!: Labour's Traditional Right in the 1970s and 1980s* (Manchester: Manchester University Press, 2005), p. 132

44 Shore papers, Annual Dinner of the Carlisle Constituency Labour Party, 20 February 1981, SHORE/2/18, LSE

45 Hayter, *Fightback!*, p. 135

46 Shore papers, Labour Solidarity meeting, Ely, 13 June 1981, SHORE/2/18, LSE

47 Hayter, *Fightback!*, p. 137

48 Shore papers, Labour Solidarity at Transport House, Cardiff, 5 June 1981, SHORE/2/18, LSE

49 Ibid.

50 Shore papers, Labour Solidarity meeting, Glasgow, 13 September 1981, SHORE/2/18, LSE

51 Shore papers, Labour Solidarity meeting, Old Bury Sandwell, 21 September 1981, SHORE/2/18, LSE

52 Shore papers, *Weekend World*, London Weekend Television, 12 June 1983, SHORE/13/170, LSE

53 Interview with Lady Shore, St. Ives, 15 December 2016; Interview with Dr Cris Shore

54 Shore papers, Labour Solidarity meeting, Northern Region Conference, 28 March 1981, SHORE/2/18, LSE

55 Shore papers, Cambridge Union, 11 June 1981, SHORE/2/18, LSE

56 Interview with Lord Rodgers, London, 3 October 2018

57 House of Commons debate, vol. 994, col. 572, 27 November 1980

58 P. J. Beck, 'The Future of the Falkland Islands: A Solution Made in Hong Kong?', *International Affairs*, vol. 61, no. 4 (1985), pp. 647–8

59 House of Commons debate, vol. 995, col. 128–34, 2 December 1980

60 D. M. Bruni, *The British Political Parties and the Falklands War* (London: Palgrave Macmillan, 2018), pp. 84, 92

61 'Mr Foot stays out', *The Guardian*, 4 May 1982

62 Shore papers, American Chamber of Commerce, London, 12 May 1982, SHORE/13/112, LSE

63 Bruni, *The British Political Parties and the Falklands War*, pp. 105–6

64 Shore papers, *Weekend World*, London Weekend Television, 23 May 1982, SHORE/13/64, LSE

65 P. Shore, 'Let the Islanders be free to choose', *Daily Telegraph*, 6 June 1982

66 V. Bogdanor, *Politics and the Constitution* (Aldershot: Dartmouth, 1996), p. 65

7: THE 1983 LABOUR LEADERSHIP CONTEST

1 A. McSmith, *John Smith: A Life, 1938–1994* (London: Verso, 1993), p. 102

2 'Shore opens bid for leadership', *The Times*, 17 June 1981

3 *The Guardian*, 6 September 1982

4 Shore papers, *Weekend World*, 12 June 1983, SHORE/13/170, LSE

5 Interview with Jack Straw, London, 20 March 2017; Gould, *Goodbye to All That*, p. 153

6 Quoted in R. Harris, *The Making of Neil Kinnock* (London: Faber & Faber, 1984), p. 216

7 Ibid., p. 216

8 Interview with Nick Butler

9 Shore papers, 'Socialist and Strategist', 1983 Labour Leadership Election Leaflet, SHORE/2/20, LSE

10 Shore papers, 'Why we lost', Sheffield Town Hall, 17 July 1983, SHORE/2/20, LSE

11 Shore papers, 'Strategy for Survival', Central London Fabian Society, 20 July 1983, SHORE/2/20, LSE

12 Shore papers, 'The New Earning Classes', Chesham and Amersham CLP, 24 July 1983, SHORE/2/20, LSE

13 Hattersley, Heffer, Kinnock and Shore, 'Labour's Choices', pp. 16–17

14 P. Shore, 'Put people before purity', *The Times*, 12 July 1983

15 Shore papers, 'Multilateralism', Lambeth Town Hall, 1 August 1983, SHORE/2/20, LSE

16 Shore papers, 'International Economic Crisis', Toynbee Hall, London, SHORE/2/20, LSE

17 Shore papers, 'British Industry and the Common Market', Wakefield, 18 August 1983, SHORE/2/20, LSE

18 Shore papers, 'British Economy', Southampton and Area Labour Parties, 1 September 1983, SHORE/2/20, LSE

19 Shore papers, 'Values and Ideas', Brotherhood Hall, Letchworth, 3 September 1983, SHORE/2/20, LSE

20 L. Baston, 'Roy Hattersley' in K. Jefferys (ed.), *Labour Forces*, p. 228

21 Shore papers, 'Face the Press' Transcript, Channel 4, 25 September 1983, SHORE/13/170, LSE

22 A. Sofer, 'Diary', *London Review of Books*, vol. 5, no. 16 (1 September 1983), p. 21

23 'A new wizard, but the same old tricks?', *Sunday Standard*, 19 June 1983

24 'Why Shore must make a stand – if he is to stand again', *The Times*, 1 August 1984

25 Shore's candidature was supported by the following Labour MPs: Jack Ashley (Stoke-on-Trent South); Betty Boothroyd (West Bromwich West); Don Coleman (Neath); Laurence Cunliffe (Leigh); Denzil Davies (Llanelli); Gwyneth Dunwoody (Crewe & Nantwich); Harry Ewing (East Falkirk); Frank Field (Birkenhead); John Forrester (Stoke-on-Trent North); Reg Freeson (Brent East); John Gilbert (Dudley East); Bryan Gould (Dagenham); Walter Harrison (Wakefield); Ted Leadbitter (Hartlepool); Roy Mason (Barnsley Central); Michael McGuire (Makerfield); Maurice Miller (East Kilbride); Bob Sheldon (Ashton-under-Lyme); Nigel Spearing (Newham South); Roger Stott (Wigan); Jack Straw (Blackburn); Tom Torney (Bradford South). Shore papers, SHORE/13/66, LSE

26 Shore papers, 'Face the Press', 25 September 1983, SHORE/13/170, LSE

27 Interview with the Rt Hon. Dame Margaret Beckett MP

28 Interview with David Cowling

29 Interview with Nick Butler

30 Harris, *The Making of Neil Kinnock*, p. 237

31 Shore papers, Letter from Callaghan to Shore, 22 September 1983, SHORE/13/169, LSE

32 Sofer, 'Diary', p. 21

33 A. Watkins, *The Road to Number 10: From Bonar Law to Tony Blair* (London: Duckworth, 1998), p. 166

34 Interview with the Rt Hon. Dame Margaret Beckett MP

35 Quoted in P. Cosgrave, 'Lord Shore of Stepney', *The Independent*, 25 September 2001

36 P. Shore, 'Dream Ticket', *London Review of Books*, vol. 5, no. 18 (1983), pp. 3–4

8: THE MILITANT TENDENCY AND THE BATTLE FOR STEPNEY

1 *Marxism Today*, August 1982

2 Interview with Christine Sibley, London, 30 September 2018

3 J. Rentoul, *Tony Blair: Prime Minister* (London: Faber & Faber, 2013), p. 72

4 Interview with John Spellar, West Bromwich, 3 January 2019

5 Interviews with John Biggs and Nick Butler

6 Interview with John Biggs

7 Interview with Nick Butler
8 Interview with John Biggs
9 Quoted in 'Why Shore must make a stand – if he is to stand again', *The Times*, 1 August 1984
10 Quoted in Sofer, 'Diary', p. 21
11 H. Wainwright, *Labour: A Tale of Two Parties* (London: Hogarth Press, 1987), p. 40
12 R. Kilroy-Silk, *Hard Labour: Political Diary of Robert Kilroy-Silk* (London: Chatto & Windus, 1986), p. 67
13 Tower Hamlets Local History Centre, S/Lab/K/6/7
14 Interview with John Spellar
15 I. Mikardo, *Back-bencher* (London: Weidenfeld & Nicolson, 1988), p. 196
16 Interview with Lord Kinnock
17 Quoted in Hayter, *Fightback!*, p. 111
18 Ibid.
19 Interview with John Spellar
20 Ibid.
21 By 1985 one fifth of Britain's 100,000 Bangladeshi community was based in Tower Hamlets. D. Widgery, *Some Lives: A GP's East End* (London: Simon & Schuster, 1993), p. 201
22 'Why Shore must make a stand – if he is to stand again', *The Times*, 1 August 1984
23 Ibid.
24 Email from John Rentoul, 31 May 2019
25 Interview with Derek Gadd

9: THE BACK BENCHES, EUROPE AND THE LORDS

1 Quoted in M. Westlake, *Kinnock: The Biography* (London: Little, Brown, 2001), p. 254
2 McSmith, *John Smith*, p. 102
3 Quoted in Westlake, *Kinnock*, p. 254
4 'Opposition chooses its team', *The Times*, 9 July 1987
5 Shore, *Leading the Left*, p. 171
6 Ibid., p. 174
7 *Sunday Mirror*, 9 August 1987
8 Shore papers, 'Beating the Blues' Conference on Labour's Defence Policy, Southbank Polytechnic, 5 December 1987, SHORE/2/24, LSE
9 Ibid.
10 Shore papers, Tower Hamlets Campaign for Nuclear Disarmament, 13 June 1988, SHORE/2/25, LSE
11 House of Commons debate, vol. 177, col. 795, 6 September 1990
12 House of Commons debate, vol. 183, col. 798, 15 January 1991. The 1975 Indonesian invasion of East Timor, which occurred while Labour was in power, would be another example.
13 R. Hill, *The Labour Party's Economic Strategy, 1979–1997: The Long Road Back* (Hampshire: Palgrave, 2001), pp. 180, 189

14 McSmith, *John Smith*, p. 171

15 Labour Party, *Looking to the Future* (London: Labour Party, 1990), p. 7

16 Shore papers, Labour Common Market Safeguards Committee, 12 December 1990, SHORE/2/19, LSE

17 House of Commons debate, vol. 175, col. 496, 28 June 1990

18 Shore, Speech to The Bruges Group, Reform Club, 24 July 1990, in *Shared Thoughts, Shared Values* (London: the Bruges Group, 1990), pp. 25–31

19 Shore papers, Campaign for an Independent Britain, 7 April 1990, SHORE/2/19, LSE

20 Shore papers, Oxford Speech, 22 May 1990, SHORE/2/19, LSE

21 P. Shore, 'Europe – the meaning of unity', *House Magazine*, 25 June 1990

22 P. Shore, 'Whatever happened to the opposition?', *London Evening Standard*, 27 August 1992

23 House of Commons debate, vol. 224, col. 140, 4 May 1993

24 Minutes of the party meeting held on 17 February 1993 at 11.30 a.m. in Committee Room 14. Quoted in M. Stuart, *John Smith: A Life* (London: Politico's, 2005), pp. 282–3

25 Shore, *Leading the Left*, pp. 186–7

26 'Shore's criticism dismissed', *The Herald*, 24 September 1993

27 Shore, *Leading the Left*, pp. 186–7

28 Ibid., pp. 191–2

29 Interview with Dr Cris Shore, London, 18 January 2017

30 Rentoul, *Tony Blair*, p. 85

31 Ibid., p. 87

32 C. Mullin, 'Diary Entry – Tuesday 14 January 1997', *A Walk-On Part*, pp. 210–11

33 Quoted in 'The Pursuit of Power', BBC 2, 18 December 1995

34 Mullin, 'Diary Entry – Tuesday 14 January 1997', *A Walk-On Part*, pp. 210–11

35 Quoted in *Daily Mail*, 12 August 1996

36 P. Shore, 'The deadly gap left by Labour', *Tribune*, 8 July 1994

37 Shore papers, Labour Economic Policy Group at Labour Party Conference, 30 October 1996, SHORE/16/173, LSE

38 P. Shore, 'Britons deceived: We can vote out Tony Blair when we get fed up with him but not the president of the European Bank', *The Guardian*, 6 January 1999

39 Shore papers, Normand & Sherbrooke Branch of the Fulham Labour Party, 14 November, SHORE/16/173, LSE

40 P. Shore, 'Why as a democrat I had to vote against my own party', *Independent on Sunday*, 22 November 1998

41 P. Shore, 'Never underestimate New Labour's determination to take us into the euro', *The Times*, 16 November 2000

42 P. Shore, 'Why Blair must oppose the euro', *Sunday Times*, 27 December 1998

43 Shore, 'Never underestimate New Labour's determination to take us into the euro', *The Times*, 16 November 2000

44 Shore, *Separate Ways*, pp. 118, 120–21

45 P. Shore, 'Traitors to their nation', *The Guardian*, 28 November 2000

46 Shore, *Separate Ways*, p. 120

47 P. Shore, 'European Union Takeover of UK' in K. Sutherland, *The Rape of the Constitution?* (Thorverton: Imprint Academic, 2000), p. 298

48 Interview with Stephen Pollard

49 Shore, *Europe*, p. 25

50 Shore, 'Traitors to their nation', *The Guardian*, 28 November 2000

51 Ibid.

52 Shore, *Separate Ways*, p. 118

53 Ibid., pp. 224–38

CONCLUSION

1 Pearce, 'Lord Shore of Stepney', *The Guardian*, 26 September 2001

2 Lord David Lipsey, Baroness Goudie, Gwyneth Dunwoody MP, David Bean QC, Stephen Pollard, Simon Crine, David Cowling, *The Guardian*, 27 September 2001

3 Dalyell, 'Obituary: Lord Shore of Stepney', *The Independent*, 26 September 2001

4 Interview with David Cowling; Interview with Stephen Pollard; Interview with Nick Butler

5 Cosgrave, 'Lord Shore of Stepney', *The Independent*, 25 September 2001

6 N. Clark, 'Peter Shore, Labour's forgotten prophet', *The Guardian*, 24 September 2011

7 Quoted in Crick, 'Peter Shore, 1924–2001', *Dictionary of National Biography*

8 Karen Blick, 'Letters: Peter Shore', *The Guardian*, 27 September 2001

9 Ibid.

10 Shore papers, 'This house believes that Europe has more to lose than to gain in political union', 22 May 1990, SHORE/2/26, LSE

11 Shore, 'European Union Takeover of UK' in Sutherland, *The Rape of the Constitution?*, pp. 305–6

12 Shore, *Separate Ways*, p. 124

13 Interview with Dr Cris Shore

14 Shore papers, Oxford Union Debate 1975, 3 June 1975, SHORE/16/173, LSE

15 Shore, *Separate Ways*, p. 150

16 'Everyone's second choice', *Sunday Times*, 19 October 1980

17 Ibid. John of Gaunt – 'England that was wont to conquer others, Hath made a shameful conquest of itself'

18 House of Commons debate, vol. 473, col. 176, 11 March 2008

19 Interview with David Cowling

20 V. Bogdanor, 'Constitutional Reform' in A. Seldon (ed.), *The Blair Effect* (London: Little, Brown, 2001)

21 M. Glasman, J. Rutherford, M. Stears and S. White (eds), *The Labour Tradition and the Politics of Paradox* (London: Soundings, 2011), available at https://www.lwbooks.co.uk/sites/default/files/free-book/Labour_tradition_and_the_politics_of_paradox.pdf, accessed 3 October 2019

INDEX